the Unoff

Guide™ to
Adopting a Child

Andrea DellaVecchio, MA, M.Ed.

IDG Books Worldwide, Inc.
An International Data Group Company
Foster City • Chicago, IL • Indianapolis, IN
New York, NY

IDG Books Worldwide, Inc.
An International Data Group Company
919 E. Hillsdale Boulevard
Suite 400
Foster City, CA 94404

For general information on IDG Books Worldwide's books in the U.S., please call our Consumer Customer Service department at 800-762-2974. For reseller information, including discounts and previous sales, please call our Reseller Customer Service department at 800-434-3422.

ISBN: 0-02-863494-2

Manufactured in the United States of America

10 9 8 7 6 5 4 3 2 1

First edition

To my husband, Tony,
and our two daughters, Jessalyn and Stephanie.

Acknowledgments

I would like to thank the following people for making it possible for me to write this book: Judith Bush, for her extensive knowledge of adoption and post-adoption issues as well as her personal guidance and support; Kris Fehr, my development editor, for her generous words of encouragement and direction; all the adoptive parents who have shared their experiences and personal wisdom with me over the years, especially Judy Ashkenaz for the many hours we have spent discussing the reality of it all; and all the professionals in the various fields that touch adoption who have kindly shared their knowledge and experience with me. Finally, a special thanks to my family who has been extremely understanding and patient; especially Mousse, who has missed so many walks by the river.

Contents

The *Unofficial Guide* Reader's Bill of Rights

We Give You More Than the Official Line

Welcome to the *Unofficial Guide* series of Lifestyles titles—books that deliver critical, unbiased information that other books can't or won't reveal—*the inside scoop.* Our goal is to provide you with the *most accessible, useful* information and advice possible. The recommendations we offer in these pages are not influenced by the corporate line of any organization or industry; we give you the hard facts, whether those institutions like them or not. If something is ill-advised or will cause a loss of time and/or money, we'll give you ample warning. And if it is a worthwhile option, we'll let you know that, too.

Armed and Ready

Our hand-picked authors confidently and critically report on a wide range of topics that matter to smart readers like you. Our authors are passionate about their subjects, but have distanced themselves enough from them to help you be armed and protected, and help you make educated decisions as you go through your process. It is our intent that, from having read this book, you will avoid the pitfalls everyone else falls into and get it right the first time.

Don't be fooled by cheap imitations; this is the *genuine article Unofficial Guide* series from IDG Books Worldwide. You may be familiar with our proven track record of the travel *Unofficial Guides*, which have more than two million copies in print. Each year thousands of travelers—new and old—are armed with a brand new, fully updated edition of the flagship *Unofficial Guide to Walt Disney World*, by Bob Sehlinger. It is our intention here to provide you with the same level of objective authority that Mr. Sehlinger does in his brainchild.

The Unofficial Panel of Experts

Every work in the Lifestyle *Unofficial Guides* is intensively inspected by a team of three top professionals in their fields. These experts review the manuscript for factual accuracy, comprehensiveness, and an insider's determination as to whether the manuscript fulfills the credo in this Reader's Bill of Rights. In other words, our Panel ensures that you are, in fact, getting "the inside scoop."

Our Pledge

The authors, the editorial staff, and the Unofficial Panel of Experts assembled for *Unofficial Guides* are determined to lay out the most valuable alternatives available for our readers. This dictum means that our writers must be explicit, prescriptive, and above all, direct. We strive to be thorough and complete, but our goal is not necessarily to have the "most" or "all" of the information on a topic; this is not, after all, an encyclopedia. Our objective is to help you narrow down your options to the best of what is available, unbiased by affiliation with any industry or organization.

In each *Unofficial Guide* we give you:

- Comprehensive coverage of necessary and vital information
- Authoritative, rigidly fact-checked data
- The most up-to-date insights into trends
- Savvy, sophisticated writing that's also readable
- Sensible, applicable facts and secrets that only an insider knows

Special Features

Every book in our series offers the following six special sidebars in the margins that were devised to help you get things done cheaply, efficiently, and smartly.

1. "Timesaver"—tips and shortcuts that save you time.

2. "Moneysaver"—tips and shortcuts that save you money.

3. "Watch Out!"—more serious cautions and warnings.

4. "Bright Idea"—general tips and shortcuts to help you find an easier or smarter way to do something.

5. "Quote"—statements from real people that are intended to be prescriptive and valuable to you.

6. "Unofficially..."—an insider's fact or anecdote.

We also recognize your need to have quick information at your fingertips, and have thus provided the following comprehensive sections at the back of the book:

1. **Glossary:** Definitions of complicated terminology and jargon.
2. **Resource Guide:** Lists of relevant agencies, associations, institutions, Web sites, etc.
3. **Recommended Reading List:** Suggested titles that can help you get more in-depth information on related topics.
5. **Important Statistics:** Facts and numbers presented at-a-glance for easy reference.
6. **Index.**

Letters, Comments, and Questions from Readers

We strive to continually improve the *Unofficial* series, and input from our readers is a valuable way for us to do that. Many of those who have used the *Unofficial Guide* travel books write to the authors to ask questions, make comments, or share their own discoveries and lessons. For lifestyle *Unofficial Guides*, we would also appreciate all such correspondence, both positive and critical, and we will make best efforts to incorporate appropriate readers' feedback and comments in revised editions of this work.

How to write to us:

Unofficial Guides
Lifestyle Guides
IDG Books Worldwide, Inc
1633 Broadway
New York, NY 10019

Attention: Reader's Comments

About the Author

Andrea DellaVecchio, MA, M.Ed., is the coordinator of the Vermont Adoptive Parent Support Network. She is currently involved with several projects in her home state of Vermont dedicated to giving voice to parents of challenging adopted children and to teaching the community how to help these children. Ms. Della-Vecchio is also a member of the Court Improvement Project of the Vermont State Initiative on Protecting Abused and Neglected Children. In conjunction with Casey Family Services, a post-adoption program, she has developed an educational curriculum to help teachers who work with children with Reactive Attachment Disorder and is participating in training workshops statewide. She has worked with the Federation of Families for Mental Health to develop a video for the secondary caregivers of adopted children with attachment issues.

A 20-year veteran of teaching middle-school English in the United States, Ms. DellaVecchio spent two years teaching English to educators in Asia. She is the author of numerous articles for a variety of professional journals and newspapers such as the Glens Falls Business Journal and the Saratogian. She and her husband, Tony, are the parents of two daughters who were adopted.

The *Unofficial Guide* Panel of Experts

The *Unofficial* editorial team recognizes that you've purchased this book with the expectation of getting the most authoritative, carefully inspected information currently available. Toward that end, on each and every title in this series, we have selected a minimum of three "official" experts comprising the "Unofficial Panel" who painstakingly review the manuscripts to ensure: factual accuracy of all data; inclusion of the most up-to-date and relevant information; and that, from an insider's perspective, the authors have armed you with all the necessary facts you need—but the institutions don't want you to know.

For *The Unofficial Guide to Adoption,* we are proud to introduce the following panel of experts:

Leo J. Farley Mr. Farley is the manager of the Adoption Subsidy Unit of the Massachusetts Department of Social Services. His work includes the design and implementation of state subsidy policy and coordination with federal agencies.

Panel of Experts

Prior to his work with the subsidy unit, Mr. Farley conducted reviews for the quality of care received by foster children in the care of the Massachusetts Department of Social Services—Boston Unit. He started his career with MDSS investigating child abuse allegations and also served as an adoption specialist, developing and implementing adoption plans for a case load of 20–30 children.

Mr. Farley received an A.B. degree in psychology from Bishop's University in 1978 and an MSW from Salem State College in 1999.

Mary Gambon   Ms. Gambon is the Director of Foster Care and Adoption Services for the Massachusetts Department of Social Services. She develops and implements new policy, case practice standards, and quality assurance measures in the areas of adoption and foster care. She provides statewide consultation, training, and support in the areas of adoption and foster care placement and permanency services.

Ms. Gambon began her career with MDSS as an area office supervisor, managing area-based adoption and foster care programs. She rose to Adoption Contract Manager in the Office of Clinical and Placement Services before becoming Director of Adoption Support Services, where she oversaw a 13-member staff, a $65 million budget, and 5 statewide programs including Adoption Contracts, Adoption Subsidy and Guardianship Subsidy, Adoption Search, Post-Adoption Services, and the Birth Certificate Program.

Ms. Gambon holds a bachelor of arts degree in sociology/social work from Regis College in

Weston, Massachusetts, an M.A. in Human Development/Psychological Counseling from Appalachian State University, and a graduate certificate in advanced treatment of children from Boston College. She also attended the McCormick Institute of Public Policy at the Univeristy of Massachusetts in the Women in Government Graduate Program.

Linda Lach   Ms. Lach has been an attorney for 22 years and since 1984 has limited her practice to adoption. She currently lives and practices on the island of Kauai, Hawaii, where she moved in 1992. Prior to that, she practiced law in California and in Washington state.

Ms. Lach holds a J.D. from Georgetown University. Before becoming an attorney, she received a bachelor's degree in business and an MBA from Babson College in Massachusetts.

Ms. Lach estimates she has completed over 500 adoptions in her career, and currently handles between 30 and 50 per year. In most of her cases, she finds the birthmother for her clients. She is a member of RESOLVE, and has spoken at its meetings and symposia several times. When she's not working, she enjoys the beauty and serenity of Kauai, the beach, and reading.

AnnaMarie Merrill   Ms. Merrill began volunteer work in intercountry adoption in 1972. She is currently one-third of the executive board of International Concerns for Children, where she serves as publications coordinator and fundraiser. One of her most important projects for ICC has been the Report on Intercountry Adoption, which, since its inception in 1975, is the only definitive and comprehensive publication in intercountry adoption agencies available to the United States. When ICC incorporated in 1979, it expanded its services to include a photolisting of waiting children in other countries, and for the next 18 years, until the increased use of the Internet, it was the only such venue in the United States.

ICC is a member of JCICS, AEA, and NACAC. It continues to assist local parent groups with intercountry adoption questions, as well as answer questions and advise callers from around the United States.

Ms. Merrill has received numerous awards, including the NACAC Friend of Children in 1998.

Introduction

Americans don't know the truth about adoption.

In 1997, The Evan B. Donaldson Adoption Institute in New York commissioned a survey called The Benchmark Adoption Survey. The survey, conducted by the Princeton Research Associates, found that while most Americans view adoption very favorably or somewhat favorably (90 percent), many Americans (64 percent) have never considered adopting a child, and about half (49 percent) believe that adoption is not quite as good as raising one's own biological child. Almost half the people in America believe that raising an adopted child is second best!

According to the same survey, college-educated Amercians, women, and Caucasians are more supportive of adoption than those with a high-school education, men, or African-Americans. Half of all those surveyed believe that those adopted from other countries are more likely to have emotional problems and less likely to be physically healthy.

Americans are equally divided over whether it is better for pregnant teenagers to place their babies for adoption or raise them themselves. They are also divided over whether the government should promote adoption as an alternative to welfare.

Most Americans believe open adoption (an adoption in which there is some contact between the birth family and the adoptive family) is a good idea, but only in a limited number of cases. The bottom line is that only one in five Americans thinks it is a good idea for birthmothers to maintain contact with the children they have placed for adoption, according to the Benchmark Adoption Survey.

Americans are unsure if searching for and finding birthparents is a good idea. Most believe that adoptees are the most likely of the triad (the birthparent, the adoptive family, and the adoptee) to benefit from contacting birthparents.

Where does the average American learn about adoption? Almost half (45 percent) say that they learn about adoption from family and friends; 30 percent report getting their information from news sources; and 16 percent say they get their information from magazines.

The public needs to be educated.

Curtis R. Welling, an adoptive parent and president of the board of The Evan B. Donaldson Adoption Institute, concludes, "With these survey results in mind, we need to embark on a public education initiative to educate and provide balanced information about adoption. Adoption has been an important service for children whose birthparents cannot rear them and will remain so only if adoption is viewed positively by prospective adoptive parents." It sounds like a simple solution, but who is going to do the educating and what is going to be taught? Obviously, if the public has been uneducated and misled, the public needs to know the truth.

And the truth is...?

The truth is that many couples and singles do adopt children and subsequently build strong, happy families. The truth is that there are literally hundreds of thousands of children who need and deserve good homes. The truth is that there are thousands of adults who want to adopt these children.

What is *not* true is the belief many Americans hold about how readily these happy families come together, a belief based loosely on *Annie* of Broadway and Hollywood fame: A child is adopted from an orphanage where the child had been placed because both birthparents were tragically killed in an automobile accident; the child, too young to remember the birthparents and so grateful to have a warm and loving home, lives happily ever after.

If this ever was the truth, which is highly unlikely, it is certainly not today. In fact, nothing could be farther from the truth, both here in the United States and in other countries around the world. The world has changed, and so has adoption.

Today, the vast majority of children know from an early age that they have been adopted; therefore, both they and their adoptive parents have to deal with all the ramifications of that knowledge. Both parties have to acknowledge that adoption involves loss—a loss that can be an ongoing struggle not only for the adoptee, but also for the adoptive parents.

Many adoptees must deal with the consequences of traumatic experiences in their early lives. Children adopted from our domestic foster care system and from orphanages and other situations in countries around the world who have experienced neglect and abuse sometimes struggle with lasting, and often severe, mental and physical challenges. Some families adopting these children have had their lives turned upside-down, faced financial disaster, compromised existing relationships, and found no place to turn for support.

It is also the truth that adoption is teeming with controversy. Even the experts do not agree on what the problems are, never mind the solutions. Few are aware of *all* the complexities involved in the process of adopting and raising a child.

There are people who do not agree that inter-country adoption should be an option for Americans who are interested in adopting a child. People both here in the United States and in other countries feel that these children could be better served in the country of their birth.

Others are embroiled in the debate over open adoption. A relatively new phenomenon with many degrees of openness possible, many experts don't even agree on the definition of open adoption. More importantly, there are those who do not agree that open adoption is beneficial to any member of the triad—the birthparents, the adoptive parents, or the adoptee.

Despite the fact that only between two and four percent of all adoptees search for birthparents, controversy also surrounds the issue of adoption records. Years ago, original birth and adoption records were sealed, resulting in what was known as closed adoptions. Today, many adoptees want to find out about their personal histories. They feel they have the right to know certain medical and other non-identifying information. Others take a much stronger stand, demanding the right to search for members of their birth families. Not all birthparents agree that adoptees have this right. Many maintain that they signed contracts guaranteeing anonymity and have a right to expect these contracts to be honored. Compromise doesn't seem to satisfy either side, and many states are grappling with the issue in the courts and legislatures.

The need for change

Fortunately, most of the experts have not been living in a complete vacuum over the last several years. Many are clamoring for reform, which has resulted in a multitude of new laws and court edicts. This in itself has led to further problems.

Adoption laws are legislated on the state level. Those involved in the legal areas of adoption have seen this as a problem and have called for a uniform set of adoption laws. There are no easy answers, as the call for reform has simply opened another Pandora's box of controversy, which has lasted for years and could continue on indefinitely.

The efforts of adoption activists have resulted in two national policy changes—the Adoption and Safe Families Act and the Adoption 2002 initiative, which calls for the placement of more than 200,000 children in permanent situations. These changes have had a great impact on the American domestic adoption community. Both have caused a flurry of activity in every state social welfare office as social workers are galvanized to place foster children in permanent homes as soon as possible. While both address the plight of the thousands of children languishing in the foster care system, neither mandates provisions for the support of the families and individuals who will adopt these children. Again, it has been left up to the states to legislate. A few states have responded with positive legislation, often spearheaded by adoptive parent groups. In these states, legislation has been passed that sets aside large sums of money for post-adoption support. However, in most states, there has been no such legislation.

Truth in statistics

Statistics don't lie, but statistics also don't tell the whole story. This is especially true for adoption statistics, which are regrettably incomplete. According to the National Adoption Information Clearinghouse (NAIC), no one in the public sector or in the private sector is attempting to collect comprehensive national data on adoption. Although sporadic attempts have been made throughout the past 50 years to gather complete information, none of these efforts has been successful. The most comprehensive data was gathered by the National Center for Social Statistics from 1957 through 1975, when states voluntarily reported on all finalized adoptions. The NAIC emphasizes that only limited statistical information is available with the most recent complete picture of adoption being provided between 1990 and 1995 by Carol and Victor Flango at the National Center for State Courts in Williamsburg, Virginia. Their findings are at least five years old and already outdated.

The good news is that with the passage of the Adoption and Safe Families Act of 1997, provisions have been made under the Adoption and Foster Care Analysis and Reporting System (AFCARS) for each state to collect and track data on adoptions finalized in the state. The states have a few years to comply with these provisions, and complete statistics are not yet available.

But even when statistics and data are available, the story is not complete. Statistics measure with numbers, and human experience often cannot be measured with numbers. We need to hear the voices of experience in order to make informed judgments about adoption. The first large group of individuals who were raised in open adoption situations, for example, is just coming of age. They have not had the opportunity to speak as adults about their experiences and needs.

We also need to hear from experienced adoptive parents in order to make the changes that will help parents after they have adopted. The truth is that not every adoption is a happy-ever-after story. Many adoptive families are in desperate need of financial help along with an experienced and understanding support system.

Spreading the truth

As we mentioned earlier, 45 percent of Americans say they learn about adoption from family and friends. Chances are they get anecdotal information that presents adoption as either positive or negative, depending on the experience of the individual. Or they see and hear what the adoptive family wants the public and even relatives to see and hear. Family life is a private matter. Few are willing to air the details. It's human nature to share our joys and keep our problems to ourselves.

Even more Americans (46 percent) get their information about adoption from news sources. As with any news topic, coverage of what goes wrong in adoption receives a disproportionate amount of attention, making objective conclusions difficult to reach. This is made even more difficult as the line between news and entertainment blurs.

Recently, talk-show host Oprah Winfrey dedicated an entire program to honoring adoptive mothers. The stories told by the adoptees from various countries were both heartwarming and encouraging, and certainly brought tears to many eyes. The television news program *20/20* recently presented a story about the many children in orphanages in Eastern Europe. The stories and videos of the plight of the children were so graphic and heart-wrenching that the telephone lines were literally jammed with people inquiring about how they could adopt these children. In another *20/20* documentary, a divorced mother with two adopted boys with extreme behaviors was struggling to keep her life together. At one time or another there have been stories or news documentaries about Reactive Attachment Disorder (RAD), the right to search, the right to privacy, tragic stories about the abuse of children in the foster care system, stolen children for sale in some faraway land, and more. The images of extreme examples of each situation may increase the ratings but do little to promote a clear, balanced understanding.

While there have been some attempts to educate the public, mostly on the local level, most Americans are still unaware of the reality of the modern adoption experience. How then can prospective adopters make informed decisions about adoption if they are not adequately informed?

Why you need this book

We are convinced that there is a need for a book about adoption that tells it like it is—a book that does not gloss over the hard parts or paint a picture of adoption as seen through rose-colored glasses. *The Unofficial Guide to Adoption* is that book. It gives the prospective adoptive parent a clear picture of not only the joys of adopting a child, but also of the potential pitfalls and hardships that are a part of adoption.

We have put together a "how to adopt" book that discusses in detail subjects that other books on adoption barely mention or, even worse, fail to mention at all. Our intent is not to discourage any prospective adopter from making the decision to adopt, but rather to give every prospective adopter an introduction to all the facts needed to make informed and lasting decisions in a less-than-perfect world.

In the chapters on the specific types of adoption, we have given both the pros and cons of that kind of adoption. We feel that in the end, it is your decision, probably one of the most important decisions you will ever make. You deserve to know the truth so you can weigh the pros and cons and make the decision that is right for you, your family, and the adopted child.

We devote an entire chapter to discussing Reactive Attachment Disorder and its potential impact on adoptees and adoptive parents. An estimated 80 percent of the children adopted from our foster care system and countless others adopted from other countries have some level of this disorder, but if it is detected and treated early, children with attachment issues can be helped. We have offered suggestions on how to determine if a child is at risk, how to detect it early so that treatment can begin as early as possible, how to raise a child with RAD, and how to find help.

We also tackle a subject that other adoption books don't even touch—parents parenting their children's children. This fast growing segment of the population is not only forgotten by popular adoption writers, but also often by the experts and others in the public sector. We tell these grandparents how to get help from an agency and find public assistance.

We tell you the truth about what it's like not only to build a family through adoption, but also how to handle those who are less than kind in their evaluation of you and your children. We give you hints on how to educate the educators about adoption. We truthfully discuss what it's like to add birth relatives to your own extended family.

In a recent poll, prospective adopters responded to the question, "What is the most difficult part about adoption?" Almost half, 44 percent, responded, "finding enough money." We have dedicated another chapter to all the financial aspects of adoption. Not only do we tell you how much to expect to pay, we also tell you how to find the money to pay it.

In the same poll, 26 percent of you said that "understanding how to adopt" is the most difficult aspect of adoption. We take you step-by-step through the adoption process. Although each agency's procedures and adoption language vary slightly from agency to agency or area to area, we have armed you with enough information to be prepared for whatever you will encounter.

The Unofficial Guide to Adopting a Child is filled with the most up-to-date information available in the field of adoption. After you have finished reading this book, you will be prepared to begin your search for your child. We have included a list of recommended books, publications, and a selected list of support groups throughout the United States. Armed with all this information, you will know if you are ready to make the decision that will change your life forever!

It's All About
Making Choices

PART I

GET THE SCOOP ON...
Choosing your adopted child's age, race, and
sex ▪ Are you ready to adopt? ▪ Deciding if your
family is ready ▪ The high costs of parenting
and adoption

Describing Your Dream

If you are thinking about adopting a child, especially an infant, you are not alone. Five hundred thousand women inquired about adopting a child in 1995, according to the National Survey of Family Growth, up from 204,000 in 1988. In 1997, the National Center for Health Statistics reported that of the 500,000 women inquiring about adoption, only 20 percent had actually applied to adopt.

Approximately 130,000 adoptions were finalized in the United States in the Federal fiscal year 1998. Approximately half of these were adoptions by relatives; 15,774 were intercountry adoptions, according to the Joint Council on International Adoption; and the remainder were domestic adoptions by non-relatives. About half of the children adopted by non-relatives were infants. No reliable statistics are available regarding the ages of children adopted internationally, but it is likely that the majority were infants.

Trends in adoption have changed dramatically over the last several decades. Today's prospective adoptive parents are older, young, gay, lesbian, straight, or single, in addition to married couples; and they are pursuing open, international, special needs, and interracial adoptions. Although any adoption involves a certain amount of risk, and the wait can be long for any child (up to five years for a healthy infant, in some instances), the good news is that you can minimize both the risks and the waiting period by learning about the business of adoption.

This is a very personal time in your life, a time when only you (and your partner, if you have one) can make the correct judgments about your future. You are thinking about taking one of the biggest steps of your life, and you must make an educated decision rather than an emotional one. If you decide to proceed with the adoption process, you will probably be required to participate in a home study, which involves filling out many forms and going through a series of interviews. (Most states require a home study; see Chapters 2 and 8 for details.) You will need to have your answers ready, but before that, you will need to be sure *you* are ready for all of the wonderful—and challenging— changes that adoption will bring into your life.

While it will be the job of the agency, social worker, intermediary, or birthmother to decide if you are a good match for the child in question, only you can determine if the child is the right child for you. As a prospective adoptive parent, you have the unique opportunity to envision many things about the child who may eventually share your home and life with you. As you think about the following factors, keep in mind that the phone could ring one day soon, and the caller will ask you if you would be interested in a particular child. You will give an answer that will change your life forever. You need to be prepared for that moment.

Imagining your child

Begin by describing the child you want to parent. This might feel selfish or awkward at first. As you discuss it with friends or family, you might even get some criticism from those who think that this is not a "natural" thing to do. The truth is that it is neither selfish nor unnatural, but rather an act of good judgment, to be able to describe the child who will fit best into your present family. Imagining the child you want to parent is the basis of all your other decisions, and it will help you determine where to look as well as who can help you find your child. There are many children waiting to be adopted, both in the United States and in other countries, including infants and older children of all races and cultures. The options are limitless.

Oh boy, or girl?

Although there are only two choices, parents have huge debates over the boy/girl issue. It's easier to make a decision if you are single, but if you are a couple, and the two of you don't agree, you will have to work it out. In infant adoptions many prospective parents will accept the first infant that is made available, no matter what the sex of the baby. Perhaps that will be your philosophy also. Independent adoption experts in this country forewarn prospective adoptive parents that specifying gender can significantly slow down the independent adoption process. Therefore, some adopters choose to adopt a child from another country in which more infants in their desired gender are available.

While kids today engage in fewer gender-specific activities, there are still some differences when it comes to raising boys and girls. Think about the following:

> **"**
> We told our social worker that we wanted a girl around five years old. When she called asking if we would be interested in biological sisters ages two and three, without a moment's hesitation I told her yes. Four months later, we were a family of four.
> —Janice, adoptive mother
> **"**

Unofficially...
There are an estimated 3.3 adoption seekers for every actual adoption, according to the 1988 National Survey of Family Growth.

- If you are a single parent, can you provide opposite-sex role models in your child's life?

- If you have other children, are they willing to work to make the new child feel welcome and part of the family, especially if the newly adopted child is of the opposite sex?

- Have you always dreamed about teaching a daughter to quilt or a son to play football and cannot imagine teaching those things to the opposite sex?

- Do you firmly believe that raising a girl is easier than a boy, or vice versa?

Tiny, terrible twos, or beyond?

When you are considering the age of a child you can best parent, look at the entire age continuum. Not everyone feels the need to cuddle and coo over a baby. Perhaps you would prefer to start with a child who is already out of diapers, maybe even in school. Slightly older children may better fit into your lifestyle. While some might shudder at the thought of starting parenthood with a teenager, if you are particularly fond of adolescents, there are many children over the age of 10 who would love to find a good home. Often, older children have psychological or physical problems as a result of being in foster care and orphanages. If you consider an older child, be prepared to deal with some of the challenges that are discussed in Chapter 12. When deciding what age child is best for you to parent, consider the following:

- If you have other children, determine what age would blend in best with your existing family. In placing children, social workers take the needs of the adopted child into consideration and often make a judgment about placing the child into a family with older, younger, or no other children.

- Decide if you can or cannot deal with the issues that many older children have, resulting from years of abuse, neglect, and traveling from foster home to foster home. Some of these issues can be life-altering for these children and the parents who adopt them.

- Decide how long you want to actively parent children. Do you want to space your children far enough apart so that you are actively parenting for 30 years or more?

- Have a clear picture of what is involved in parenting an adopted child at every stage of development. (I'll discuss this in Chapter 10.)

A rainbow of choices

The diversity of children available for adoption is endless. You can adopt from many different countries in the world or from many different cultures and ethnic groups in the United States. Some prospective adoptive parents feel linked to a particular race or culture because of their ancestry or through personal experiences such as travel or military service.

You may wish to adopt across cultures or races for one of these reasons, or you may simply like the idea of reaching out to children in need, no matter what their nationality or ethnic background. However, not everyone—including some adoptees—believes that intercountry or transracial adoption is a desirable option. I will discuss more about the negative sides of these adoptions in Chapters 4 and 11.

Watch Out! People who adopt older children with special needs require accurate information about them. The termination (disruption) rate for these adoptions is estimated to be as high as 20 percent, 10 to 20 times higher than the failure rate in infant adoptions. Do your homework—see Chapters 2, 11, and 12.

Taking a child of a different race or ethnic group into your family is not something that can be done without a great deal of thought and preparation. On the other hand, adopting a transracial or transcultural child can be a richly rewarding experience if you are willing to do the following:

- Readily acknowledge to the general public the fact that you are an adoptive family, and be prepared to answer many questions concerning that fact.

- Acknowledge discrimination and teach your children to cope with the racial and cultural intolerance that exists in every neighborhood and school today.

- Have friends of different races and ethnic groups, go to multicultural festivals, eat ethnic foods, and celebrate holidays that are different from your own.

- Provide role models who are of the same race or ethnic group as your child.

Watch Out!
In any adoption, find out about any other siblings who have been freed for adoption. While they may not be important factors in your child's life at the time of the adoption, later on they may become important in both your lives.

The magic number

You can adopt children one at a time or in non-sibling or sibling groups of two or more. Sibling groups are easier to adopt because they are conversely more difficult to place. Sometimes, single children and sibling groups of two have been separated from a larger sibling group, or after the group has been split, the biological mother gives birth to more siblings.

While it would be ideal to keep all children from one family together, you need to judge how many children you are able to adopt based on practical considerations. Here are a few things that you should be thinking about:

- The total number of children you wish to have in your family, both now and in the future

- The possibility of adding more children to your family in the future

- Whether or not you would be overwhelmed at even the thought of having more than one child join your family

- The logistics of handling more than one child at once

- The financial demands of supporting more than one child, including medical expenses, childcare, vacations, a larger car, two or more college tuitions to pay, and so on

- The physical space in your existing residence or the costs involved in moving to a larger space

Special needs children

Agencies call children with emotional or physical challenges either special needs children or waiting children. While no children, whether biological or adopted, are completely without problems, special needs or waiting children are usually older children who have had some of their needs identified. They are often called special needs children because of physical limitations or psychological scars left by abuse and neglect. The wait to adopt these children is shorter because there are fewer people willing to adopt a child with obvious physical or emotional needs. I will be discussing in detail many of the emotional challenges these children and their adoptive parents face in Chapter 12. For now, it's important to understand that you could adopt a special needs child if you can do the following:

- Understand that while your child is in desperate need of love, love alone will not solve your child's problems.

- Prepare yourself and your family for some challenging behavioral problems and/or demanding physical problems.

- Understand that your child may not respond immediately to your love and that it will take time to build the bond between you and the child and the rest of the family.

- Be willing to negotiate with the agency to provide the special services your child will need both now and in the future.

- Rearrange your lifestyle to accommodate your child's need for services such as doctor's visits and therapy appointments.

- Consider the possibility of giving up your career altogether if your child needs you to be a stay-at-home caregiver in order to nurture and bond successfully.

Are you ready?

It's easy to say *now* that you are willing to do anything and change anything for the sake of the child that you want to have join your family. In reality, it's less selfish to think it through thoroughly and be absolutely sure that you are willing to do what is necessary now or several years down the road.

Many of the issues in this section are relevant to all parents, adoptive or not. But some issues that are unique to adoptive parents must be addressed first. Contrary to the beliefs held by many in the general population, adoption is not "the easy way" to create a family, nor is adoptive parenting just like any other

Timesaver
To find more of what you need to know about international adoption, log on to the Internet at www. rainbowkids.com, where you'll find all kinds of information concerning intercountry adoption.

kind of parenting. Prospective adoptive parents must consider many issues when they think about adoption. Some of them are:

- *Will I be able to love a stranger? Will this stranger be able to love me?* The truth is that we are able to love people who are not our biological relatives. In an overwhelming majority of adoptions, a loving bond is formed.

- *Will we be able to form the bond? How will we do it? How long will it take?* There are no easy answers to these questions. It depends on the history of the child and the willingness and abilities of the adoptive parents.

- *Will I be able to adjust to a child with a radically different personality from my own?* The truth is that many biological children have very different personalities from their parents, and their parents find ways to cope.

- *How much of a role will genes and parenting play in the development of my child?* This nature/nurture debate is discussed in Chapter 10.

- *Will I be able to help my child deal with the issues of loss that all adoptees feel?* Chapter 11 will help you learn about these issues and suggest ways to deal with them.

Adoption, at your age?

Age limits for adoptive parents vary from agency to agency and country to country. In an adoption in which a birthparent chooses the adoptive parents, the age of the adoptive parents is determined by the preference of the birthparents. Many of the age limits and issues surrounding them will be discussed in detail in later chapters under each type of adoption.

Unofficially...
Many people who adopt are not infertile, including most singles, lesbians, and gay men. People have other reasons for adopting, including medical reasons, a preference for an older child, and a belief that it makes more sense to adopt a child who needs a loving home rather than give birth to a child.

At this point, though, it's safe to say that a persistent adult of any age, even those in their seventies, can pursue adoption.

How prepared are you to take on the responsibilities of raising a child at your age? If you are in your twenties or early thirties, here are some of the things that you should consider:

- Your ability to handle an indefinite future, a loss of your job, a change of career, a transfer, or a downsizing, with the added responsibilities of a child

- Your willingness to make the necessary changes in your lifestyle to settle down and accommodate the needs of a child

- Your readiness to share your life with a child who may have needs and challenges that are not immediately apparent

If you are a person in your late thirties and forties whose "biological clock" is telling you it is time to settle down and have a family, you may need to consider many of the same things, with a few more age-related issues such as the following:

- Your ability to do the walking, lifting, and carrying that goes along with infants: diaper bags and baby carriers, as well as 30-pound toddlers who must be lifted into cars and chairs

- Your ability to keep up with a child and the child's activities

- Your readiness to look (and feel) older than every other parent in your child's class, and to have your child tell you that you are

- Your concern over how old you are going to be when your child graduates from high school

▪ Your willingness to postpone your early retirement plans in order to send your child to college

Today, it is not unusual to have children later in life. Many people in their forties and older are deciding to shift emphasis from career to family. According to the National Center for Health Statistics, in 1994 there were three times as many women having their first baby over the age of forty as there were in 1980.

Would your child resent being adopted by older parents? No one has studied adopted children specifically, but researchers have studied non-adopted children who grew up with older parents. The results of this research indicate that while children of older parents often feel embarrassed by the appearance of their parents, they are also aware of the benefits of their parent's maturity and experience. Children of older parents may need some help sorting out their feelings about this issue, but it is certainly not a reason to forego adoption.

What if you are gay, lesbian, or single?

Over the last several decades, a more nontraditional view of what constitutes a family has emerged in the United States. As a result, single men and women, as well as lesbians and gay men, have attained the legal right to adopt children in an increasing number of states. While in the past, most parenting experts were against allowing singles or gay/lesbian couples to adopt children, today many feel that marital or sexual status is not important, as long as the adoptive parents are capable of raising the child in a safe and loving environment. (Note, however, that while adoption by single parents is legal in all states, adoption by gay/lesbian couples is not allowed in all

Bright Idea
If you are interested in spending time with other people who are considering adoption, consider a cruise! There are several cruises for people interested in adopting children. Check with your local travel agency.

states, and that laws in this area are changing frequently. See Chapter 6 for a review of the changing laws and the chapters about each type of adoption for more details on how to build the nontraditional family.) Because individuals, lesbians, and gays have been willing in the past to adopt children who were otherwise designated as "unwanted," such as HIV-positive and drug-addicted infants, many feel they have effectively proven their ability to parent.

I do, or don't

While you can't predict what your life will be like 10 years from now (or even two years from now), you must examine the status of your current relationship and try to anticipate how an adopted child will affect any changes you make in the future.

If you are a single person considering adoption, but a relationship could be in your future, consider the following before you adopt a child:

- How you will meet other single people in your role as a parent

- How you will feel about the lack of potential partners who are willing to take on a ready-made family

- How you will afford baby-sitters when it's time to date

- How having one or more children in your life will affect your future romantic relationships and how this will affect your attitude toward your child or children

- Your child's ability to accept another new person at some point and how you can help the change be a positive one for your child

Even if you are a happily married couple, you should think about the possibility of divorce and

Watch Out!
Children do not fix bad relationships; therefore, you should not even be considering adoption if your relationship is less than solid.

how it might impact your adopted child. No one plans to marry and get divorced, but it happens in almost 50 percent of the marriages in the United States.

The stress of adopting children who have presented unpredictable challenges has put an unbearable strain on even apparently good marriages. Even though you cannot predict the future of your marital status, you can assess your ability to go it alone with the added responsibility of a child. You need to determine if you have the strength and support of enough people in your life to carry on after an unanticipated event such as a divorce or death.

Navigating family politics

Probably the most important consideration in adopting a child is how the adoption will affect those already in the family. Everyone in the family will need to adjust to a stranger who is brought into the home. No one can handle the challenges of adoption without the cooperation and understanding of both the immediate and extended family. In Chapter 9, I will discuss how to prepare family members to accept a new child in their lives.

The future grandparents of the child can be a wonderful source of love, support, guidance, and childcare for the family. It's important to bring them into the discussion of adoption as soon as possible. Often, including them early in the process will not only help alleviate some of their concerns, but give you the advantage of their parenting experience.(See Chapters 9 and 14 for more ideas on how to win over your extended family.)

You and your family are ready to adopt if:

- You and your partner have discussed at length the pros and cons of adoption, and you both

Timesaver
Have family members make a list of what concerns them about adopting a new child. Copy these lists and distribute them to all members of the family before a family meeting. This will give everyone an opportunity to think about the issues before the family discusses them.

have a clear picture of how adoption will affect your life.

■ You have discussed in depth how each family member feels about adding a new child and everyone has had the opportunity to express their hopes, doubts, and fears.

■ Each member of the family accepts the idea of sharing with the new family member. Perhaps a sibling will have to share a room as well as games, the computer, and more. Be sure each person understands completely how his life will be altered.

■ You have explored with your parents and your partner's parents the role they will play in your child's life.

The price of parenthood

For most people, the cost of adopting a child will put a significant dent in their budget. (See Chapter 7 for some creative hints on how to finance your adoption.)

But that is just the beginning: Raising a child can be an extremely expensive endeavor. The costs involved can be a shock to those who have never raised a child before. It's best to be prepared ahead of time.

What it costs to raise a child

Assuming that your child will not have any special needs or unexpected medical expenses, even the simplest everyday expenses can add up. Some typical expenses include:

■ Three meals a day including school lunches, which can average $3 per day per child

- Clothing for growing children who will need new clothes every six months to a year
- Sports equipment and athletic wear
- Routine medical expenses such as regular checkups and dentist visits
- Health coverage, including coverage for braces and glasses
- Transportation, including a car large enough to carry your children and their friends, and car insurance
- "Child-proofing" your home
- Books, games, and toys
- Activities, clubs, and camps
- Music lessons and/or tutoring
- Movies, including the cost of candy and other entertainment offered in some movie theaters
- Dinners out (fast-food prices are no longer cheap, costing as much as $30 for a large family)
- Vacations
- Allowances
- Holiday and birthday celebrations and gifts
- Saving for college or vocational school
- Saving for a post-school interdependent period of young adulthood
- Traditional weddings and religious events

As you can tell from this long but incomplete list, you can spend a huge amount of money on your child. But one of the largest expenditures that you will make will be on childcare. It is so significant it needs to be discussed as a separate issue.

Unofficially...
According to 1995 figures from the U.S. Department of Agriculture, it costs the average, middle-income family in excess of $145,320 to raise a child from birth through the age of 17. This does not include the cost of education beyond high school.

Unofficially...
According to Ann
Douglas, author
of the *Unofficial
Guide to
Childcare,*
Macmillan, 1998,
childcare may
cost anywhere
from $400 to
$4,000 a month
per child,
depending on
the type of
childcare you
choose.

The lowdown on the cost of childcare

If you are like most parents in the United States, you don't plan to give up working in order to raise your family. Unfortunately, most working parents face a childcare crisis. Not only is it difficult to find quality childcare, it's almost impossible to find affordable childcare. You will need to make yourself aware of what kinds of childcare are available in your community and how much it is going to cost.

Before you make a final decision about childcare, be sure to do the following:

- Investigate all the childcare options in your area and decide which will best fulfill your needs.

- Consider the cost of this childcare in relation to your own budget and determine that you can afford it.

- Remember to include the fees that childcare centers often add on, such as late fees and field trips.

- Figure in the cost of a special caregiver on the days that your child is ill and cannot attend an out-of-home childcare center.

- Research government and employer childcare subsidies as well as tax breaks that you can receive for your childcare payments.

Juggling job and family

To work or not to work? This is a question that many prospective adoptive parents in two-parent families struggle with, although for many more families, there is no choice.

While most adoption arrangers don't require you to be a stay-at-home parent, many adoption experts recommend that one parent remain at home for at least the first six months to a year to successfully bond with the child.

Experienced adoptive parents maintain that it is not only in the best interests of the child for one parent to be home for at least the first six months, but it may also be financially feasible, even for single parents. Network with adoptive parents who have already managed to do it.

To work or not to work is an issue that you (and your partner if you have one) should settle prior to adopting. If you have not wrestled with the childcare issue before, network with other adoptive parents to find out how they manage. Experienced working single adoptive parents or adoptive couples in which both partners work can offer suggestions, including:

- Use the time it takes to take your child to and from childcare to sing with your child and talk about your respective days. As soon as you get home, make it a ritual to sit quietly together and hug and play.

- Make sure that the time you spend with your child when you are not at work is quality time in which your child receives attention.

- Involve your child in your work around the house. Children love to help cook supper or clean next to you if you make it fun.

- Make arrangements for what to do when your child is sick and you cannot miss work. You might arrange a babysitting trade with another working parent, or you might find an older neighbor who would be willing to watch your child for a fee, or for an exchange of services.

- If possible, telecommute to your job and/or work at home at least part of the time.

- Evaluate your job duties. If your job does not permit you time away for your child's special activities or it requires you to travel, reassess the value of spending your time at home and consider a job change.

If you have children already, you have most likely worked out these issues. Many parents make the mistake of believing that adding one more child to the family will have little impact. Few are ever fully prepared for the reality of the situation until they have experienced it. As a mother of two toddlers reported, "I had no idea how overwhelmed I could feel after we adopted our second child. It was far more than twice as hard."

Life will never be the same

For the most part, the practical changes that you as an adoptive parent will make in your life will be no different from the changes that any prospective parent would have to make. You will be planning your every trip—even running a quick errand to the store—so that your child is not left alone. You will enter a world that offers two choices: Either you take your child with you or you hire a baby-sitter. Neither of these options is stress-free, no matter what the age of your child.

Moneysaver
Assume that you will spend more money than you were told to expect. It would be wise to open an adoption savings account now and save as much as possible. If you don't use it for the adoption, you are sure to use it later.

There will be many other changes in your lifestyle. You will be trading candlelit dinners for candles on birthday cakes, and romantic vacations for trips to the local theme park. You will become outraged at all the inappropriate language and programming on TV that you never noticed before. You may learn every theme song to every children's show by heart. You will experience the pure pleasure of seeing your child get a goal or basket, hit the right note in a concert, or hit the mark on stage. Most importantly, you will feel the pure joy that a hug from a happy child will bring to you.

You're going to be a parent!

No matter how long you have waited and planned for the arrival of your new family member, you can never be fully prepared for the feelings you will have when your child spends the first night in your home. Most likely the joy of the moment will be mixed with the awesome sense of the commitment that you have made to this child. Sometime in the first week, the unqualified magnitude of the job you have taken on will hit you. You will be struck with the full range of emotions that plague every parent. These emotions may not be new to you, but the intensity and rapidity with which you experience them will astound you. You will be ready to be a parent if you are ready to have the following emotions, shared by most parents, on a regular basis, sometimes all at once:

- *Love.* Love just goes with the territory. It's the one emotion that makes it all worth it.

- *Guilt.* Not that adoptive parents have the edge on guilt, but some do tend to try harder and second-guess themselves more than other parents. It's OK to remind yourself that you are a good parent.

- *Worry.* This is second only to guilt and goes hand in hand with fear. You will worry about absolutely every aspect of your child's life. You will find new things to be afraid of on a daily basis.

- *Joy and sadness.* You will be amazed at how many times a day your feelings will fluctuate between these two emotions.

66

The second night after my two boys had been placed permanently in our home, they were in the bedroom sleeping. I was in the living room winding down. Suddenly, I felt a shudder of fear. It was the first time I actually realized what a frightening responsibility I had taken on.
—Susan, adoptive mother

99

- *Anger.* This will take on a new importance in your life. You will be angry at your child at times. Then, you will be angry at yourself for being angry at your child, which will bring you back to guilt. Pretty soon, you'll develop a good sense of humor about it all.

I think you get the picture. Raising a child is a very emotional experience. Hopefully, the emotional highs will outweigh the emotional lows, and they most likely will, as long as you can hold onto your perspective.

Just the facts

- Describe the child or children you wish to adopt, including age, sex, race or nationality, and special needs, if any. This will help you to narrow your search and save you time.

- Be prepared to truthfully explain yourself, your family, and your needs to the various people who will be making decisions in your adoption.

- Every member of the family needs to be taken into consideration when making the important decision to adopt a child.

- Every aspect of your life will change when you adopt a child into your family. You need to be prepared.

- Adoptive parenting is different. Adoptive parents may have to deal with many of the challenging issues discussed in this book. But, as with every type of parenting, adoptive parenting has many rewards.

GET THE SCOOP ON...
The advantages and disadvantages of using an
agency ▪ How to choose the right agency ▪ The
advantages and disadvantages of independent
adoption ▪ Finding the right attorney

Making More Decisions—Agency or Independent?

Chapter 2

Once you have decided that adoption is for you, you are ready to proceed with the adoption process. How you proceed will be determined by focusing on the child you want, and by weighing the options available to you.

Some prospective adoptive parents cringe at the thought of putting their lives in the hands of strangers, and they choose to complete their adoptions independently. Others find an agency to be a safety net, offering needed counseling and experience. They prefer to be guided through each step by an experienced social worker. According to the National Adoption Information Clearinghouse (NAIC), in 1992, private adoption agencies completed 47 percent of the total number of adoptions, public agencies completed 16 percent, and independent adoption arrangers completed the remaining 37 percent.

Before you can make an informed choice—agency or non-agency—you need to know who the agencies are and what they can do for you. You also need to be aware of the benefits and potential pitfalls in arranging your own adoption. In this chapter, I will discuss the ins and outs of using an agency or an adoption attorney, or arranging an independent adoption on your own.

What does an agency do?

Simply put, an agency matches the right child with the right parent, although each agency may have different methods and requirements.

The three types of agencies are public, non-profit private, and for-profit private. Public agencies are funded by tax dollars and are the local branches of state social service agencies. Most public agencies handle only special needs adoptions and do not do international adoptions. Private agencies, on the other hand, do both domestic and international adoptions, although an agency may choose to specialize in one particular area of adoption.

Private agencies are either non-profit or for-profit institutions. Non-profit agencies often serve the needs of children who are considered challenging to place. Non-profit agencies also contribute to the welfare of these children by making financial contributions to the orphanages with whom they arrange adoptions, although many for-profit agencies do as well. All adoption agencies are required to be licensed in the state in which they are operating.

A domestic agency has access to children either through the foster care system or through birthparents. The agency takes applications from prospective adoptive parents, screens them, and interviews them. Once it accepts the applicants, the agency

Unofficially...
In many states, adoption attorneys do everything an agency does to guide people through an adoption. They find the birthmothers, arrange for counseling, and make the necessary medical and financial arrangements.

educates them in all aspects of adoption; completes a home study, which includes a great deal of paperwork for the applicants; and, after an indefinite waiting period, arranges a match. (See Chapter 3 for more details on domestic adoption.)

An international agency has access to children in other countries either through direct contact with birthmothers, government agents, or orphanages in the foreign country. Some agencies work exclusively with one country while others will work with two or more. Some international agencies employ representatives in the other country, usually English-speaking natives, who aid with the adoption details in the country itself. In some cases, the government or orphanage provides an English-speaking representative either to aid in the adoption process locally or to escort the child to his or her new home.

The international agency's screening process and educational programs are very similar to those of a domestic agency. An international agency will also help the applicant compile the various documents for the required official dossier and advise the applicant on what needs to be done to have the documents authenticated for the foreign country. The agency will help the family fulfill any additional requirements in the child's country or in the adoptive parent's state and will assist in post-placement visits with the agency's social worker. (See Chapter 4 for more details on international adoption.)

The advantages of agency-assisted adoptions

Although many prospective adoptive parents say they would never adopt without the assistance of an agency, this choice is often made for the wrong reasons:

■ They erroneously believe that an independent adoption is illegal.

■ They may not be aware that an international adoption can be done independently in some countries.

■ They are wrongly convinced that agency adoptions involve fewer risks.

■ They mistakenly believe that they will have a better chance of getting a healthy child.

None of these reasons is a good reason to use an agency. Independent adoptions are legal and possible in many countries, and things can and do go wrong in agency adoptions. Nevertheless, experienced adopters agree that there are some valid and rational reasons to seek the help of an agency.

Experience counts

Agencies are experienced in finding children, matching them with parents, and satisfying the necessary legal requirements. Because they already know how to do these things, they can expedite the process, are less likely to make mistakes than someone who is adopting without the guidance of a professional, and will do much of the time-consuming legwork.

Counseling through the bumps

Another major advantage of using an agency is the counseling it can offer. A good agency will be able to counsel the adoptive parents, the birthmother, and any older children involved. Often, the social worker and the adoptive parents establish a relationship that will support the adoptive parents through the complex emotional, legal, and practical issues that arise in all types of adoption.

The disadvantages of agency-assisted adoptions

The most obvious disadvantage is the large fee that some private agencies charge for their services. Agency fees can range from $10,000 to a staggering $35,000 or more in some cases, according to the NAIC. (See the section "The bottom line" in Chapter 3 for a breakdown of these fees.) The fees vary due to a variety of factors:

- The kind of adoption being arranged
- The area of the United States where the adoption is arranged
- The country in which an international adoption is arranged
- How the agency determines its fees—based on family income or a flat rate

If you decide to adopt a waiting child through a public or social service agency, in most cases you will not be required to pay a fee. While the amount of money an agency charges should be a consideration, there are other reasons prospective adoptive parents give for choosing to adopt a child without the involvement of an agency.

Go to the end of the line

Most private domestic agencies report that they have a long list of prospective parents and a short list of children waiting for placement. This is especially true if the parents want a healthy, white infant. Therefore, agencies can be very selective when adding parents to their lists. Private agencies turn people away for a variety of reasons. Agencies will sometimes:

- Set an upper limit to the parent's age by determining a ratio of the parent's age plus the

Bright Idea
Log on to the Internet or check your local newspaper for photolistings of waiting children. These photolistings are provided by adoption exchanges, regional, national, or international non-profit organizations that serve waiting children and families.

child's age, or simply state that persons over 40 may not adopt.

- Limit their placements to couples who have been married at least three years.

- Set a minimum standard for annual income.

- Set rigid health, religion, and family size requirements.

- Require that the couple have no other children and be unable to give birth.

- Require that one parent not work outside the home for at least six months after placement.

- Require that parents fulfill a specified residency requirement in the state.

On the other hand, not all agencies have such strict requirements. See Chapter 5 for hints on how to find an agency that will work with people who are building a nontraditional family.

Too much "lag time"

"Lag time" refers to the waiting period between the birth of an infant and permanent placement in the adoptive home. Agencies often prefer to wait to place children until all the necessary papers and legal concerns have been settled. Because of this, the agency places children in foster homes until all the paperwork has been completed. While this placement is intended to last only a few days, it's not unusual for the placement to drag into weeks. The amount of lag time depends on the amount of red tape involved and the period of time in which a birthparent has the legal right to change her mind, which varies from state to state.

Many parents, wanting to give the child a secure and loving environment as soon as possible, choose to adopt independently to avoid the lag time between birth and placement in their home.

Today, some agencies attempt to solve this problem by creating a type of adoption called "legal risk placement," in which they place the child in the adoptive home immediately after birth. If either or both of the birthparents want the child back before their rights have been legally terminated, the adoptive parents must give up the child. How risky is this? Read Chapter 3 for details.

Selecting the right private agency

Next to finding the right child, professionals in the field of adoption maintain that if you choose to use a private agency, finding the right one is the most important step you will take in the adoption process. The agency should become your ally. You could be working closely with a social worker from this agency for several years, so you need to know from the beginning that your social worker is a person you can trust to do what is best for you. Because the social worker will be getting to know you and your family (if you have one) on a personal basis, asking personal questions, and visiting your home, you need to feel comfortable talking and working with this person.

A prospective adoptive mother who had been waiting for a newborn for several years called her agency often to find out if there was any news of a child. "I knew they would call me as soon as they knew anything, but I needed to have that contact with my social worker," she said. "I know she was just doing her job, but she was so kind and understanding. She made me feel like she was my friend. She became part of the support group that got me through the frustrating wait."

❝
My husband and I had a difficult time deciding if we should go through an agency or try to do an independent adoption. We knew there were risks in both types of adoption, but felt that a 'legal risk' placement through an agency was the right compromise.
—Leigh, an adoptive mother
❞

With over 3,000 agencies in the United States, how do you decide which agency is best for you? Experienced adoptive parents report that the additional time spent in the beginning searching for the right agency can save many hours and dollars down the road. It can also save much heartache if you can avoid hiring a disreputable agency that is after your money (see Chapter 6).

Making the phone calls

Your first call should be to the National Adoption Information Clearinghouse (NAIC), which can identify agencies in your area. You can reach it by calling (888) 251-0075 or (703) 352-3488, or log on to the Internet at naic@calif.com. The NAIC can also give you the number of your state adoption specialist and a local adoptive parent support group. You should be able to gather enough information from these people to compile a list of agencies from which to choose.

You can also call your state's department of human or social services to ask for the telephone number of the state adoption specialist. Your state's adoption specialist can answer all your questions regarding adoption laws and procedures in your state. If you are adopting a child from another state, contact the state adoption specialist in that state through that state's department of social or human services.

Once you have a list of agencies, you can make preliminary calls to learn more about their services. In the first phone call, ask if the agency has any prohibiting requirements such as age, health, or others mentioned previously. Pay attention to their general attitude and willingness to work with you in this initial phone call. Once you have chosen two or three

Timesaver
The National Adoption Information Clearinghouse publishes the National Adoption Directory, which is an excellent resource for adoptive parents. It has most of the up-to-date resources that you will need now and in the future.

likely candidates from the list, you're ready to do some more investigating.

Checking the credentials

As I mentioned earlier, all adoption agencies are required to be licensed in the state in which they are operating. State organizations check adoption agencies on a regular basis, including on-site inspections to check records and operating procedures, so call your state licensing board to check on the credentials of the agencies you are considering. The board's representative can tell you if there have been any licensing violations, or if it has received any major complaints against the agency.

You may also be able to obtain some information about an agency from your state's department of social services. Finally, check with your state or local department of consumer affairs, state attorney general's office, or the Better Business Bureau.

Evaluating the agency

Once you have determined that the agency appears to have an untainted reputation, ask to be sent some literature. Good agencies know the most commonly asked questions and will address them in their materials. This will give you an opportunity to study and compare the agencies in your own home.

If you are looking for an international agency, check to see if the agency is a member of the Joint Council on International Children's Services (JCICS). According to its mission statement, JCICS "is the oldest and largest affiliation of licensed, non-profit international adoption agencies in the world. Membership also includes parent groups, advocacy organizations, and individuals who have an interest in intercountry adoption." The JCICS member agencies subscribe to the Standards of Practice, which the membership designed to protect the rights of children, birthparents, and adoptive parents. The standards address a variety of issues including education, home study, placement, post-adoption support, and interagency relationships.

After you have done your reading, you are ready to call the agency to request an in-person interview. Ask if the agency has a free orientation program. Following is a series of questions that any ethical agency should be able to answer in the interview or at the orientation.

Ask about the agency itself:

- How long has the agency been in business?
- Is it a for-profit or non-profit agency?
- What are the qualifications of the people who actually arrange for the adoptions?
- How much experience has the agency had in the type of adoption you are seeking?

Ask about finances:

- Are the agency fees reasonable for what is offered?
- What type of payment schedule does it offer? Most agencies do not require full payment at the beginning of the process. Fee payments are scheduled with the bulk of the money payable right before the placement is completed. Application fees can range from $500 to $1,000. If the agency is asking for all the money up front, find another agency.
- What if the adoption is not completed? Is there a contingency fee schedule for incomplete adoptions?

- If more than one adoption falls through, will the agency continue to work with you until an adoption is completed?

- Is the agency willing to give an estimate in writing of the total cost of the adoption?

Ask about the process itself:

- What restrictions or limits does the agency itself place on acceptance of applicants? You should have covered this in your initial phone call, but it's best to double-check.

- How much time can they spend with you? When will they be available to see you personally, take your calls, and answer questions?

- Can the agency estimate how long the entire process will take? If it sounds too good to be true, it probably is!

- Will you be given complete medical records for your child?

- If the health of the birthmother changes after the adoption, and it's something you should know for your child's sake, will the agency notify you of the change?

Ask about counseling and support:

- What kind of pre-adoptive counseling and preparation does the agency provide for the birthparents and adoptive parents? Does the counseling fit your type of adoption? Each type of adoption has different risk factors and emotional stresses.

- What kind of post-adoptive counseling and support are offered for the birthparents and adoptive parents? Some agencies don't offer this

Moneysaver
Shop around for agencies. They may charge different fees but offer the same services. Some have a sliding scale based on income. Don't forget to factor in the cost of transportation to and from the agency and the cost of phone calls before you make your final decision.

Bright Idea
Ask agencies to send you their initial information prior to the first meeting. Smaller agencies with phones staffed by volunteers or busy employees may not be able to answer your questions over the phone.

kind of help for adoptive parents, but good agencies do. Also, ask how long this post-adoptive counseling is available. Some adopted children appear to be doing fine until they reach their teens. How long will the agency be willing to help you and your adopted child? (See Chapter 12.)

- Who will be handling your case? Ask to meet this person. You need to determine early on that you can establish a rapport with this person. Will the same person handle your case through-out the process?

Ask about international adoption:

- How many adoptions has the agency completed with the country that interests you?

- Has someone from the agency actually traveled to the country and, if they place children who have been living in orphanages, has someone visited the orphanages?

- Does the agency specialize in only one country? If so, what will the agency do if something happens in that country and adoptions are discontinued? Are they prepared to work with another country?

- Will you receive photographs of the child and information regarding the child's background? If you need more information, will the agency assist you in getting it?

- Can the agency guarantee that it will do all the required paperwork both here and in the foreign country?

- Can the agency give you a realistic estimate of the traveling expenses to the country? Will you be required to carry a specific amount of money while you are traveling in that country?

- Does the agency brief you on the country you will be visiting? Does it help with the traveling arrangements? Does it have a representative who will be in the country to assist you?

- If you have relatives or other connections in the country, will the agency allow you to use these people to facilitate the adoption?

These are by no means all the questions you will need to ask, but they will get you started. Once you've decided which agency will work best for you, you will be ready to start the actual adoption procedure.

Steps in agency adoption

The actual steps in the process will vary somewhat depending on the type of adoption you are considering, but no matter what kind of adoption you have decided to pursue, your agency will require you to submit certain documents and certificates as well as an extensive application form. Most agencies will provide some kind of educational program, and most agencies will have a waiting list.

It might be tempting to register with more than one agency in the hope that it would double your chances of having a child placed with you quickly. Some experts emphasize the need for good counseling and building a rapport with your social worker and believe you will benefit more from establishing a solid relationship with a single agency. Others encourage registering with more than one agency. It's a matter of personal choice based on many factors, including the amount of work and money you are willing to invest.

Watch Out!
If an agency claims that it has never had any problems with any adoptions and can guarantee good results, the agency is either very inexperienced or not telling the truth. Adoption is a risky business; a good agency will admit to having difficulties and failures.

Timesaver
As soon as you have chosen the agency, gather all your own paperwork, such as your birth certificates and marriage license. Line up your references. Schedule a health exam. Get your financial records in order. You will need to submit these with your application.

Doing the paperwork

You may be invited by an agency to attend an agency-sponsored group education session. In these sessions, you and other applicants will learn about the procedures of your particular agency, learn something about the children available for adoption, and receive your application forms. You may be required to pay an application fee ranging from $100 to $500. (For a complete breakdown of expenses for each type of adoption, see "The bottom line" sections in Chapters 3 and 4.)

It could take several weeks to several months for the agency to review your application and accept you as a client. You will be asked to pay a registration fee after the agency has officially accepted you as a client.

The next step is the home study, during which you will be asked to complete a series of forms and questionnaires. (I'll talk more about the actual home study in Chapter 8.) The home study can usually be completed within several months, and if a child has already been identified for you, it can often be completed even more quickly.

Back to the classroom

All good agencies, including public agencies, offer some kind of educational program for prospective adopters. Some use a group approach requiring their applicants to take a series of classes that will realistically prepare them for adoptive parenting and help them identify the child they wish to adopt. This can be a lengthy process in some public agencies. Because some public agencies will not start the home study until the applicant has completed the classes, it could add a few months to the entire process. On the other hand, once you have completed the classroom work and home study, the wait for a child is usually shorter with public agencies because they normally place the "waiting" children from their own foster care system. In other agencies, the educational process is completed on a personal level with the assistance of the social worker. Generally, the educational portion of the process lasts several months and may run concurrently with the home study.

Hurry up and wait

The most commonly asked question is, "How long will I have to wait for my child?" The answer from both professionals and adoptive parents is, "Be prepared to wait a long time." The time it takes for an agency to place a child depends on the type of adoption and many unforeseeable circumstances. If you wish to adopt a Caucasian infant, you will probably have to wait at least a year from the completion of the home study, but it is not unusual to wait two to five or more years. African-American applicants wishing to adopt African-American babies will have to wait around six months. An international adoption can take anywhere from 6 to 18 months. The placement of a waiting child can take from 4 to 18 months.

As required by law, a domestic agency adoption is not finalized until six months to a year after the child has been placed in the home. Some international adoptions have been finalized before the child leaves the country of birth.

A word about the home study

No matter what type of adoption you use, in every state but Hawaii, Maine, Maryland, and Wyoming, a prospective adoptive parent will be evaluated

Unofficially...
According to the American Public Human Services Association, currently there are over 500,000 children in the foster care system in the United States, with 110,000 eligible to be adopted. The process for adopting these children can be as short as six months.

through a process called a home study. This is a confidential, interactive process that includes both office and home visits. Where legally required, the home study must be conducted by an agency or social worker located in the prospective adoptive parent's state. Usually, the home study is done by the agency assisting you with your adoption, and the cost is part of the adoption fee. However, you would hire a local agency or certified social worker to do the home study if you choose to do one of the following:

- Use an international adoption agency that is not in your state.

- Do an international adoption independently.

- Seek an independent, domestic adoption without the assistance of an agency or other licensed intermediary.

An agency or a certified social worker in private practice may charge $500 to $2,000 or more for the home study and post-placement services. Be sure to ask for the total cost of the study before you hire anyone. Also, determine if the fee can be paid in installments.

To find a good home study agency, follow the same guidelines given in "Selecting the Right Private Agency."

The advantages of being independent

In an independent adoption, the parents arrange the adoption of a child without the assistance of an agency. In some independent adoptions the adoptive parents make all the arrangements, but in others another person, such as an attorney, a doctor, or a clergy person, actually brings the two parties together.

Watch Out!
A few international adoption agencies have contracts in each state with certain agencies and will require you to use these agencies. This means you will not be able to shop around to get a good price. Ask if you can choose the home study agency.

Don't confuse independent adoptions (adoptions in which an agency is not making the placement decision), with open adoptions. Open adoptions, those in which the birthparents and adoptive parents are identified to each other, can be initiated through an agency (domestic or international) or independently. All kinds of adoptions can be pursued independently. (See Chapter 3 to find out where to find birthmothers.)

Keeping it personal

Some adoptive parents explain that they chose to arrange their adoptions themselves because they did not like the idea of strangers meddling in their lives. Especially in open adoptions, those where there is direct contact between the adoptive parents and the birthmother, prospective parents often feel it's less risky to arrange the adoption directly with the birthmother. Others feel that they don't need the help of an agency or other intermediary. As the mother of a four-year-old girl recently adopted from Colombia explained, "I can speak Spanish fluently, as does my husband, who travels a great deal in South America. Between the two of us we were able to arrange the adoption through an orphanage in Colombia. The entire procedure took less than a year and cost little more than the actual traveling expenses to Colombia. It could have taken years if we had gone through an agency here in the United States." While it might not have taken years, 18 months is the average for an agency-assisted intercountry adoption, so this couple was able to save some time. Obviously, you would need to be able to speak the language fluently, or find a trustworthy, English-speaking attorney in the country, in order to be sure you have followed all the laws of that country.

Watch Out!
As of January 1999, the American Bar Association has verified that independent adoptions are not legal in Connecticut, Delaware, Massachusetts, and Minnesota.

While there are risks, adoptive parents have reported several advantages to completing independent adoptions.

Speeding up the process

One very good reason for choosing to do an independent adoption without the help of an agency or other intermediary is the time it saves. You can speed up the process by, in effect, skipping to the front of the line and doing most of the leg-work yourself. You will not be put on an agency's waiting list, which might be several years long, or even worse, be turned down by an agency because you did not meet its rigid criteria. Many people who could not otherwise adopt follow the independent route.

Saving money

Independent adoptions can save money, especially in international adoptions. It is possible to contact an attorney or other adoption arranger in another country without the aid of an agency here in the United States. Many adopters have completed successful intercountry adoptions without the assistance of an adoption agency and therefore, without paying agency fees. Needless to say, this involves some risk and is not for the feint of heart. Contact your local adoption support groups to find out how others have accomplished independent intercountry adoptions.

In an independent domestic adoption, however, it is not unusual for the expenses to equal those in an agency adoption. It is customary for the adoptive parents to pay the following expenses:

- A home study conducted by a certified social worker or licensed agency

Bright Idea
If you plan to go out of state to locate a child, check the Interstate Compact on the Placement of Children (ICPC) to be sure you are complying with applicable adoption laws. Call your state social services division for the telephone number of the ICPC office.

- Their own legal expenses
- The birthmother's medical and legal expenses
- In some states, the birthmother's living expenses and clothes
- Counseling, which is required in some states

Persons who wish to pursue an independent adoption can try to minimize their financial risks by:

- Deciding ahead of time how much they wish to spend on the adoption. This budget should include money for the unexpected.

- Arranging and finalizing an adoption in a state where prospective adoptive parents are not allowed to pay the living expenses of the birthmother.

- Working with a birthmother who has health insurance or Medicaid.

- Purchasing adoption cancellation insurance, which provides some financial protection if an adoption effort fails due to the change of heart of a birthparent.

Being open

Many agencies offer only closed and semi-closed adoptions and will not provide information about birth or adoptive parents even if both sides agree to an open adoption.

Open adoption is a hot topic in the adoption world today. (See Chapter 3.) Because agencies offering open adoptions are still limited, those who wish to have an open adoption may seek an independent adoption for the following reasons:

- They believe open adoption relieves the stress and worry of not knowing medical history, genetics, and other details.

Watch Out!
As of this writing, only agency adoptions are allowed in Poland. To make sure independent adoptions are allowed in a country, check intercountry adoption requirements at the U.S. Department of State Web site at www.state.gov.

- Because they know the birthmother personally, they believe they will not have to fear that someday the birthmother or another birth relative will claim rights to their child.

- The child will benefit by growing up with fewer unanswered questions and misconceptions.

The disadvantages of being independent

Many adoptive parents who adopt independently once, hire an agency for subsequent adoptions, although the reverse is also true. They report that the incredible amount of work involved and the unexpected expense were not worth the effort.

One adoptive mother said, "It seemed that I was constantly on the phone with one person after another. Most of the calls were dead ends. I could not help feeling that if we had gone to an agency, someone else would be following the dead ends, and I would hear only the positive news. What should have been a very exciting time in our lives became very depressing. I became more and more emotionally stressed as time went on. By the time we finally succeeded, I was exhausted."

The stress and hard work of adopting independently are not the only risks. There are some other very serious considerations.

Breaking the law

Every state has its own laws regarding independent adoption. In all states it is illegal to buy or sell a baby.

Check the laws in your state and the state in which the mother lives and in which the birth will take place to be sure that:

- You can legally pay medical expenses for the birthmother.

- You can legally pay for living expenses such as food, housing, and transportation during the pregnancy of the birthmother.

- You can legally pay for the legal fees of the birthmother.

- Your state does or does not require counseling for the birthmother.

All states allow the adoptive parents to pay reasonable costs that are specifically related to the cost of the adoption. As laws are constantly changing, check with your state to find what it regards as "reasonable." Most states require all the expenses to be itemized and approved by the court before the adoption is finalized.

Needing support

Many experts who oppose independent adoption feel that the participating members of the triad—adoptive parents, birthmother, and older children—do not receive the proper amount of counseling. Some prospective adoptive parents and birthparents believe that counseling is not necessary or too expensive. Others have chosen independent adoption because it speeds up the process, and they feel that counseling would slow it down. As a result, almost 15 percent more independent adoptions fall apart because one of the participants is not psychologically ready to follow through. Usually, it is the birthmother or birthfather who is not prepared for feelings of loss and depression. The prospective parents are sometimes overwhelmed by the stress that is involved in an adoption. Older children can find the entire process traumatic, and they need to be prepared for the transition as well. Furthermore, some states prolong the duration in which birthparents can change their minds in independent adoptions, which puts the adoption at an even greater risk. (See Chapter 3 for more information on counseling in adoption.)

How to find the right attorney

When looking for the right attorney, you are looking for someone who is experienced in handling adoptions and can provide competent services. A good place to start looking for an attorney is with your local adoptive parent support group. Another place is with the American Academy of Adoption Attorneys. You can call for a referral at (202) 832-2222. The Academy also maintains a Web site at www.adoption-attorneys.org. When hiring an attorney, ask the following questions:

- What are your credentials and your experience?
- Do you offer counseling for both the birthparents and adoptive parents?
- What is the average cost of the adoptions that you handle?
- Do you require a retainer fee?
- If the adoption falls through, what happens to the retainer?
- Do you charge a flat fee or by the hour?
- If you charge a flat fee, does it include the home study, birthmother fees, legal fees, counseling services, and advertising?
- Are there any separate fees for preparing documents, photocopying, mailings, or telephone calls?
- What type of payment schedule is offered?
- Are you willing to give an estimate of the total cost of the adoption in writing?

Moneysaver
If you choose to work with an attorney who charges by the hour, be organized for each meeting and prepare a list of all of your questions in advance.

- Can you give an estimate of how long the adoption process will take?
- Will you be given complete medical records with your child?

The compromise: identified adoptions

An identified adoption, also known as a designated or parent-initiated adoption, is one in which the prospective parents have found the birthmother on their own, or the other way around, and have then asked an agency to finish the process. In this way, the parents don't have to put their names on the long waiting list at the agency, but can still take advantage of the agency's experience and counseling services. Identified adoptions furnish an option to adopters in the few states that do not allow independent adoptions. Also, persons who do not live in states where independent adoptions are legal may travel to a state that allows independent adoptions.

What is a facilitator?

In some states, it's legal to hire a facilitator to help you find a birthmother, write adoption resumes, and arrange birthmother meetings along with the many other details in arranging adoptions. After you have determined it is legal to hire a facilitator in your state, be sure to ask the same questions you would if you were hiring an attorney.

Just the facts

- An agency adoption is legal in all 50 states and the District of Columbia and provides prospective adopters with an experienced staff of professionals to complete their adoption.

- In some independent adoptions, parents arrange for the adoption without the use of an

I don't know how we would have managed without the help of an agency. About halfway through the process, it became obvious to us that the birthmother needed some counseling. We immediately applied to an agency who successfully completed the process.
—LeeAnn, recent adoptive mother

agency, saving time and, sometimes, money. In most states parents must have a home study done by a licensed social worker or an agency.

- You must do your homework and investigate an agency carefully to be assured that it is providing the best possible legitimate services.

- The financial and emotional risks of adoption can be minimized with careful preparation, counseling, and education.

The Business of
Finding a Child

PART II

GET THE SCOOP ON...
How open adoption can benefit your child
- How to find a birthmother independently
- What to ask when adopting an older
child - The cost of a domestic adoption

The Ins and Outs of Domestic Adoptions

A couple wishing to adopt an infant placed this "Dear Birthmother" advertisement on the Internet: "We have much to offer a child—two loving parents, a great home, educational opportunities, security, and lots of laughter and hugs...open to keeping you in contact with your child...visit our Web site to learn more about our home in the Midwest; our active lifestyle; John, our one-year old; our relationship with John's birthmother; and the warm, loving extended family waiting excitedly to nurture a new member of the family and help make a safe place for a new little soul."

Are these people desperate, or is this the way to find a child today? Do you have to be a good marketer to adopt a child, or are there other ways to do it? If you want an older child, do you have to visit an orphanage here in the United States? How do you adopt "the waiting children" in state-funded foster care? How much contact should you have with the birthparents before, during, and after the birth of your child?

49

While no magic formula exists for finding the child for you, you increase your odds of finding the right birthmother or situation by understanding how your search will affect your child's well-being long after the adoption is finalized.

Contact in adoption

In adoptions that are arranged today, there is a continuum of contact between the adoptive parents and the birthparents ranging from no contact at all to a close relationship among the birthparents, adoptive parents, and the adoptee. It will be up to you to choose the amount of contact you wish to have with the birthparents, and then find birthparents who are willing to agree to the same amount of contact.

While there are no statistics currently available for independent adoptions, researchers have indicated that 69 percent of adoptive parents using public and private agencies now choose to have some contact with birthparents. The terms used by the adoption community—closed, semi-open, and open—refer to the level of contact that ordinarily occurs among the birthparents, adoptive parents, and the child both during the adoption process and after the adoption is finalized. These terms vary greatly from agency to agency and area to area. Make sure you ask your adoption arranger for a definition of the terms to be sure you are discussing the same level of openness.

- Closed (also known as a confidential or traditional adoption). The birthparents may or may not pick the family to adopt the infant, but most frequently they do not. There are no names exchanged, nor do the two parties meet. The only information exchanged is medical information provided at the time of placement. The birth family does not have anything to do with the adoptive family before or after the birth of the infant. In this type of adoption, the birth family may consent to being found when the adoptees are adults, but usually not. This level of adoption is usually arranged by an agency or an attorney.

- Semi-open (also known as a mediated adoption). In this level of adoption, the birthparents usually choose the adoptive parents, but agencies or attorneys may choose the adoptive family for the birthparents. Often, only first names are given to identify the individuals involved. Pictures and letters may be exchanged, but usually only for the first year. Customarily, the birthparents will keep their records on file with the agency or attorney who arranged the adoption, allowing the child to find them later in life.

- Open (also known as a fully disclosed or cooperative adoption). Again, the birthparents choose the adoptive parents, but in this type of adoption the two sets of parents have personal contact. Often, the adoptive parent(s) have provided financial aid to the birthmother and are present at the infant's birth. Contact among the triad— the birthparent, adoptive parent, and child—is maintained at agreed-upon levels throughout the child's life. This contact may consist of letters, pictures, telephone calls, and visits.

Open adoption is also a term used in reference to the adoption of older children. Families who adopt older children are provided with the necessary information and histories of the child in order to deal with any emotional or behavioral problems that arise due to prior abuse or neglect.

Unofficially...
Experts believe that a trend is developing toward birthmothers placing their children with higher-income families. They tend to choose the better-educated and more affluent families because they think this will be best for their baby.

Many families who adopt older children determine that it's in the best interests of the child to maintain contact with certain members of the birth family such as siblings or other extended family members. As one adoptive mother explained, "We adopted our two sons when they were five and six years old. They had been removed from their birthparents' home because of severe neglect. They had an older brother who had previously been removed. My boys had distinct memories of their older brother; we could not take those memories away. Over the years they exchanged letters and had a few telephone calls. It was very helpful to the boys to have positive memories of their past."

The facts about open adoption

Open adoption first appeared about 20 years ago as a protest to the restrictions of traditional adoption. Prior to that, most adoptions were kept confidential, not only from the community, but also from the adopted child. Professionals believed that keeping adoptions confidential protected both the birthmother, who was usually unwed, and the adoptee from the intolerant attitudes of the public. Early laws such as the Minnesota Act of 1917 required that adoption be kept confidential and that birth certificates and adoption records remain permanently sealed. By the early 1950s, almost every state had amended its adoption laws to ensure complete confidentiality.

By the early 1970s, research demonstrated a direct relation between the psychological problems observed in some adolescent and adult adoptees and the secrecy of adoption. Researchers also found that birthparents and adoptive parents sometimes suffered psychological problems related to this secrecy.

At the same time, birthparents began to unite and speak out against traditional adoption practices. In 1973, Lee Campbell founded Concerned United Birthparents (CUB) as a support group for birthparents. This group was instrumental in directing the adoption process toward more openness, especially as advances in birth control and changes in societal attitudes toward single mothers were made and the number of healthy white infants available for adoption began to decrease. Suddenly, birthmothers had more power to negotiate their roles in the lives of their birthchildren.

Adoptees were also unhappy with traditional adoption. Many reported that not knowing why they were placed for adoption left them feeling rejected and struggling to find an identity, especially during their adolescent years. Others spent their entire lives searching for answers, and many have suffered serious mental health consequences as a result. Although adopted children make up less than 2 percent of the population, they make up about 5 percent of the outpatients and 15 percent of the inpatients at psychiatric institutions, according to the NAIC. (See Chapter 12 for more about the challenges adoptees and their adoptive parents may encounter.)

Throughout the movement toward open adoption, adoptive parents were the most ambivalent of the adoption triad. Those who adopted traditionally were afraid that they would lose their children to the birthparents. Many refused to support their children in the search for their past. Others felt that it was necessary for their children to find the answers to the questions that had haunted them for so long.

Open adoption is still a very controversial issue. Social workers and attorneys who believe in open adoption are convinced that it is the only way to

Unofficially...
In the first half of the 20th century, many hospitals stamped the birth certificate of the child of an unwed mother with the word "illegitimate" in large red letters. When the child was adopted, a new birth certificate was issued.

adopt; social workers and attorneys who endorse closed adoptions are equally convinced that they are right. It will be up to the prospective adoptive parents to find adoption workers who will arrange the type of adoption they have chosen.

The pros

Supporters of open adoption are convinced that it is beneficial to all members of the triad, but especially to the adoptees because it provides answers to the inevitable questions that they will ask. Supporters have also argued that if the process were more respectful of the birthparents' rights and concerns, the number of infants available for adoption might increase. Other arguments supporting open adoption include:

- If adoptees are aware of their racial and national origins, they will have a sense of who they are. In fully disclosed adoptions, the adoptees are also aware of their family history, to the extent that information is available and secured from the birth family. Lack of this knowledge can lead to what sociologists and psychologists call "genealogical bewilderment." Because people generally talk about things that make them proud, the secrecy concerning their past leads adoptees to believe that there is something terrible about their birth family.

- If adoptees have the knowledge and understanding of why their birthparents placed them for adoption, they will not fear that their birthparents thought they were too ugly or terrible to keep, or even hated them. They will know that they are loved by those who gave birth to them.

Sadly, it can be very helpful for a child to understand that it was a deficiency in the parent and not the child that resulted in an adoption plan.

- The adoptees will have their medical history, to the extent that is known to the birth family.

- An adoptee can have a relationship with the birth family both as a child and as an adult.

- Adoptive parents will be able to help their child deal with the problems surrounding the issues of adoption. They will be able to answer the difficult questions.

- Adoptive parents may have more of a sense of security if they are acquainted with at least one of the birthparents.

- The birth family can become part of the extended family.

- Birthparents are more willing to place their children with people they have met. They are also more likely to place children if they know they will have the opportunity to be a part of the children's lives.

While reliable statistics are not available, most open adoption programs report that they can help a couple adopt within six to 18 months. The wait for an infant in conventional adoption programs can be as long as seven years.

The cons

Opponents of open adoptions maintain that confidentiality is very important in adoptions. One of the strongest opponents is William Pierce, president of the National Council for Adoption, who sees it as potentially harmful to all members of the adoption triad. Other experts point out that many adoptees

Watch Out!
Not everyone agrees that open adoption is the best option. There are mixed opinions in the adoption community. Even proponents of open adoption admit that it is not the perfect solution. You need to do your homework to be sure it is right for you.

work through their identity issues without any contact with the birth family and go on to lead happy, productive lives. Some of the concerns expressed by opponents of open adoption are:

- Exchanging pictures, letters, and other information may cause the birthparents to regret their decision and encourage them to try to get their child back.

- If the birthmother knows who the adoptive parents are, what they look like, and even where they live, she may track them down and demand the baby back.

- It is a form of coparenting. The adoptive parents will not feel that they have clear entitlement to the child. There will be no clear definition of who the "real" parents are.

- Birthparents do not always follow the original agreement. What if they want more or less contact? What if they want more say in how the child is raised?

- Adoptive parents don't always follow the original agreement and may refuse contact after the adoption is final.

- Adding birthparents to the extended family often does not work for other members of the family. Adoptive grandparents, aunts, and uncles may not be as open to the idea as the birth- and adoptive parents.

- The extended birth family may also have differing ideas of how much contact is appropriate and acceptable.

What the research reveals

As I mentioned, open adoption is relatively new, so research has not determined its long-term effects. In its online publication, "Open Adoption," the NAIC reports the conclusions of a longitudinal study on open adoption by Harold D. Grotevant and Ruth G. McRoy. Between 1987 and 1992, 190 adoptive families and 169 birthmothers were studied 4 to 12 years after placement. Grotevant and McRoy drew the following conclusions:

Unofficially...
According to the experts, just as many birthmothers change their minds in closed adoptions as in open adoptions. Because the details are hidden from the adopters in a closed adoption, the adopters do not know when a birthmother has changed her mind.

- Adoptive parents who have fully disclosed adoptions do not fear that birthparents would attempt to reclaim their children or otherwise intrude on adoptive families' lives.

- Openness does not interfere with adoptive parents' emerging sense of parenthood.

- Having a fully disclosed adoption does not guarantee successful grief resolution, as is evidenced by the broad range of grief resolution ratings among birthmothers across all adoption arrangements in this study.

Arranging an open adoption

The type of adoption that is best is the one that suits the individuals in question. The degree of openness should be based on the comfort level of each member of the triad. Many adopters begin with one choice and decide another level of openness is best after the child is placed; for example, families may start with little contact and later open the adoption to allow more contact for the child's benefit. In cases where there has been abuse and neglect, contact may never be established.

If you are considering arranging an independent open adoption without the assistance of a lawyer or other adoption arranger, you are the one who will need to find a birthmother and create an agreement that will meet the needs of both of you.

How to find a birthmother

If you are arranging your own adoption, the most difficult part of the process is the search for a birthmother who is willing to place her baby for adoption. The lack of consistency in state laws, and in the interpretation of laws in different courts within the same state, complicates the search. While prospective adoptive parents may choose to search throughout the country for a birthmother, local judges may not approve of the adoption. "The judge in the area of Georgia where we lived said it was immoral for anyone to use an agency in another state to find a baby for us. She called it 'baby-selling.' We were forced to find a baby in our own state which took us longer," recalls one adoptive mother. (See Chapter 6 for more about adoption law.) Be sure to investigate the situation in your area by networking with those who have successfully completed an open adoption.

As of this writing, it's legal in 32 states to advertise for a birthmother. Ads can be placed in the classified sections of local newspapers and have proven successful in bringing prospective adoptive parents and birthmothers together. If you are uncomfortable writing your own ad, an adoption attorney can give you information on where or how to advertise. You can also use an adoption advertising consultant who will charge you a fee for the service. Finally, there are some sites on the Internet that will post your advertisement. When advertising in any media, including the Internet, be sure to protect your privacy by using a post office box number or non-identifying phone number.

Once you have determined that it's legal to place a classified ad in the newspaper in your state, think about placing your own advertisement. The best way

Moneysaver
You can place a classified ad on many sites on the Internet. Some charge a small fee; others are free. Check with the National Adoption Information Clearinghouse's guide to the Internet, "Adoption Web Sites: How to find reliable information" to make sure these sites are legitimate. (See Appendix B.)

to learn how to word your ad is to read the ads placed by other couples who are also looking for a birthmother. Be sure to include relevant information that will make your ad stand out from the others. If you believe there is something special about you and your family, be sure to include it in the ad. When placing an ad, remember the following:

- You will be able to get the word out to more people.

- Advertisements in newspapers are usually brief due to the cost. Advertising can become very expensive.

- You may get many unwanted calls and be easier to scam.

It will be helpful to have a list of questions near the telephone. These questions will help you screen the calls and should give you enough information to determine if you wish to refer the birthmother to your attorney, talk to the birthmother, or arrange a meeting with the birthmother. You should also be ready to answer some questions about yourself. Some of the information exchanged in the first phone call may include:

- Ages
- Due date
- Marital status
- Ethnic background
- Medical history
- Reasons for choosing an adoptive placement

Always check your state to see if the laws have changed. As of this writing, the following states do not allow adoption advertising:

California	Maine
Delaware	Massachusetts
Florida	Montana
Georgia	Nevada
Idaho	North Carolina
Kansas	Ohio
Kentucky	Texas

Both Oregon and Washington require the prospective adoptive parents to have a home study before they place an advertisement.

Other ways some adoptive parents have used to locate a birthmother include the following:

- Contacting obstetricians, school guidance counselors, college health services, ministers, and adoption attorneys. Send a resume that includes a picture of you (and your family and pets) and briefly describes you (and your family) and what you have to offer a child.

- Using networking tools such as pins and tee shirts that announce your desire to adopt.

- Using business cards to announce your adoption plans. Distribute them to anyone with whom you come in contact.

- Distributing flyers with your adoption message.

- Volunteering at local agencies such as youth centers and YWCAs. Being at the right place at the right time can help.

Evaluating each other

Once you and the birthmother have agreed to work together, you may decide to maintain a telephone relationship for several months, or you may decide to arrange a meeting immediately. This depends on

Bright Idea
Set up an 800 number just for replies to your advertising. In this way, no one will have access to your home or work address, but be aware that some birthmothers may think that only attorneys or agencies use toll-free numbers.

the preferences of both parties and the situation. Both of you should decide when and where to meet. Some birthmothers might be too intimidated to meet in your home and would prefer to meet in neutral territory. Others might want to see where the child will be living.

Experts agree that birthparents and adoptive parents need to agree on an adoption plan that is in the best interests of the child. (Because more birthfathers are choosing to be part of the adoption process, in this section it will be assumed there are two birthparents participating.) Therefore, you will need to take the time and effort to build a great deal of trust with the birthparents. It can be helpful to remember that this is an emotional and difficult time for all involved.

Be completely truthful and willing to follow the agreement you reach with the birthparents. If you automatically agree to all that is required by the birthparents just to have the baby placed with you, you will set yourself up for problems in the future.

When you meet and/or talk with each other, you are all deciding if this adoption arrangement can work for all members of the triad, especially the child. Each of you will have questions that must be carefully and truthfully answered.

What the birthparents want to know
The birthparents may ask you questions to help them determine if you will be the right parents for their child. They will also evaluate your enthusiasm for parenting their child, your sense of humor, and evidence of the loving home you can provide. You may have several meetings with them; it's up to you to decide when you will answer which questions. Keep in mind that the more information you give

them, the more information they will have available to help them make their final decision. Their questions might include:

- Why do you want to adopt my child?

- Will one of you be staying home full-time to care for the baby? If not, what are the arrangements for childcare?

- What do you do for a living? Where do you work?

- What religion are you?

- What do you do for entertainment and fun?

- Are there other children in your family?

The birthparents may also ask you questions about money. They might ask questions about your salary and what the financial arrangements of the placement will be. These are fair questions, but experts advise using caution when answering questions like them. Laws vary from state to state, and what is legal in one state may be a felony in another. They advise adopters to leave the financial arrangements to an experienced adoption arranger. Be wary if the first questions the birthparents ask are about finances, and if they push for answers right away.

Birthmothers have expressed a variety of reasons for placing their child with a certain couple. In some cases, the birthmother made the judgment based upon how the couple conducted themselves in the interviews. Some have required that their baby have a full-time mother; they rejected couples if the mother planned to continue working. Others have rejected couples who seemed like they would expect too much of their child or couples in which the father did not seem to be invested in the process.

What you should ask the birthparents

You will also have an opportunity to ask questions of the birthparents to determine if a match can be made. Be careful when asking questions of the birthmother. It may be a very emotional time for her, and she may be reluctant to answer some of the more personal questions. Naturally, you will need the answers to these difficult questions, but you may have to wait for another meeting. Some of the questions you need to ask are:

- What would you like to know about us?

- Why have you chosen an adoption plan?

- When is the baby due?

- Have you had regular doctor's visits?

- Have you had any medical problems concerning the pregnancy? Have you had any medical problems not related to the pregnancy? Have you had any mental health problems in the past?

- Have you taken drugs, consumed alcohol, or smoked during the pregnancy?

- Have you had any previous pregnancies?

- Does your family support your decision to place your baby for adoption?

- What are your plans for your life after the birth of the baby?

If the birthfather is not present, some of the questions you should ask are:

- Who is the father?

- Does the father support your decision to place your baby for adoption? Does his family support the decision?

- Why is the father not involved in the adoption plan?

Bright Idea
Bring a photo album to the first meeting. Also bring a biography of you (and your family) to give to the prospective birthparents. Include in it what you can offer their child and why you believe you would be a good family for their child.

Timesaver
Sometimes, a birthmother or birthfather may feel intimidated when you are questioning them. Some experienced adopters suggest making a list of your questions and giving them to the birthparents ahead of time. This may not only facilitate meetings, but also put the birthparents at ease.

- What is the medical and mental health history of the birthfather?

The case for counseling in open adoption

Experts agree that counseling is an essential ingredient in a successful adoption. A counselor can help both the birthparents and adoptive parents through each step of the adoption process. Counseling can provide the following reassurances for the birthparents and help them maintain their commitment to the adoption by providing them with someone who will:

- Guide them through the periods of doubt preceding the birth. A counselor can assure them that their misgivings are normal.

- Help them through the normal feelings of loss and grief after the birth.

Counseling can provide a similar support system for you:

- If you have been frustrated in your efforts to become a parent, a counselor can help you rebuild a positive attitude and trust.

- A counselor can ask the difficult questions at your meeting with the birthparents.

- A counselor can support you in whatever decision you make, especially if you decide that it is not a good match. The counselor can reassure you that another opportunity will arise.

- A counselor can support you through a failed adoption attempt.

Making an agreement

Most professionals agree that the key ingredient in an open adoption is the agreement that clearly states the conditions and expectations of the placement for both sets of parents. Get it in writing! All parties involved need a legal contract stating the terms of contact in the future.

What if they change their minds?

If the birthparents change their minds and decide to parent the baby, or even to reclaim the baby after adoption, experts are unanimous in stressing that the well-being of the child must always be placed before all other considerations. That is not an easy proposition for the adoptive parent, especially if the baby has been living in the adoptive parent's home for any length of time. In the latter situation, the adoptive parents' first impulse is to fight the birthparents legally, but this is not necessarily the best choice.

Experts encourage adoptive parents to seek the help of a mediator to facilitate a quick resolution rather than struggle for years in legal battles that will only result in increased pain for all parties, especially the child. They also encourage adoptive parents to mourn the loss of the child they had hoped to parent or had actually parented for weeks or months, rather than to vent their anger at the birthparents. If the adoptive parents are able to recognize their feelings of loss, they may be able to relate to the feelings of the birthparents.

What about the children in foster care?

Available statistics indicate that there are approximately half a million children in state-funded foster care placements throughout the United States. (Many states have not submitted complete data.) In 1997, the U.S. Congress passed the Adoption and Safe Families Act (ASFA) to promote more timely decision making concerning the permanent plans for all children in foster care. In other words, ASFA has mandated states speed up the process and provide permanent placements for children in foster care within a reasonable amount of time. (See Chapter 6 for more about ASFA.) Permanency can mean a return to the birth family, a permanent guardianship, or an adoptive placement. According to some estimates, the number of children in the foster care system available for adoption will rise from the 20 percent currently available (about 100,000) to more than double that amount.

According to the Children's Bureau of the U.S. Department of Health and Human Services, based on data collected by the Adoption and Foster Care Analysis and Reporting System (AFCARS), ages of children in foster care in 1996 were as follows:

- 4 percent were under one year old
- 29 percent were age 1 to 5
- 27 percent were age 6 to 10
- 25 percent were age 11 to 15
- 14 percent were age 16 to 18

Of these children, 51 percent were male and 49 percent were female; 62 percent were of minority background and 38 percent were white.

Who are these children really?

That is what the demographics say about the children in foster care, but who are they really? They are children whose parents for one reason or another were found to be incapable of caring for them. In some cases, the parents themselves decided that they could not care for their child or children adequately and voluntarily terminated their rights. In other cases, the courts terminated the parents' rights because they abused and/or neglected their child.

Watch Out!
With more people searching for birthmothers independently, scams are increasing. One of the most common is the practice of birthmothers taking money from more than one couple at a time. See Chapter 6 for more information on scams.

Because many of these children were abused and neglected, they carry both physical and emotional scars from their pasts. Often, they have been moved from one foster home to another.

Public agencies call children in foster care who are waiting for adoption "the waiting children" or special needs children. All children in foster care do not meet the legal definition of special needs. In the adoption world, a special needs child is defined at this time as a child who meets one or more of the following criteria:

- A child with a diagnosable physical, medical, mental, or emotional handicapping condition

- An "older child," usually over age five in most states but defined as over two in some states

- Siblings (two or more children) who must be placed together, although twins are not automatically considered special needs

Special needs or waiting children desperately need a permanent adoptive home. Fortunately, there are people who are eager to give these children homes, sincerely believing that love and caring will make the difference.

But experts caution that love alone is not enough to help these children, and prospective adoptive parents need to become informed about the issues involved in raising challenging (special needs) children. At a recent support group for challenging adopted children, an adoption social worker complained, "We try to prepare prospective adoptive parents in our classes for some of the challenges they might encounter in the future. I know they are not listening to the facts. They are convinced that all these children need is a loving home.

Bright Idea
To learn more about children in the foster care system, provide respite care or foster care for them. Contact your local community mental health agencies or state social service agencies for information on how to provide these services.

Our intent is not to dissuade them from adopting, but rather to help them learn how to adjust to the realities of the challenges they will encounter."

In *Adopting the Hurt Child: Hope for Families with Special Needs Kids, A Guide for Parents and Professionals* (see Appendix C), Gregory C. Keck and Regina M. Kupecky suggest that parents considering adopting from the foster care system educate themselves as much as possible by reading everything available on the subject and speaking with as many experienced people as possible.

Keck and Kupecky also urge prospective parents to ask the following questions:

- Why was the child originally removed from the birth home?

- When did the initial removal occur and how old was the child?

- How many reunification attempts have there been, and why did they fail?

- How many placements has the child been through, and why did they end?

- How does the child do in school?

- How well does the child get along with others?

- Does the child have any dangerous behaviors— e.g., a history of setting fires, animal abuse, sexual abuse of other children, injuring others?

- Does the child have any diagnosed conditions— e.g., dyslexia, Attention Deficit Disorder, Reactive Attachment Disorder? Is there any reason to suspect that any such conditions exist that have not been diagnosed?

- Did the child's parents have addictions to drugs or alcohol?

- Is it likely the child's mother used drugs or alcohol while pregnant?

- Has the child been tested for communicable or hereditary diseases?

- Does the child have any other health issues that should be of concern?

- Are there any genetic issues that may affect the child later?

- Does the child have brothers or sisters? How many? How old? Where are they? Why aren't they being placed together? Will they visit?

- Are there any birth relatives, foster parents, or others who have a significant positive impact on the child? Are they willing to remain in touch with the child after adoption?

- What does the child like to do?

- Does the child enjoy any particular hobbies?

- Does the child have any favorite toys, foods, or television shows?

- Does the child attend religious services, and if so, what kind?

- Does the child participate in any sports or scouting activities?

- Are there any photos available of the child in his birth home or foster homes that he can bring to his new home?

- Does the child have any treasured possessions that should come with him?

- Does the child have a pet that he would like to bring along?

- How do his caretakers discipline him? Is this method effective?

- Is there anything about the child we should know to ease his adjustment to his new home?

In Chapter 12, I'll discuss in detail the importance of the first three years of a child's life. The following questions refer to the first three years:

- Is there any reason to suspect the child was abused, neglected, or abandoned?

- Was there anyone who provided consistent loving care?

- Were the child's needs met satisfactorily and on a consistent basis?

- Was the child seriously ill or in pain?

As you can see, an incredible amount of information needs to be gathered in order to have a full picture of the child in question. Keck and Kupecky suggest you use the following sources:

- Pay close attention to everything said about the child.

- Ask questions of the adoption worker.

- Read the child's file.

- Talk to the child's therapist.

- Talk to the current and former foster parents.

- Talk to any social workers who have been involved in the case.

- Talk to any available birth family relatives.

In the past, agencies were very reluctant to disclose any information regarding the histories and needs of the children in foster care. The good news is that today agencies are increasingly realizing that adoptive parents must have full knowledge of the challenges that they will face in raising their children. With this knowledge, they will be able to do

Timesaver
Because children adopted from other countries could have had similar traumatic histories, or have been raised in orphanages, these questions should be asked when arranging an intercountry adoption also.

what is best for their children. In a recent survey of adoptive parents who adopted special needs children as recently as 10 years ago, the parents reported a need for full disclosure of information. A common response to the survey was, "Had we known what to expect with our child, what his needs were, we could have found the appropriate help much sooner. This would have saved both him and us much anguish and pain."

Today, special needs adoptions generally include more extensive training and preparation for the adoptive parents before the adoption. Adoptive parents in the survey also reported a need for ongoing post-adoption support and services from the agencies. Some states are responding to the need with the creation of adoption preservation programs. (See Chapter 12 for a complete discussion of the challenges of special needs adoptions.)

As I mentioned, nearly 62 percent of the children in foster care are children of a minority background. See Chapter 4 for more information on the ins and outs of raising adoptive children with a transracial or transcultural background.

The facts about foster adoption

As suggested earlier in this chapter, another option available to prospective adoptive parents is foster parenting. Children are placed with foster parents while their parents are given time to get their lives together and receive the appropriate counseling and services. In the past, only half of the children adopted from foster care were adopted by their foster parents.

Two factors will radically change the focus of state agencies' adoptions from the foster care system. First, recent scientific research has proven that abused and neglected children suffer further damage by multiple placements while waiting to be reunited with birthparents or adopted. Second, passage of ASFA, the law passed in 1997 by the federal government, has limited the amount of time that children can remain in foster care. In order to implement this law, the state agencies will be looking for more people who are willing to foster/adopt. (In some states, this is also referred to as legal risk adoption.) In this type of pre-adoptive situation, a child is placed with the family that is considering adopting the child. During this time, the goal remains a return to the birth home, but there is a strong probability that this will not be accomplished.

As the name implies, there is risk in this type of arrangement. It takes a very special person to be able to parent a child while waiting to see if the child will be reunited with the birthparents. Some of the issues to consider are:

- Will you be able to parent a child for a period of time with the knowledge that it is maybe in the best interest of the child to be returned to his birthparents?

- Will you be able to work on a daily basis toward reunification with the child's parents?

- Will you be willing to facilitate meetings with the birthparents and reinforce the importance of the birth family on a consistent basis?

- Will you be able to handle the grief of the loss of the child should that child be returned to the birthparents?

The bottom line

What can you expect to pay for domestic adoptions? It depends on the type of adoption and how the

Unofficially...
The good news is that the wait for special needs children is usually quite short. The entire process can be arranged in less than a year from initiation to placement in an adoptive home.

adoption is arranged. The National Adoption Information Clearinghouse breaks down the cost of each adoption discussed in this chapter as follows:

	Low	High
Agency Fees:		
Application fee	$ 100	$ 500
Home study	$ 700	$ 2,500
Post-placement supervision	$ 200	$ 1,500
Parent physical (each)	$ 35	$ 150
Psychiatric evaluation	$ 250	$ 400
Attorney fees:		
Document preparation	$ 500	$ 2,000
Petition and court fees	$2,500	$12,000
Advertising	$ 500	$ 5,000
Birthparent expenses:		
Medical expenses	$ 0 (insurance)	$20,000
Living expenses	$ 500	$12,000
Legal representation	$ 500	$ 1,500
Counseling	$ 500	$ 2,000

In the case of special needs adoptions, fees are not usually charged by the agencies. Also, adoption subsidies are available for those children meeting certain guidelines discussed in Chapter 7.

Just the facts

- Whether you find the birthparents yourself, with the help of an attorney, or through an agency, be prepared to ask the right questions as well as provide the right answers.

- Despite the fact that it is a rapidly growing trend in this country, not all experts agree that open adoption is the best choice. Many experts, however, believe it is the best arrangement for the child.

- In an open adoption, it is the birthparent(s) who make(s) the final decision concerning the placement of the baby.

- In the end, an independent adoption can cost as much as an agency-arranged adoption.

- It is estimated that by 2002, almost twice as many children in foster care will be available for adoption.

- Prospective adoptive parents need to carefully investigate the challenges that could be encountered when adopting special needs children.

GET THE SCOOP ON...
The pros and cons of international adoption
■ What the most popular countries require ■ The
bottom line on paperwork and costs ■ Tips to
make the trip easier

The Lowdown on International Adoptions

Chapter 4

In an international/intercountry adoption, U.S. citizens adopt children who are citizens of other countries and bring them back to the United States. This type of adoption has been popular in the United States since the 1950s, but the number of those adopted internationally has increased dramatically in the 1990s. In 1992, there were 6,536 international adoptions; in 1997, that number more than doubled to 13,620. In 1998, the number rose to 15,774 with even more expected in 1999 and 2000. As a result of the increased availability of children born in other countries, international adoption is becoming a big business.

Sometimes intercountry adoption is also big news, as it was with the situation in Romania in the early 1990s. Stories of corruption in the adoption industry appeared in the news media around the world. But experts caution that corruption usually occurs when a country is new to the intercountry adoption idea, and there are no rules and regulations to govern intercountry adoptions. According to a social worker experienced in intercountry adoptions, "It was a feeding frenzy as folks from many countries sought to rescue those kids without regard to whether they were actually free for adoption or whether they had been stolen, etc. Finally, Romania told us all to go home and don't call us, we'll call you, which they eventually did after they got their act together."

How can you avoid becoming involved in a political situation? How do you choose the country? What is the procedure for adopting from another country? In this chapter, I'll answer these questions and more. While adopting a child from another country can be a very rewarding experience, it is necessary for prospective adoptive parents to know all the facts before they proceed with the arrangements.

Intercountry adoption— what you need to know

Experts agree that intercountry adoption can be more complicated than domestic adoption. It's necessary to deal not only with the bureaucracy here in the United States, but also with a bureaucracy in another country, which results in a large amount of red tape. Often, the prospective adoptive parents are required to travel to the country itself, which can be expensive and stressful, but also rewarding and valuable. Nonetheless, there are advantages to adopting internationally which for many outweigh the disadvantages and risks involved.

The steps in intercountry adoption

To complete a private (independent) or agency-assisted adoption, you will have to follow a number of steps which I describe in this chapter.

You should take the following steps to complete an agency-assisted intercountry adoption:

- Find an agency using the guidelines in Chapter 2.

- Complete the home study.

- Put together your dossier (the documents you will need in order to arrange an international adoption). I'll discuss this in more detail later in the chapter.

- Request INS forms I-600A and I-600. Complete and mail I-600 to the Immigration and Naturalization Service (INS). These will be returned to be included in your dossier.

- Certify your dossier documents with the appropriate Secretary of State and authenticate the documents at the consulate of the birth country of your child.

- Accept a referral of a child from an agency (adoption proceedings begin in foreign court, and includes decree, birth certificate, relinquishment or abandonment certificates).

- Arrange travel; establish contact with translator, escort, or attorney.

- Go to court to accept placement and custody (may include adoption finalization depending on laws of the country).

- Get passport for child in country of birth, get visa photos.

- File documents and I-600 at U.S. Embassy for issuance of visa and travel documents.

- Participate in required post-placement services.

- Finalize adoption in the United States if required or desired.

- Request and file forms and participate in naturalization.

You should take the following steps to complete an independent (private) intercountry adoption:

- Choose country and check country/procedures with experienced families or support groups.

- Establish contact with an attorney, orphanage, or child welfare agency in the country of choice.

- Check contact's references in the United States through the embassy and other parents.

- Check with the U.S. Embassy in the country for complaints against the contact and for the country's political attitudes toward adoption.

- Select an agency to do the home study for an international adoption.

- Request INS forms as listed earlier.

- From the contact, get specific list of documents and authentications needed by the country.

- Begin collecting and authenticating documents.

- Send the documents to the contact via Federal Express.

Once you have the referral of a child, the procedure is the same as the one I listed for the steps of an agency adoption.

The advantages

Speed is the biggest advantage in intercountry adoption. You can bring home a relatively healthy infant from a foreign country in less than one year.

If you are older, you will find another advantage in the more generous upper age limits set by some countries for prospective adoptive parents. While most domestic adoption agencies set an age limit of

35 to 40 because of the competition for infants in this country, many other countries allow people in their forties and even fifties to adopt children of all ages.

You will also find less competition for infants and younger children in international adoptions. Because of this, foreign countries are more open to nontraditional adoptions, welcoming not only older adopters, but single men and women as well. One single adoptive mother, explaining why she chose to adopt internationally rather than in an open domestic adoption, said, "I had to compete with other prospective parents who were trying to sell themselves to the birthparents. This made me uncomfortable with the open adoption process. It was too much like a business deal."

The disadvantages

The disadvantages associated with international adoptions include:

- The tendency to be more expensive than domestic adoptions.

- The frequency with which adoption policies in foreign countries change. It is possible for an adoption attempt to fail because of a policy change.

- The requirement for one or both of the adopting parents to travel at least once to the country in which the adoption is arranged. The duration of the visits vary from country to country.

- The fact that you may not get important medical and family history for your child.

- The uncertainty about obtaining more information about your child for health reasons, should you need to know more.

Unofficially...
Experts have noted that since U.S. birthparents have been given more choice about where they place their infants, many seem to prefer couples under the age of 40.

> **"**
> While it might be a financial strain, traveling to the birth country of your child offers you a wonderful opportunity to see where your child is really 'coming from,' which you can tell your child later in order to establish a sense of past and continuity.
> —An intercountry adoption arranger
> **"**

- The uncertainty of financial aid available to you if you discover after the adoption has been finalized that you have a adopted a child with special needs.

- The risk of Reactive Attachment Disorder (see Chapter 12) if your child was severely neglected in an orphanage.

- The reluctance of some adopted children to be raised in a different culture.

The risks

Beyond the disadvantages, which for the most part can be overcome, a few serious risks are worth noting.

United States consular offices in many countries report that they continue to receive and investigate complaints from people adopting in their countries. While payments to adoption arrangers are part of the process in many countries, one of the main complaints is about adoption arrangers who take too much money to arrange an adoption. Another common complaint is about people who take money to arrange an adoption but never place the child. A couple who recently adopted their son in Romania reportedly paid a fee to a Romanian facilitator. "We don't know how much she got in the deal," the adoptive father said, "but it had to be significant. She made some cash."

"Black market" trafficking schemes in foreign countries also exist, and although rare, they provide babies and older children to unsuspecting adoptive parents. When these schemes are uncovered in a country, it is not unusual for officials in the country to search for these children throughout the world and require that they be returned to the birthparents.

As one adoptive mother explained, "We chose to adopt here in the United States because we felt it was a safer option. In the late 1980s, we were living in an Asian country where adoption of infants was extremely easy. It was simply a matter of making an application, paying a relatively small fee, and waiting a few weeks for the infant. Fortunately, as we were about to go to the appropriate government office with our completed application and our money, we saw the headlines of the Western newspaper published in the country. The newspaper story stated that the Asian parents of babies who had been stolen or coerced from them were joining forces to 'find their babies and force those who had illegally adopted them to return them to their birthparents.' We decided to wait until we returned to the United States to arrange a domestic adoption."

A recent report on television's *20/20* told a similar story. According to *20/20*, a judge in Sao Paulo, Brazil, was taking children from impoverished parents after alleging abuse and neglect. The parents claimed that these were false allegations. These children were quickly freed for adoption and adopted by parents throughout the world. Prior to the airing of the story, some children had been successfully traced, while others had reestablished contact with their birthparents in Brazil. The birthparents vowed they would fight to get their children back. The judge was removed from his position after the *20/20* investigation.

Incidents such as these, although rare, have not gone unnoticed by international adoption officials. In 1992, child welfare experts held a meeting in Manila, Philippines, to discuss "Protecting Children's Rights in Intercountry Adoptions and

Preventing the Trafficking and Sale of Children" and agreed on the following:

- If a child cannot be raised by his or her parents, the first step is to place the child with extended family.

- If an extended family placement cannot be made, every effort should be made to place the child domestically.

- The final option should be international adoption.

The Hague Convention

The Hague Convention on Inter-Country Adoption is a treaty being considered by the legislatures of countries around the world, including the U.S. Congress. If implemented, each signing country will create a Central Adoption Authority to preside over its adoption process and to work with the Authorities of other countries. Private adoption agencies would have to be certified by the Authority, as well as by the states in which they operate. The goals are to bring a level of protection to parents searching for an agency and to better protect children as well.

Avoiding the pitfalls

There are two ways to avoid placing unnecessary financial and emotional strain on yourself (and your family) if you are pursuing an international adoption.

The first is to put yourself in the hands of the experts at an agency. There are over 200 agencies in the United States handling international adoptions. Some agencies specialize in one particular country, while others arrange adoptions in two or more countries. Agencies are very familiar with the laws, trends, and attitudes in the countries in which they specialize. (See Chapter 2 to review how to find the right agency.)

If you choose to arrange the adoption yourself, you should become an expert on your country of choice. Not only do you need to know all the laws and regulations concerning adoption here and in the other country, you also need to know the predominant attitudes and trends of the chosen country. Network with as many people as possible who have adopted in that country. Try to find someone who has been to the country and, if you are adopting from an orphanage, who has visited the orphanage. Join a support group that might lead you to contacts in that country, attend classes and seminars, learn as much of the language as possible, and read.

Where the children are

It is almost impossible to determine at any given time where the most children available for adoption are located in the world. No international organization can provide reliable statistics. On the other hand, it is possible to determine which countries have been most popular with Americans in the past based on the number of orphan visas issued for intercountry adoption. For the years 1996 through 1998, the countries with the most children adopted by U.S. citizens were China, Russia, South Korea, Guatemala, Romania, and Vietnam, together accounting for about 75 percent of the total international adoptions.

In 1996, the children adopted internationally were:

- 64 percent female; 36 percent male
- 54 percent under one year old

Bright Idea
Once you have identified the country in which you plan to arrange an adoption, take courses at your local college or university that will give you insights into the culture and history of the country or area. If no courses are available to you, read everything you can find on the country.

- 35 percent 1 to 4 years old
- 8 percent 5 to 9 years old
- 3 percent over 9 years old

Remember, rules and regulations in various countries change often. While one day it may be legal to adopt in a certain country, the next day the same country will place a moratorium on all intercountry adoptions. It can also work the other way around.

International Concerns for Children, Inc., publishes annually the Report on Intercountry Adoption, which includes ten monthly updates. The report is a comprehensive and up-to-date compilation on international adoption and includes costs, waiting periods and types of children available for adoption. The report costs $20 and can be ordered from International Concerns for Children, 911 Cypress Drive, Boulder, CO 80303-2821, by telephone at 303-494-8833, or on the Internet at www.fortnet.org/icc.

The following is a brief overview of some of the rules, regulations, and requirements of some of the more popular countries as of this writing.

Programs in Eastern Europe
Russia

In 1990, children who were in institutions in Russia became available for international adoption. Since that time, approximately 15,000 children have been adopted from Russia and other former Soviet Republics. In 1998, Russia was the most popular destination for those seeking an international adoption, with 4,491 immigrant visas issued to orphans from that country.

According to the results of a recent survey conducted by the Cradle of Hope Adoption Center and

18 other adoption agencies, adoptions from Eastern European orphanages are "overwhelmingly successful." The surveys were mailed to 2,159 families with adopted children ranging in age from 1 month to 16 years, and 1,246 families returned the survey, reporting the following:

- Almost all (95 percent) of the families reported that their children's overall adjustment was good.

- The parents also reported that upon arrival their children's physical health (89 percent), their emotional health (87 percent), and their cognitive development (87 percent) were as they had expected.

- At the time of the survey, most children had mild or no developmental delays in their motor skills (95 percent), emotional maturity (88 percent) and physical size (85 percent).

- At the time of the survey, 90 percent of the younger children were reported to have good attachment to the family; 72 percent of the older children were reported to have good attachment.

Russian adoptions have received bad press over the last few years. A woman in Colorado was accused of killing her three-year-old Russian son who was diagnosed with Reactive Attachment Disorder. The woman claimed that he was self-destructive and killed himself. In another incident, two adoptive parents were convicted of beating their two Russian adopted daughters on the flight back from Russia. These reports and others in Russian newspapers have caused tension between the two countries in the adoption arena.

Experts emphasize that a small percentage of adopted children have suffered severe emotional and physical problems as a result of living in an institution for even a short period of time. The media has repeatedly reported on both the abuse and neglect in international orphanages. Recent research has also emphasized the importance of the first three years of a child's life. These facts cannot be ignored. There are families who have adopted children from Russia (as well as other countries and the United States) who will need a great deal of support in raising their adoptive children. (See Chapter 12 for more on the challenges of parenting abused and neglected children.)

More details on adopting in Russia:

- Couples must be married at least one, preferably two, years.
- Single women may adopt, and single men are considered.
- There may not be more than 45 years between the adoptive mother and the child.
- Parents may have been previously divorced and/or have children already.
- The time frame for a completed adoption is six to nine months after the documents have been completed.
- Children of all ages are available, including infants, as are sibling groups. The children have Caucasian, Asian, Gypsy, and Mediterranean appearances.
- Adopting parents may adopt two children who are not related.
- All adoptions must be finalized in a court in Russia.

- Usually, two parents travel for one week to 10 days. In some territories it's necessary to make a second trip if required by the court.

The details about adopting in the Ukraine:

- Couples, single men, and single women may adopt. Age is flexible, although you must be under 45 to adopt an infant. You may also adopt if you have biological children.

- Available children are over one year old (under one year with special needs are sometimes available).

- The travel required is one trip of three weeks, or two trips of four to five days each. Adoption is finalized abroad.

The details about adopting in Romania:

- Couples married three years or singles (single men on case-by-case basis) may adopt. Singles should be flexible concerning the age of the child they will adopt. No more than 45 years between the ages of adopting parents and the child is allowed.

- Available children are 18 months or older and of Caucasian and/or Gypsy ethnicity.

- Travel is required by one parent only, with a stay of one to two weeks. Parents may meet the child before accepting the child, which is not necessarily true in other countries. If the parent is unable to return to pick up the child, an escort will be available to travel with the child to the United States. Final adoption is abroad.

At this time, other countries in Eastern Europe are offering children for adoption. They include Kazakhstan, Bulgaria, Hungary, Belarus, Latvia,

Bright Idea
Keep a journal of your trip. Fill it with details of your trip, observations, and the names of people you meet. It will help those who stayed behind feel included in the journey, and it will be part of your adopted child's history.

Lithuania, Moldova, and to a much lesser extent, Albania and Poland.

Programs in Asia
China

In the last two years, China has been second only to Russia in the number of children adopted by Americans. In order to control the rising population and terrible famines of the 1950s and 1960s, the Chinese government passed laws to limit the number of children each family could have. Because of these laws, Chinese women who are unmarried or who already have the allowed number of children abandon infants in the hopes that they will be found and placed in loving families. Chinese culture and tradition emphasize the importance of the male child; therefore, far more female babies are abandoned than male babies. Experts who have visited Chinese orphanages report that they are adequate and improving.

More details about adopting from China:

- Married couples and singles (both male and female) may adopt from China. You may be divorced.

- China has recently lowered the minimum age requirement to 30 years old. Now people from 30 into their 50s may adopt.

- Most adoptions can be completed within a year with all the fees known in advance.

- Available children include infants, toddlers, and older children. Ninety-eight percent of all the children are female.

- There are no sibling groups, and only one child may be adopted at a time.

- You may have other children in your home, but China requires you to have at least one other child in your home if adopting a special needs child.

- One or both parents may travel to China. A special power of attorney is needed for the non-traveling parent.

- The stay in China is 10 days to two weeks. Your child will be with you much of the time.

- Fees and donations to the Chinese government are less than $5,000, with a required $3,000 donation to the adoption orphanage from which you adopted the child. (See "The bottom line—what it really costs" at the end of this chapter to figure additional costs.)

Vietnam

Vietnam has been open for intercountry adoptions for a number of years, but it has not been a popular destination until recently. Agencies that have programs with the country report that it is one of the easiest countries in which to adopt a child.

- Couples and single women may adopt, but they must be at least 20 years older than the child.

- Only one parent must travel to complete the paperwork. There is a two- to three-week stay if the parent waits to bring the child home or a travel time of one week to complete the paperwork only if the child is to be escorted back to the U.S. by someone other than the adoptive parent.

- Adoption is finalized abroad.

South Korea

Korea has been open for intercountry adoption since the 1970s. Children are not put in orphanages

Moneysaver
According to experienced travelers, take plenty of new $1 and $5 bills for buying things in Hanoi. The street vendors will only accept very clean, new-looking currency.

Watch Out!
According to the experts, certain agencies in South Korea require that neither parent weigh more than 30 percent over the normal weight for his or her height! Not all Korean agencies require this.

but are housed with foster parents. Unlike most other countries outside the United States, Korea does not prohibit the search for birthparents. The records will be made available to the adopted child if the child decides to search. Other requirements:

- Married couples must be married for at least three years. One divorce per member of the couple is allowed. No singles are accepted. You must be no more than 45 years old at the time the child is placed in your home.

- Your family income must be at least 125 percent of the poverty level, and there may be no more than four children already in your home.

- You are not required to travel to Korea; an escort is available to transport your child to the United States.

Other programs in Asia are available in Cambodia, India, Hong Kong, the Philippines, Taiwan, and Thailand. There are also programs in Japan and Nepal.

Programs in Latin America
Guatemala
Guatemala was the fourth most popular country for intercountry adoption in 1997 and 1998. The children are placed in foster homes soon after birth. They are usually of Hispanic, Indian, or Mestizo (a mixture of Spanish and Indian) origin.

Probably one of the reasons Guatemala is so popular is the fact that there are very few restrictions. There are no age requirements, and both married and single men and women may adopt. There is no limit to the number of children already in the home.

The typical wait is six to eight months. If parents choose to travel, the stay is only three days. An escort is available. Adoption is finalized abroad.

Other programs in South and Central America are available in Mexico, Bolivia, Peru, Ecuador, Chile, Colombia, Brazil, El Salvador, Haiti, and Honduras.

Choosing the right program for you

With so many adoption programs available throughout the world, how do you find the country that is right for you? Talk to as many people as possible to find out as much as you can about each country that interests you. Here are some points to consider:

- The country's requirements, such as age, divorce, and others mentioned previously. You may eliminate the country if you cannot meet the requirements.

- The children who are available. They vary according to age, sex, special needs, and appearance.

- The expenses involved and what is included.

- The political situation in the country. How stable is it? Does the program have a long history of success?

- Does the travel requirement appeal to you, or does it make you apprehensive? Remember this is your child's homeland. It's likely that your child will want to travel there again someday.

- Consider the language barriers, or the language that you might have in common. Some older children speak English as a second language.

Timesaver
Don't bother to submit an adoption application to St. Lucia unless you own land there. You do not have to be a resident, though.

Watch Out!
Be sure to do
your homework.
Countries
offering
programs and the
requirements for
individual
countries change
often. One good
place to find
information is in
the State
Department Web
site at
www.state.gov.

The documents you will need

The documents you will need in order to arrange an international adoption are referred to as your dossier. In general and depending on your situation, you will need three copies of each of the following documents:

- A valid, favorable home study by an agency or social worker licensed in the state in which the child will reside. Your social worker will have it notarized for you.

- A certified birth certificate for each adopting parent.

- A certified marriage certificate.

- A divorce decree for each divorce from the clerk of the court or a death certificate from a previous marriage if applicable.

- A financial statement including your assets, bank balances, and salaries. You and your spouse must sign it in front of a notary.

- A letter from your employer on company letterhead stating your position, salary, and length of employment. If you are self-employed, an accountant must write this up on his or her stationery and it must be notarized.

- Medical letters from your doctor stating that after a basic physical you are in good health. This must be on the doctor's stationery and notarized.

- A statement from the police stating that you are not a criminal. The INS requires fingerprints for the adoptive parents and anyone else in the household who is 18 years or older. (See later in this chapter to find out how to have your FBI criminal check completed.)

- Approval from the INS.

Some countries require legalization of documents. This legalization is called authentication. According to the State Department, "Generally, U.S. civil records such as birth, death, and marriage certificates must bear the seal of the issuing office, state capitol, then by the U.S. Department of State Authentications Office. The U.S. Department of State Authentications Office is located at 518 23rd Street, N.W., State Annex 1, Washington, D.C. 20520, tel: (202) 647-5002. Walk-in service is available 8 a.m. to 12 noon, Monday–Friday, except holidays. The Department charges $4.00 per document for this service, payable in the form of a check drawn on a U.S. bank or money order made payable to the Department of State."

INS requirements

You must apply to the Immigration and Naturalization Service to bring a child into this country. Call (800) 870-3676 to request the forms. Ask for two fingerprint cards (two sets for each person to be fingerprinted) with the forms. Identify the country in which you are arranging the adoption. They will send you the following:

- I-600A application for advance processing of orphan petition for use prior to identification of the child

- I-600 petition to classify the orphan as an immediate relative once you have identified the child

- Form I-864 affidavit of support

- FD-258 fingerprint cards

Bright Idea
You can download your passport application and INS forms on the Internet at www.lapa-nnj.com. Maintained by the Latin America Adoptive Parents Association, this Web site provides information on adopting and parenting Latin American children.

FBI criminal check

The INS requires that every prospective adoptive parent have an FBI criminal check. You must also have your fingerprints taken by the INS. When you submit your completed I-600A, you should do the following:

- Submit $25 for each prospective adoptive parent and for each adult member of the household over 18 years of age along with the $405 filing fee. The total fee may be in one check. Do not submit the completed fingerprint cards with the forms.

- After receiving your forms, the INS will send you appointment letters with the date and location for all the required members of the household to be fingerprinted. Read the instructions carefully and be sure to take all the necessary forms with you.

- Call to confirm the processing charge because it changes frequently. Call (202) 324-3000, the Fingerprint department, to obtain the charge.

Contact letter to the source

If you are arranging your own adoption without the help of an agency, in a country where such arrangements are legal, you may have to write a letter to the source indicating your interest in adopting to initiate the adoption process. The source is the person or agency who is arranging the adoption in the country. Sources include orphanages, government agencies, attorneys, facilitators, and agencies. Sources vary from country to country and program to program. Experts suggest your letter be around two pages in length, neatly handwritten or typed on quality stationery. Be sure to check to determine if

Timesaver
Be sure to advise the INS of the total number of individuals to be fingerprinted with the original applications. Failure to do so may cause weeks or months of delay.

the letter should be written in English or in the language of the country. Along with your personal feelings about the adoption, your letter should include the following:

- Your name, address, and telephone number

- Your age(s) and if applicable, the number of years married

- Information on other children in your family

- General health

- Religious affiliation if relevant to adopting a child in the country of your choice.

- Extended family members and their feelings about the adoption

- The reason you are seeking to adopt a child from this country

- The status of your home study

- Photographs of your home, children, and yourselves

- Affirmation of your desire to have or add to your family

- A statement that you will follow their requirements

- A statement that you have begun to read about their culture so that your child will know his or her heritage and be proud of the country of birth

If in two months you have not heard from this source, write again or call. It's recommended that you write to more than one source.

Making the trip

Be prepared! That's the consensus of those who have made the trip to another country to pick up

Watch Out!
Don't spoil it for those who follow. After you have selected to arrange your adoption with a particular source, notify other sources you contacted that you will not be working with them. This helps maintain goodwill with these sources.

their child. Even experienced adopting parents describe their emotions at the moment they receive their notification to travel as sheer panic, although it is mixed with profound joy.

There are usually several months between the time you receive your referral (notification that your child has been identified) and your notification to travel. Use that time to:

- Make sure your passport and visa are in order.

- Make sure that all your adoption papers are completed correctly. Put all your papers in a safe place that only you can easily access.

- Decide which clothes you'll be taking. You may need business clothes for court. Don't plan to wear shorts or loud clothes. Take comfortable walking shoes.

- Leave some room in your suitcase (or pack an extra duffel bag) for clothes you may buy for your child in the country. Also, leave room for things your child might not want to leave behind, such as a favorite toy or special blanket.

- Pack a camera and plenty of film. Register the camera with U.S. Customs before departure at the airport.

- Arrange to have ample money available either through your credit card or with traveler's checks. Do not take large amounts of cash.

Packing list for your new child

Assume that your child will need everything new. In this way, you will feel confident that you will have everything necessary to bring your child home comfortably. If you are adopting an infant, include the following:

- Some clothes for your child, including under-wear, socks, a cap, bibs, and pajamas

- Diapers (7 to 10 a day) and baby wipes

- Soy formula, since that is likely to be what the baby has been eating

- A "huggy-pack" and lightweight stroller for an infant; a lightweight stroller for a toddler

If you are adopting an older child remember to include:

- Several outfits, including shoes

- Underwear and socks

- Age-appropriate games (that don't require a knowledge of English) and toys for times in transit

Moneysaver
Remember, your child is growing and sizes will be difficult to judge. Take just enough clothes for the remainder of your stay in the country and the trip home. Check your local consignment shop for some great bargains.

Are we there yet?

In Chapter 9, I'll discuss the pros and cons of taking your other children along with you for the adoption. It's a great challenge to keep the children occupied during the long waits involved in the trip and in the hotel rooms. In case you do decide to take them along, experienced adoptive parents have compiled the following suggestions for items to include on your list:

- Crayons, coloring books, small toys, and stuffed animals

- Books, small compact games especially made for traveling

- Radio/tape player with tapes, batteries, and headphones

- Homework, crossword puzzles, a deck of cards

Getting there and back

Find a good travel agency in your area long before you know the exact dates of your trip. Some agencies specialize in adoption travel and may know how to save you money. The cost of the plane tickets depends on the day of the week you travel, the duration of your stay, and advanced booking. A savvy travel agent may be able to arrange to obtain waivers for some of these airfare rules.

You will, of course, need round-trip tickets for you and anyone traveling with you. For the child you will be adopting, you will need the following:

- Infants under two will need a ticket (10 percent of the adult fare) between the city of departure and the first point of entry in the United States. In the United States an infant under two can travel free.

- A child age 2 to 11 will need a ticket (two-thirds of the adult fare) between the city of departure and home. You may need to pay full fare if traveling in the United States. Check with your travel agent.

You can purchase the tickets either in the United States and carry them with you, or you can pick them up in the country as a prepaid ticket. Check with your travel agent.

Your travel agent can also recommend a hotel or other place to stay while you are in the country. If you are arranging the adoption through an adoption agency, the agency may make arrangements for you to stay at a hotel, a host family, or the orphanage.

Customs and Immigration

Before you enter the country in which you are arranging your adoption, you will go through that

Bright Idea
Confirm your reservations at least 72 hours before returning to the United States. If you do not, the airline may cancel your reservations.

country's Immigration control. This simply means that you will show your passport and Tourist Card, if you have received one on the airplane. The Immigration official will stamp your passport.

When you return to the Unites States, you will go through Immigration again. At this time, you will need to show the agent the packet of papers that you received for your child. The U.S. Immigration officials will stamp your child's passport with a temporary stamp indicating that your child is a legal resident alien. Your child will receive a permanent "Green Card" later. This is not a permanent citizenship. You must file for citizenship later. (See "What happens after you adopt?" later in this chapter for details.)

You will also be required to go through Customs. Here, the officials may or may not inspect your luggage. Be sure you know what you can bring into the country. Check with your travel agent or adoption agency prior to traveling. You can also find information on the Internet at www.customs.ustreas.gov.

Travel tips

The following are a few of the many traveling tips that experienced adopting parents have offered based on their own trips to a foreign country to adopt a child. It's important to network with experienced adoptive parents who have traveled to the country of your choice.

■ Remember that you are traveling to your child's homeland. Be sure you read all you can about the country and its culture before you go. While there, learn as much as you possibly can about the country and the people. Go to local markets, restaurants, and other places. This will help you answer your child's questions in the future.

- Arrive a few days early to adjust to the different culture and local customs. Be patient and remember you are a visitor in their country.

- Take your own over-the-counter medicines and prescription medicines.

- Take small gifts for the children in the orphanage if you will be visiting one, although you may be asked to leave these gifts in the office of the orphanage.

- Take a camera which develops the pictures instantly so you can hand out pictures to the children in the orphanage if it is allowed.

- Fax updates to the people at home. Faxes are much cheaper than phone calls.

- Because pretzels travel better than saltines, pack them to eat in case you start to feel sick.

- Take a measuring cup to measure your baby's formula.

- Before you go, make an appointment with your doctor for each member of the family who travels to have the necessary shots before you travel and a complete physical after your return.

What happens after you adopt?

In most cases, you will have finalized the adoption of your child before you return to the United States. Re-adoption is not required. If your spouse does not travel with you to pick up the child, it may be necessary to re-adopt your child in the United States.

Most parents do re-adopt their child in the United States because it creates a paper trail of your adoption. A court official takes notice of the adoption and initiates the process of issuing a birth certificate and adoption decree for your child.

Adoption professionals experienced in international adoption strongly recommend re-adopting in the United States.

If you do choose to re-adopt, you may need to have a post-placement home visit completed. This is simply an update of the original home study. Usually, the social worker from the agency who did the original home study will revisit your home about 30 days after your return to the United States. If your child has integrated into the family without any obvious problems, a post-placement report will be issued indicating that you be allowed to re-adopt in the United States.

As previously mentioned, your child will be issued a Green Card upon entry into the United States. Neither the Green Card nor re-adoption automatically makes your child a U.S. citizen. You must apply for and obtain U.S. citizenship for your child as soon as possible after returning home. You will need to submit to the INS Form N-643, the Application for Certificate of Citizenship. You can contact the INS directly, download the form from its Web site (http://doj.ins.gov), or obtain the form from your adoption agency.

Despite the fact that adopted children of U.S. citizens are supposedly considered "expedited cases," it could take up to three years to obtain citizenship.

The bottom line—what it really costs

It is very difficult to estimate the final cost of an international adoption. The costs vary according to many factors:

- Whether the placement entities in the foreign country are government agencies, government-subsidized orphanages, charitable foundations,

Unofficially...
The 1996 Immigration Act includes a provision requiring the deportation of non-citizen immigrants who are convicted of a felony charge. In one case, an adoptee was convicted as a felon and deported in March of 1996. His adoptive parents had never applied for his citizenship.

attorneys, facilitators, or any combination of these

- Whether the foreign country requires translation and/or authentication of the dossier documents
- Whether the U.S. agency requires a "donation" to the foreign orphanage or agency
- Whether the foreign country requires one or both of the adoptive parents to travel to the country for interviews and court hearings; could be more than one trip and of varying length

Agency fees could range anywhere from $10,000 to $30,000. (For a breakdown of agency fees, see the section "The bottom line" in domestic adoptions in Chapter 3.)

Along with agency fees, add in the following:

INS/State Department fees

Filing fee: I-600, I-600A	$405
Filing fee: N-643	$125
Immigrant visa application fee	$260
Immigrant visa issuance fee	$60

The following expenses vary from country to country:

- Travel expenses (transportation, hotel, meals)
- Foreign agency placement fee
- Foreign attorney legal and placement fee
- Foster and medical care for the child
- Use of translation and escort services by U.S. agency representative in the foreign country
- Foreign court filing fee and document fees (birth certificate and adoption decree)
- Required "donation" to the orphanage or agency

- Translation and escort services provided by the foreign agency
- Passport office fees
- Child foster care (usually in South and Central American adoptions)
- Child's medical care and treatment (occasionally in South and Central America)

The following is a sample of adoption travel expenses for a trip to Vietnam by two people, not including airfare:

Eighteen nights in a hotel	$840
Eighteen days meal expenses	$510
Transportation within the country (taxis, trip to and from airport)	$130
Bottled water, diapers, laundry, and similar items	$180
Food and drink while traveling	$100
Souvenirs	$450
Miscellaneous	$100
Contingency for emergency	$250
Grand total	**$2,560**

Naturally, the costs will vary depending on the country in which you are arranging the adoption and the agency that is assisting you with the adoption. The costs listed here will give you a general idea of what to expect if you pursue an international adoption.

Just the facts

- International adoptions can be quicker and the requirements for adoptive parents can be more flexible than in domestic adoptions.

- There are many risks involved in adopting internationally, but if you do your homework you can avoid most of them.

- You can make the trip to pick up your child easier by preparing well in advance.

- The costs of intercountry adoption vary according to a variety of factors, including fees and travel.

GET THE SCOOP ON...
Successfully arranging a single-parent adoption
▪ The ins and outs of gay/lesbian adoption ▪
Tips for adopting in the military ▪ How to do a
stepparent adoption ▪ Saying yes or no to
parenting your children's children

Ways to Build a Nontraditional Family

There's no such thing as an average adoptive family: More than 80 percent of the adoptive families formed today are nontraditional families. These include single-parent families, gay/lesbian families, kinship families, unusually large families, families in which at least one member has physical challenges, and various combinations of all the above. The good news is that if you can demonstrate a desire and the ability to raise a child, you will probably have the opportunity to adopt a child.

The two most critical requirements for successfully building a nontraditional family are determination and perseverance. While trends are evolving and nontraditional adoptive parents are proving their abilities to be good parents, you may still encounter old attitudes. Some social workers and attorneys in adoption still need to be convinced that nontraditional families not only work, but in many cases can be the best option for a child in need of permanent placement. If you are trying to build a nontraditional family, this chapter will explore the advice experts in the field have for you.

Single-parent adoptions

The number of single-parent adoptions is slowly increasing in the United States. In the 1970s, 0.5 percent to 4 percent of all adoptions were completed by single persons. In the 1980s, that figure jumped to about one-third of all adoptions being completed by single persons. Nine out of ten single adopters are female, and most singles adopt special needs children who are older, minority, or handicapped.

Evolving attitudes

Research over the last two decades has shown that single-parent adoptions have been very successful. In 1985, a study by J. F. Shireman and P. R. Johnson concluded that "single-parent homes may be particularly suited for children who need intense and close relationships and thus particularly appropriate for many of the older children in foster care who are now prepared for permanent homes. For some children, such a close bond may meet a need and be a path to normal development."

Today, the number of older children with special needs available for adoption has increased, and fewer couples are interested in adopting them, so many public and private agencies are turning to single adopters for help. Subsidies are also available for these children, which eases the potential financial burden on single adopters. Some agencies find single parents a better choice than two-parent families because of the following:

- Because of the extra intense screening process they have prior to adoption, they tend to be more qualified.

- There is a one-to-one parent/child ratio, which is better for some children.

- There is a more focused nurturing, which some children need.

- Single men can be good role models for some boys in need of strong male guidance.

Overcoming the obstacles

Many agencies still do not accept applications from single men or women. Even when they do, they may hesitate to tell singles up front that birthparents tend not to be interested in single parents for their children. The single adopter may be put at the end of the waiting list, where they could stay for years. Or, they may be offered only the older special needs child or siblings, who are traditionally difficult to place.

Steps in single-parent adoption

Thirty-nine percent of single parents, compared to eighteen percent of couples, make three or more attempts to adopt before successfully completing an adoption. Some steps you might find helpful in arranging a successful single-parent adoption are the following:

- Network with as many other single parents as possible. Find out how they completed their adoptions.

- Read as much as you can find on single-parent adoptions.

- Establish a strong support network of relatives and friends who will be willing to help you in parenting your child. Find role models for your child.

- Find good childcare for your child. Be prepared to show the agency that you can afford the

Bright Idea
An excellent resource for singles is *The Handbook for Single Adoptive Parents*, which can be ordered from the National Council for Single Adoptive Parents, P.O. Box 15084, Chevy Chase, MD 20825.

childcare and will have backup if you or the child is ill.

If you choose to do a domestic or intercountry adoption through an agency, you will need to find an agency willing to work with single prospective adoptive parents. Be prepared to prove yourself to the agency. You must show the agency that you are a stable, serious individual who has thought of all the possible pitfalls in being a single parent. Some things to demonstrate to the agency:

- You have considered your future social life and all the implications. Single adopters report that this seems to be of particular concern to agencies.

- You can show your ability to balance your life with the addition of a child.

- If you are a male, you are prepared to answer questions about your sexuality, your motives, friends, and living arrangements.

- You have determined which friend or relative would be willing to take over the parenting of the child should you become too ill to do so.

Singles adopting infants

If you are interested in an intercountry adoption, you will find that many countries encourage singles to submit applications. (See Chapter 4 for details.) It's also possible for singles to arrange adoptions with birthparents domestically either through an agency or independently. (See Chapter 3.) You should remember that you will be taking the same risks as couples who arrange adoptions with birthparents, and you should be prepared to prove yourself to the birthparents in the same way you would to an agency. Keep in mind that a birthmother may

Watch Out!
Some agencies are very reluctant to accept male applicants and may require you to take a test to determine if you are a pedophile. Experts agree it is best to volunteer to take the Minnesota Multiphasic Test.

wish to place her child with a single parent for the following reasons:

- She may be angry at men because of the circumstances surrounding her pregnancy.
- She may have had a positive experience in her own life with a single parent.
- She may find a male less threatening because there will be no competition between "mothers."

Lesbian and gay adoptions

The most controversial and legally confusing type of adoption is the adoption of children by gays and lesbians. (See Chapter 7 for a discussion of the legal aspects of lesbian/gay adoptions. Many agencies refuse to accept applications from gay men or lesbians.)

In 1988, the Child Welfare League of America issued its Standards for Adoption Service. In this document, the League stated that "Gay/lesbian adoptive applicants should be assessed the same as any other adoptive applicant. It should be recognized that sexual orientation and the capacity to nurture a child are separate issues. Staff and board training on cultural diversity should include factual information about gay men and lesbians as potential adoptive resources for children needing families in order to dispel common myths about gay men and lesbians."

Despite the controversy, lesbians and gay men have adopted in the past and continue to adopt today. In the past, lesbians and gay men tended to hide their sexual orientation when adopting a child. But this is changing. As a new adoptive lesbian mother explained, "We were forewarned by others who had adopted not to lie about our sexuality if asked outright. We were told that if we did lie, we

Unofficially...
In 1970, the American Association and American Psychological Association both stated that homosexuality is not a mental illness. Further research has demonstrated that homosexuals do not choose their sexual preference.

could lose the child if our lie were uncovered. Therefore, we told the truth right from the beginning. It may have taken us longer to successfully adopt a child, but we had the peace of mind knowing that we were not jeopardizing the adoption."

Gays and lesbians are also increasingly willing to speak out about their ability to parent children and feel they have established a right to adopt children. This movement, coupled with the increased number of special needs children available for placement with good families, has brought about an increase in the number of lesbian and gay adoptions.

In states where it is legal, public agencies take applications from lesbians and gay men. As with single applicants, be prepared to prove to the agency that you are capable of effectively parenting a child and be prepared to answer personal questions regarding your sexuality and lifestyle. If you feel that your social worker is not comfortable working with you because you are gay or lesbian, request another worker. If your request is denied, consider going to another agency. You should expect questions similar to the following:

- How long have you been "out"?
- Are you comfortable with your own self-image and the fact that you are lesbian or gay?
- Do you have the support of your family concerning your sexuality and living arrangements?
- Does your family support you in your desire to adopt a child?
- Is your present relationship stable?
- Have you and your partner discussed what would happen if the two of you should terminate your relationship?

Experts stress that society has been slow in accepting lesbians and gay men as suitable parents for adopted children. While it is true that a birthmother may occasionally choose to place her infant with a gay family for the same reasons she would choose to place her infant with a single parent, it is not the norm. Often gays and lesbians are chosen to parent the children who are "less preferred" and harder to place. In *The Lesbian and Gay Parenting Handbook*, April Martin points out that "nontraditional families have unique strengths that make them excellent, and in some cases, the best homes for certain children." Martin also maintains that gay men and lesbians are uniquely capable of doing the following:

- Accepting differences
- Understanding what it's like to be in the minority
- Demonstrating flexible gender roles
- Being open about sexuality with children who have been sexually abused
- Understanding the needs of homosexual children

It is essential to network with other gay and lesbian individuals who have successfully adopted children of all ages. (Also, see Chapter 14.)

Adopting if you have a disability or illness

Experts advise potential adopting parents to hang in no matter what their physical history. If you have a history of illness or are currently disabled, you can still adopt a child. Social workers and some attorneys attempt to match a child with a person who can be of the most benefit to the child. Therefore, if you are disabled, you have something to offer a child with a disability that no one else may be able to offer—experience and understanding.

If you have been physically ill in the past and can prove that you are capable of raising a child in your present physical condition, many agencies will consider you as a prospective parent. "Few people go through life without some kind of illness," an adopting mother remarked at a recent support group meeting. "I was afraid to tell our social worker that I had been on medication two years ago for depression. When I finally told her, I was very surprised to learn that she had taken the same medication for depression in the past. It made no difference as I was no longer taking the medication."

It will be up to you to persuade the agency or birthparents that you will be able to raise the child. Be prepared to do the following:

- Search until you find an agency or birthparents willing to consider you as an adoptive parent.

- Provide a statement from your doctor indicating the status of your illness, including a statement that it is not life-threatening. (Existing suicidal tendencies or severe depression may be considered life-threatening.)

- Convince an agency that you will be a good parent for a child. The agency will have understandable concerns and questions—it's their job to keep the best interests of the child in mind.

- Be flexible. Consider special needs, transracial, or transcultural children.

Forming the half-and-half family

Parents who already have biological children may also find a need to convince agencies and birthparents

66
We were surprised to find that some agencies were reluctant to allow us to adopt because we already had eight children. We had to do a lot of convincing before they would consider us. My advice is to be prepared with an answer for every conceivable objection.
—Susan, adoptive mother of nine
99

that they should be able to adopt another child. As discussed in Chapters 3 and 4, both agencies and foreign bureaucracies have various requirements concerning the number of children that may already be in the family. They may also have restrictions that are based on whether the children already in the family are adopted or biological. Check the requirements of the agency and/or the country in which you pursue an adoption. (See Chapter 11 for ways to blend the half-and-half family.)

Adopting while in the military

The transitory nature of life in the military has kept many families from successfully completing their attempts to adopt. Agencies hesitate to begin an adoption process with the knowledge that a family could move before they could complete the process. Families have also found it difficult to meet the requirements of home ownership and mandatory meetings that most agencies require. Furthermore, families have found it difficult to prove to a new agency that the initiating agency in another state did as thorough a job as the new agency would require. Therefore, military families have been reluctant to apply to adopt, at least in the past.

This trend is beginning to change as agencies realize that they have overlooked a vast resource of prospective adoptive parents. The federal government is supporting projects designed to assist military families in completing adoptions started by adoption agencies in Pennsylvania, Virginia, Arizona, Alaska, Tennessee, and Washington, D.C. Agencies that have started to work with military families find the following positive characteristics:

- A great ethnic diversity exists in military families. Racial and cultural diversity are also present in the military and civilian neighborhoods in which they live.

- Military families are entitled to adoption benefits up to $2,000.

- Military personnel and their families are eligible for free medical care at any military medical facility.

- Military families are moving less now that the Cold War has ended, and they are better able to comply with residency requirements.

- Military personnel are not transferred to remote areas where a member of their family, including an adopted child, cannot receive specialized medical care if the need for such care is known.

- There is a huge support network when a spouse is away on a tour of duty.

If you are in the military, already stationed overseas, and wish to adopt a child from the country in which you are stationed, several agencies with bureaus abroad can help you. One agency, The Pearl S. Buck Foundation in Perkasie, Pennsylvania, works with military families throughout Asia in countries such as Japan, Korea, and Guam. Agencies in the United States that do not have intercountry resources can contact the International Social Service, American Branch, in New York City for help.

Recently, Virginia State University conducted an evaluation of the Virginia DSS' Military Family Recruitment Project. The result of the evaluation determined that there are many advantages to having military personnel adopt, but many disadvantages in the process. A focus panel made

Unofficially... If you are transferred overseas before you have completed the adoption process, inform the agency that you can still legally adopt a child from the United States through the Interstate Compact for the Placement of Children because military bases overseas are considered to be on U.S. soil.

recommendations to help facilitate adoption for military personnel. Among the recommendations were the following:

- Military families should be made aware that they can receive a humanitarian deferment (up to a year) if time is needed to finalize an adoption.

- Adoption agencies should also be made aware of the humanitarian deferment and take this into consideration when working with military families.

- Military social service staff should become more aware of post-adoption services available to families adopting special needs children.

- Support groups for military adoptive families should be established at the military bases with the assistance of state and military personnel.

For more information on adopting in the military, contact the Adoption Exchange Association, 14232 E. Evans Avenue, Aurora, CO 80014.

The adoptions that choose you

Today, almost half of all adoptions in the United States are kinship (or relative) adoptions. Kinship adoptions are adoptions by a relative either by blood or through marriage. From the years 1944 to 1975, statistics show that the number of kinship adoptions steadily increased. In the late 1980s and 1990s, there was a sharp increase in the number of kinship placements as children entering foster care were placed first with relatives. These placements were often finalized as kinship adoptions.

The vast majority of kinship adoptions are stepparent adoptions, in which the biological child of one parent is adopted by that parent's new spouse.

Also common is the adoption of a child by a relative, usually one or more of the child's grandparents. Generally speaking, relative adoptions are much easier than non-relative adoptions and require a much shorter time to complete. Many of the normal steps in adoption can be waived or consolidated because of the circumstances. In many states the adoption can be completed without the home study and the adoption hearing, shortening the waiting period considerably.

Stepparent adoptions

This type of adoption usually occurs after one biological parent dies, has never really been a part of the family, or has lost contact with the family after a divorce. The biological parent who is raising the child has remarried, and the new spouse wishes to legally adopt the child or children. As in any adoption, the welfare of the child is of primary importance, and stepparent adoption should only be considered after the emotional impact on the child has been taken into account. As Cathy Jo Faruque, a licensed independent social worker, points out in her article, "The Changing of America's Families," "Stepchildren face many problems, not the least of which is the loyalty conflict. Many stepchildren are trapped by their feelings of love and identification with the absent biological parent and the growing attachment to the stepparent. Absent parents may express feelings of rejection if their children verbalize positive feelings for the stepparent." Some of the issues that you should consider when contemplating a stepparent adoption are the following:

- Your child's potential to experience a conflict of allegiance between the birthparent and the adopting parent. You can help your child develop a strategy for coping with these feelings by talking with your child.

- Your child's potential feelings of anger, rejection, abandonment, loss, or resentment. These feelings may surface at various stages in your child's development.

- Whether or not adoption by the new parent will bring a feeling of stability to your family.

- Your desire to have the stepparent take over parental rights and duties should something happen to you.

- The birthparent's willingness to give up all legal parental rights, including rights to visit and make decisions about the child.

- Your willingness to ask the court to terminate parental rights, if necessary.

- Your willingness to give up child support payments to you and your child from the birthparent once the adoption occurs.

If a stepparent adoption seems to be the right route for your family to take, and the non-custodial parent has agreed to give consent to the adoption, the process of adopting the child can go very smoothly. On the other hand, the adoption can become quite complicated if the birthparent does not agree to give up legal rights to the child or has not been in the picture for many years. There are several ways to proceed with the adoption if the birthparent is not willing or available to give consent.

Legally terminating parental rights

You may petition the court to legally terminate parental rights because the non-custodial parent has not exercised parental rights for a period of

Moneysaver
If your state does require a home study for a stepparent adoption, check to see if your local social service agency will do the home study for little or no money.

time, usually a year in most states. The parent has not exercised parental rights if the parent has not supported the child or has abandoned the child. Abandonment usually means that the parent has not communicated with the child for over a year. You may also prove to the court that the parent is in some way an unfit parent, such as having a mental illness, and should therefore lose parental rights.

Presumed fatherhood

It may also be possible in some states to prove to the court that the father does not meet any of the tests in your state for presumed fatherhood, which will result in the court terminating his rights and allowing you to proceed without his consent. In all states, a man who is married to the woman at the time she gives birth is presumed to be the father of the child, as is a man who agrees to marry the mother after she gives birth and places his name on the birth certificate.

Who inherits what?

If a stepparent legally adopts a child while the child is a minor, the child becomes the legal heir of three parents—the two natural parents and the stepparent. If the stepparent legally adopts the child at or after the age of 18, the child becomes the legal heir of two parents: the custodial natural parent and the stepparent. Should the stepparent and the natural parent divorce and the stepparent then adopts the child as an adult, the child becomes the legal heir of only the stepparent. The child loses any inheritance from both his natural parents.

Steps in stepparent adoption

The steps in a stepparent adoption are relatively easy:

- Check out the law in your state. Experts advise hiring an attorney.

- Contact the court in your county to determine which court handles adoptions, if the court requires you to have an attorney, and where to obtain the legal forms.

- Submit the required paperwork.

- Check to see if your hearing date has been set.

- Appear in court for the hearing in which the date of the finalization of the adoption will be set.

- Finalize the adoption, which varies from state to state.

- Apply for amended birth certificates.

Unofficially...
In some states there are no laws which require you to hire a lawyer to handle the adoption of your stepchild. Especially if the other biological parent is not contesting the adoption, consider filing your own petition. It can save you thousands of dollars.

Parenting for the second time around

Another form of kinship adoption is the adoption of a blood relative. While all types of relatives do adopt other relatives, most often in America today, it is the grandparents who take over the job of raising a child when their own sons and daughters cannot fulfill their parenting obligations. The grandparents feel compelled to take over the job of raising the child in a healthy and nurturing environment. An estimated 1.3 million American children are being raised by relatives other than their own parents. The number of grandparents raising their own grandchildren has increased more than 40 percent in the last 10 years.

According to the American Association of Retired Persons Grandparent Information center, the typical grandparent/caregiver who calls his or her hotline is a female, age 59. Fifty-seven percent who call are caring for one grandchild and, on average, have cared for a grandchild (or grandchildren) for at least four years.

Kinship care is not new. The idea that "It takes a village to raise a child" had its origins in ancient African cultures, which encouraged relatives to help raise the child when the parents were not able to do so for some reason. In the past, extended family units were closer both emotionally and geographically. But family systems have changed along with the economic structure of our society. In most families both parents must work, and raising children has become very expensive. What was once "just one more mouth to feed" has become a list of costly necessities including daycare and education. The decision to adopt a relative deserves the same careful thought and consideration as any other type of adoption.

Saying yes

In recent years, social workers have been investigating the benefits of kinship care and are attempting to place children with family members before seeking other placements. As always, the welfare of the child is the first consideration. The benefits of kinship care include the following:

- Moving in with a relative may lessen the sense of loss the child will have. The child will have the same relatives, aunts, uncles, cousins, and will be able to maintain a sense of family.

- Because the child will be in a relative's home, the child will not be traveling through the foster care system, which often means many different placements.

- The child will be better able to maintain contact with the parent or parents (which may not always be desirable) and parents may be able to be included in many of the child's activities.

■ The child will be better able to maintain a connection with family and childhood history, and therefore have a better sense of identity.

Pros and cons of saying no

In many cases, grandparents make the decision to raise their grandchild or grandchildren because they are emotionally unable to let their grandchildren go to live with foster parents and eventually be placed with adoptive parents. They do not want them to live with strangers and are afraid they will not be part of their lives any longer.

Experts urge grandparents to focus on the child's best interests when considering the child's placement with them. As one adoptive mother explained, "My two girls were placed first with their paternal grandparents. They were unable to care for them, and they were returned to foster care. Next, they were placed with a paternal aunt who also decided she could not care for the girls. Finally, they were returned to the foster care system and had four more placements before we adopted them. Much damage was done by these multiple placements."

In addition to the costs of raising one or more children, consider the following:

■ Because most of these children have had some sort of family crisis, even abuse and neglect, or exposure to drugs, it may be difficult to get the appropriate help to meet their needs. Are you prepared to deal with these problems, and do you have a plan for getting needed help?

■ Without legally adopting the child, the birth-parent can return at any time to take these children out of your home.

- Will you enjoy your retirement caring for young children? Will your friends want to be around young children for more than short periods of time, and if not, are you ready to make some new friends? Will you find ways to enjoy your time as the primary care provider for young children, and will you be able to find baby-sitters for the times you need to do other things?

- Other members of your own family may not agree with what you are doing or may be jealous of all the attention you are giving to these grandchildren. Are you ready to acknowledge these emotions and help these family members through them?

- If you do not legally adopt the child, the birthparents have the legal right to make medical and educational decisions. You may even have to take care of the birthparents if they are unable to take care of themselves due to mental illness or alcohol or drug abuse.

Can you complete the job?

Grandparents must also truthfully evaluate their own health and ability to "go the distance" if their grandchildren require lengthy care. Experienced grandparents who have been successful in raising their grandchildren offer the following suggestions:

- Establish firm ground rules for both yourself and the birthparents.

- Set clear limits about who is really raising the child. If the birthparents have clear rules about who is making what decisions and agree to follow these rules, the child will have less confusion about who is really in charge. This becomes particularly important when the child reaches adolescence.

- Disengage yourself from your own children's problems and do not pass on any negative attitudes about your children to your grandchildren.

- Deal with your grandchildren as individuals.

A permanent plan

Most families raising related foster children do not choose to adopt them. Nearly 85 percent say that because they are already a family, adoption is unnecessary. But there are many reasons why arranging a permanent plan could be a better choice for you and for the child. In some cases the birthparents are deceased, or they will be forever unable to care for the child. There are several alternatives open to you if you decide to seek a permanent way to handle the situation.

Legal adoption

As in any other adoption, this form of adoption terminates the rights of the natural parents and gives the adopting relative the same rights and responsibilities as the natural parents would have. If the biological parents refuse to terminate their rights voluntarily, the relative must take them to court and prove that they have abandoned or neglected the child or that they are suffering from a mental illness. If you can prove this, and you are able to adopt the child, the birthparents will have no rights to him or her, nor will they have any responsibilities, including custody payments. If you do decide to legally adopt the child, the following will be true:

Bright Idea
You can determine who will care for your grandchild should you die by naming the appointed person in your will. The court will have to approve your selection.

- Once the adoption is final, the biological parent cannot terminate the adoption except for unusual reasons such as duress and fraud, assuming that they have consented in the manner required by your state or have had their parental rights terminated by the court.

- You will become totally responsible for the financial support of the child.

- You will be able to apply for Aid to Families with Dependent Children, temporary assistance to needy families, but they will take your income into account as you are the legal parent.

- If you adopt your grandchild, all public benefits will end with the exception of benefits to a special needs child if the child already qualifies. If you are receiving foster care benefits, they will end with the adoption.

Guardianship

There is one more option open to you if you wish to have your grandchild live in your home on a permanent basis but do not want to legally adopt him because of an existing relationship the child has maintained with one or both of the biological parents.

If the parents are unwilling to legally terminate their parental rights, and you do not wish to force them to do so in court, you may be able to establish a legal guardianship. A court investigator will interview you, the child, and the legal parents to determine if a legal guardianship is the best option. The court investigator will then make a recommendation to the court. The judge will review the case and appoint you the guardian after a hearing in court.

Legally, the financial support of the child will remain up to the legal parent or parents, but in reality, the guardian usually becomes responsible for the financial support of the child. You may pursue financial benefits for the child such as public assistance and Social Security. Often, an annual financial report will be required by the court.

The failure rate of kinship placements may in large part be due to the financial burden placed on relatives who cannot afford to raise these children. In response to this, at least 10 states have developed subsidized guardianship programs to help relatives who are willing to care for children in their family but cannot afford to do so. As of this writing, many other states are working on establishing subsidized legal guardianships in order to comply with the new federal law, the Adoption and Safe Families Act (see Chapter 6). Check to see if your state is among those that offer a subsidized guardianship.

Before you agree to becoming the guardian of a child, consider the following:

- You will be taking on the responsibilities of raising a child, including the liability for the child's actions.

- You may be monitored by the court. You may need to keep careful financial records, which you must provide to the court, and you will need to go to court to gain permission to handle certain financial matters.

- Will the guardianship have any negative ramifications on your own family, job, or health?

- Do you have the time and energy to raise the child?

Watch Out!
If a child lives with you without a legal agreement, you may have problems registering the child in school, arranging for medical care, or obtaining benefits on the child's behalf. Be sure to check the laws in your state.

- Are you willing to spend your own money on the child if necessary?

- Will there be any problems with the child's other relatives who may take issue with how you are raising the child?

- Will the child's parents (both of them) be open or hostile to the guardianship?

- A guardianship lasts until a child reaches adulthood, so be sure you can fill this role for however long that will be.

Where to find help

Parenting for the second time around presents unique challenges to grandparents. Times have changed since the first time you parented, although you have the advantage of wisdom gained from experience. You may find that the sources of support you used the first time are either no longer appropriate or available. It is extremely important for you to find the right kind of help. (See Chapter 14.)

Just the facts

- The trends in adoption have changed in the last two decades, allowing more nontraditional families to be formed.

- Adoption by singles has become increasingly accepted in the last decade, but singles may still have to work a little harder than couples to arrange an adoption.

- As early as 1988, the Child Welfare League of America supported lesbian and gay adoptions.

- Adoption agencies are becoming aware of the large number of people in the military who want to adopt and are attempting to make the process easier for them.

- You should be just as careful to do what is right for the child in a kinship adoption as you would in any other type of adoption.

Taking Care of More Business

PART III

GET THE SCOOP ON...
Understanding the new federal law ▪ How states
differ and agree on adoption ▪ Legal issues in
gay/lesbian adoption ▪ Reform movements in
adoption law ▪ Avoiding scam artists ▪ What to
do if you've been scammed

Laying Down the Law

Chapter 6

Only a few federal laws directly affect adoption today. While the federal government has a great deal of influence on the states because it stipulates how federal funds are distributed, the real power lies at the state level, where laws not only vary, but are also constantly changing. The laws change in response to new trends in adoption, to the interpretation of courts hearing cases concerning adoption, to activists and advocates for reform, and to the occasional mandates of the federal government.

Adoption law can be very confusing because laws not only vary from state to state, but may be interpreted differently from county to county within a state. I will give you a brief education in the basics of adoption law in this chapter, but I urge you to seek the advice of legal experts in your state who can guide you through your state's maze of laws and legal interpretations.

The lowdown on ASFA

On November 19, 1997, President Clinton signed into law the Adoption and Safe Families Act (ASFA).

The intention of ASFA is to provide safety and permanence to children in foster care. As a result of this law, twice as many children could be available for adoption from the foster care system by the year 2002. A complete overview of the law can be found on the Internet at www.naswdc.org/govwk/safeadop.htm.

In order to comply with the law, state legislatures, child welfare agencies, and courts have been reevaluating and changing their laws and procedures. They must shorten the amount of time a child waits in foster care to either return home or to be placed in a permanent adoptive home.

In the past, a child would be removed from an abusive or neglectful home and placed in one or more temporary foster homes, becoming part of the foster care system, where the child would languish for years. It was not unusual for a child in the foster care system to wait anywhere from two to seven years for a permanent placement. Some would "age out of the system" before ever finding a permanent home. ASFA was passed to address this serious problem.

What the law really does

The first intent of the law is to provide for the safety of children at home and in out-of-home care by requiring the following:

- Consideration of the child's health and safety as the primary concerns when removing a child from the home or returning a child to the home.

- Waiving efforts to preserve a family or reunify a family where a court determines that a child's health or safety would be endangered.

- Attention to the child's safety in case plans and reviews.

> **"**
> The intention of the Adoption and Safe Families Act is to keep the promise of safety and permanence to children in foster care according to a child's sense of time.
> —Joan Louden-Black, Massachusetts Assistant Commissioner, Placement and Family Based Services
> **"**

- Criminal record checks for final approval of foster and adoptive parents. A state may choose not to follow this provision.

The law also provides incentives to the states and individuals for adoption and other permanency options. The law encourages permanent placement of children by stating the following:

- Adoption incentive payments will be made to states that increase the number of adoptions of foster children, with higher payments for special needs children.

- Once reunification with the family is determined to be impossible, the law specifies that reasonable efforts toward permanency must be made in a timely manner.

- The law requires states to provide health insurance coverage for a child who could not be placed without it because of the child's need for medical or mental health services.

- The law requires that the time frame for the court procedure for terminating parental rights and final placement in a permanent home be significantly shortened.

- The law breaks down geographic barriers between states by prohibiting states from delaying or denying an adoption of a child when an approved adoptive parent from out of state is identified.

- The law provides for a continuation of assistance for an adopted child whose previous adoption dissolved or whose adoptive parents died.

The law also provides for the states to be accountable in developing and implementing standards of safety for children in their care. To find summaries of state legislation enacted in response to ASFA, log on to the Internet at www.ncsl.org/statefed/cf/ asfasearch.htm.

Making placements permanent

What does this mean to the individual states? It means that each state's social service agency will receive large sums of federal money if the state increases the number of adoptions of foster children in a given year. The bonuses are $4,000 for each foster child adopted and $6,000 for each special needs foster child adopted.

Among other projects, the states are redesigning programs and training social workers to satisfy the provisions of the new federal law. In order to facilitate placing children in permanent homes as quickly as possible, state social service agencies are initiating new programs such as:

- Concurrent planning (two plans in place at the same time—one to return home and one for another permanent placement) that provides a permanent goal for the child when it is unlikely that the child will return home

- Initiating a renewed emphasis on placing children with relatives for temporary foster care and permanent placement if necessary

- Implementing court improvement projects to facilitate and speed up the court's involvement in the placement of the child in a permanent home.

- Developing photolisting sites on the Internet. Thirty-seven states have developed their own sites, while all but eight states participate in national photolisting services such as The

National Adoption Exchange and/or the Faces of Adoption.

- Improving the state's capacity to comply with the Interstate Compact on Placement of Children by educating judges, attorneys, and caseworkers.

The Indian Child Welfare Act

Another major federal adoption law, The Indian Child Welfare Act (ICWA), was passed by the U.S. Congress in 1978 in response to the disproportionately large number of Indian children who were being removed from their tribes and placed in non-Indian foster care. It had become the practice of many social workers to remove children from their tribal culture with the hopes of integrating the children into the general society. As C. Steven Hager of the Oklahoma Indian Legal Services points out, "In 1977, a study by the Association of the American Indian Affairs showed that 25 to 35 percent of all Indian children had been removed from their family and placed in foster, adoptive, or institutionalized care at some point in their life. The adoption rate for Indian children was eight times higher than for non-Indian children. Ninety percent of those adoptions were to non-Indian homes."

When holding custody hearings for an Indian child, state courts must follow the provisions of the Indian Child Welfare Act. Among the provisions of the ICWA are the following:

- An Indian child must be placed for adoption by the court with a member of the Indian child's extended family, other members of the Indian child's tribe, or other Indian families.

- An Indian child must be placed in foster care or pre-adoptive care in the home of the Indian child's extended family, a foster home licensed, approved, or specified by the Indian child's tribe, or by a non-Indian licensing authority. The Indian child may also be placed in an institution approved by the Indian tribe or operated by an Indian organization.

After a child has been adopted, an Indian child has a right to search for information about his tribal culture and heritage. The court is required to give only enough information to allow the child to enroll in the tribe.

Where the power actually is

Most of the laws relating to adoption continue to be passed on the state level. Therefore, the laws vary greatly from state to state. It's up to you to know the laws in your own state in order to protect yourself from mental anguish and sorrow. The first place to look for the answers to your questions is with a licensed adoption agency or an experienced adoption attorney. If you wish to find preliminary information about your state's adoption laws, you can call a local adoption support group or your local social service agency. You can also find some information in your local library.

Experts recommend that you know the answers to the following questions that pertain to your situation before you seek to arrange an adoption. Some of the questions you might ask are:

- If you wish to arrange the adoption yourself, does your state allow private (independent) adoptions?

- Is a pre-placement home study required in your state, or can it be completed after the child is in your home?

- Is there a putative father registry in your state? (See the next section for details, and Chapter 15 for a discussion of the birthfather's rights.)

- Does your state allow the father to give consent to adoption before the child is born?

- How does your state handle an unknown father situation or a father that the birthmother refuses to identify?

- How long does a birthparent have to change his or her mind about placing the infant for adoption?

- When is the adoption finalized?

- What expenses can you legally pay in your state for the birthmother, birthfather, or birth family? What are the laws regarding this in the birth state?

- Are there any court cases or legislative activity that may change the law while you are in the process of adopting?

- If you are gay, lesbian, or single, are there any laws that will affect your ability to adopt in your state?

- Is there a law in your state requiring you to hire a lawyer to complete your adoption? Are you required to hire a lawyer for the birthparents?

- Does your state require separate counseling for birthparents and adoptive parents?

Putative father registry

In some states, a man who believes he has fathered a child may register his alleged paternity in a putative father registry. This assures the man that he will be notified if a child is actually born and will be placed for adoption. This also serves as a protection for prospective adoptive parents as they will be

Watch Out!
Adoption laws are changing constantly. State courts and legislatures are responding to the Adoption and Safe Families Act as well as to activists who are clamoring for reform. Make sure you know the law!

assured that the birthfather will be aware of the planned adoption before it is a fact. In most states with such a registry, he will not be able to claim rights at a future date if he has failed to register his impending fatherhood.

Consent

Consent is given by the birthmother and, ideally, by the birthfather for the child to be adopted. The states differ as to when consent can be given and how long the birthparents have to change their minds or revoke consent. In some states, consent may be given any time before or after the birth; in other states it may not be given until 10 or 15 days after the birth. In one state a consent may be irrevocable when signed, while in another state, the birthparent may have up to 90 days to withdraw consent.

Finalization

The states also vary greatly on the amount of time that must elapse between placement of the child in the adoptive home and the court hearing to finalize the adoption. It varies from "upon placement" in Kentucky to as long as one year in Louisiana.

The legal lowdown on gay/lesbian adoptions

The states also control laws that address the issue of gay/lesbian adoption; because of this, the law varies greatly from state to state.

As of this writing, the only states that actually ban gay, lesbian, bisexual, or transgender people from becoming foster or adoptive parents are Florida and New Hampshire, although New Hampshire will likely change its stand on gay and lesbian parenting. On March 18, 1999, the New Hampshire House of Representatives voted to lift the 11-year ban on homosexuals becoming foster or adoptive parents by an overwhelming majority. The bill still needs to pass the senate and be signed by the governor before it will become law.

Other state courts and legislatures have been grappling with the issue of gay/lesbian foster parenting and adoption:

- In December of 1997, a New Jersey court ruled in favor of allowing a same-sex couple to openly adopt a child who was in state custody. This ruling was the result of a class-action lawsuit.

- In August of 1998, the House passed a bill forbidding unmarried couples in Washington, D.C., including gays and lesbians, to adopt. The bill was dropped, but it is expected to be resurrected in 1999.

- In 1998, anti-gay/lesbian measures were introduced in Arizona, California, Georgia, Oklahoma, and Tennessee. All were defeated.

- It is expected that similar anti-gay/lesbian measures will be introduced in Indiana, Michigan, and Texas in 1999.

- In January of 1999, the Child Welfare Agency Review Board in New Jersey passed a resolution that would ban gays and lesbians from becoming foster parents and/or adoptive parents.

- In January of 1999, Arkansas and Utah became the first states to adopt regulations that in essence prevent gays and lesbians from becoming adoptive or foster parents.

This is just a small representation of the battles that are taking place in state legislatures and social service review boards. It is obvious that this is an issue that needs to be addressed and settled.

Unofficially...
Gay and lesbian activists point out that there could be as many as eight million gay men and lesbians already parenting in the United States today. Many of these are raising children from heterosexual marriages, but gays and lesbians have always adopted children.

Timesaver
Stay up to date on the frequent changes in law and court decisions on gay/lesbian adoption issues on the Internet at www. GayLawNet-GayLawNews by Subject Children.

Gay and lesbian activists also point out that there are far more children waiting to be adopted than there are heterosexual couples and singles waiting to adopt them. Adoption professionals agree that there is a shortage of those who are willing to adopt the older children, especially those who are in sibling groups.

In the past, same-sex couples were able to adopt in a roundabout manner. First, one partner in the couple would adopt as a single parent. At a later time, the second partner would do a second-parent adoption similar to that of a stepparent adoption. This is usually an easier adoption, not requiring a home study and waiting periods, but in many states co-adoption is not allowed for any non-married couples. (See Chapter 5.)

Most states allow singles to adopt a minor child as long as it is determined that the adoption is in the best interests of the child. As of this writing, no state allows unmarried couples to adopt. Since no states allow same-sex couples to marry either, no same-sex couples may adopt as couples.

In 1996, President Clinton signed into law the Defense of Marriage Act, which stated that for all federal purposes marriage is defined as a union between one man and one woman. The states can still pass laws or amend existing laws that deal with state issues. The Supreme Court in the state of Vermont is dealing with legality of gay/lesbian marriage at this time. Many gays and lesbians have found that they can travel outside their own state to adopt legally under the law of another state.

Not everyone agrees that gay/lesbian adoption is in the best interests of the child. According to Gracie S. Hsu, a policy analyst at the Family Research Council in Washington, D.C, "A recent Harris public opinion poll found that nearly two-thirds of Americans oppose adoptions by homosexuals. Only 15 percent approve of the practice." Hsu further states that "The National Committee for Adoption estimates that there are more than one million heterosexual married couples waiting to adopt...adoptive children are best served when they are placed in married-couple households (which) can provide a stable and safe environment for children..."

Be sure to check your state laws and recent court decisions when seeking to arrange an adoption in your state. At this time, according to the NAIC, the following states allow second-parent adoptions for same-sex couples: Alaska, California, Colorado, Connecticut, District of Columbia, Illinois, Indiana, Iowa, Maryland, Massachusetts, Michigan, Minnesota, Nevada, New Jersey, New York, Ohio, Oregon, Pennsylvania, Rhode Island, Texas, Vermont, and Washington. In each of these states only one court has allowed second parent adoption. In four states, Vermont, Massachusetts, New York, and New Jersey, a higher court has found in favor of second-parent adoptions, which makes it a binding law.

The need for reform

In 1978, President Carter convened a panel of experts in the field of child welfare. The panel was given the task of addressing issues of adoption reform and drafting model state legislation. The panel drafted the Model State Adoption Act that was later watered down by lobbyists in favor of sealed records in adoption.

In August of 1993, the Baby Jessica case made headlines throughout the United States. Baby Jessica was taken from a seemingly happy adoptive

Unofficially...
In 1997, the North American Council on Adoptable Children gave its Adoption Activist award to a gay Virginia father who adopted five boys.

home and returned to her birthparents. The need for universal safeguards was apparent to all involved in the area of adoption. This need became even more apparent when Baby Richard was taken from his adoptive home and returned to his birthparents in 1995.

Marcy Wineman Axness, a lecturer and writer on adoption issues, noted, "It was in the absence of these crucial ingredients of conscientious adoption practice that the seeds were sown for the anguish of Babies Richard and Jessica; neither birthmother had adequate, unbiased counseling, something that might have led them to make more considered, timely choices, including to honestly disclose the fathers' names; nor were they supported in exploring alternatives to adoption." Despite the fact that individual states tightened laws that made it more difficult for birthparents to get children back, the adoption community called for reforms on a country-wide level.

In response to this clamor for reform, the National Conference of Commissioners on Uniform State Laws drafted The Uniform Adoption Act (UAA) in 1994. The act, which was intended to unite the adoption community in the protection of the adoption triad, has opponents among many of those it was intended to unite, including the Child Welfare League of America, Adoptive Families of America, Catholic Charities USA, Concerned United Birthparents, National Adoption Center, and the Joint Council on International Children's Services.

One of the more outspoken opponents of the UAA is the American Adoption Congress (AAC), formed in 1978 with a membership consisting mainly of adoptees. The AAC stresses that any adoption law should do the following:

- Protect the right of children to grow up in the home of the birth family

- Place children with adoptive families that can meet their needs while maintaining connections to their birth families

- Protect and support the integrity of the adoptive family once formed

- Assure that financial gain is not a factor in the placement of a child

The AAC and other opponents believe that the Uniform Adoption Act of 1994 fails to protect the adoption triad for many reasons, including the following:

- The act permits adoptive parents to pay for many of the expenses incurred by the birthmother, which highlights the vulnerability of the birthmother.

- The act does not provide sufficient provisions for counseling for the birthparents nor does it indicate who will pay for the counseling.

- The act states that the birthparents have only 192 hours after the infant is born in which to change their minds.

- The act requires a pre-placement evaluation, but does not require that the evaluation be completed by a licensed agency or individual.

- The act calls for the adoptive parents to continue contact or communication with birth family members, but this is unenforceable.

- The act calls for the records to be sealed for 99 years.

- The act encourages the business of brokering infants as it allows any person to help a prospective adoptive parent locate an infant for adoption.

The discussion continues and, although various states have considered passing the Uniform Adoption Act, as of this writing, no state has done so.

The Interstate Compact

The Interstate Compact for the Placement of Children (ICPC) is an agreement among all 50 states to facilitate the transfer of children from one state to another for the purpose of adoption.

The state where the child is born is called the "sending" state. The ICPC coordinator in the sending state must do the following:

- Determine that the legal rights of the birthparents have been legally terminated.
- Gather the genetic history of the birthparents and the hospital medical records of the child.
- Give approval to leave the birth state.

The ICPC coordinator in the "receiving" state (the state in which the adoptive parents reside) must have an adoption study conducted to determine that the adoptive parents can provide a safe and nurturing home for the child.

Once the two ICPC coordinators have performed their respective tasks, approval is given for the adoptive placement. Depending on the states involved, approval can be given before the birth of the infant or within four weeks following the birth.

Who would be refused parenting papers?

The easy answer to this question is: Anyone can legally adopt a child as long as the person can prove that he or she is a fit parent. In reality, it's much more complicated. Again, each state has a different set of laws governing adoption. In some states there is a residency requirement of six months to a year. Some states require you to be a certain number of years older than the adopted child. For example, California requires adoptive parents to be 10 years older than the adoptee. In Idaho the requirement is 15 years.

If you have a criminal record, whether or not you can adopt depends in great part on the type of crime you committed. Keep in mind that you will have to prove to either the agency or the birthparents that you will be a fit parent. The same would hold true if you have a debilitating illness. While there are no laws to prohibit you from adopting, you would probably have to wait a longer time and be more flexible when you decide which child you will eventually adopt.

Your day in court

Every adoption, whether domestic or international, needs to be approved by a court. In an international adoption this is often completed while the child is still in the country of adoption. You may decide to redo the court procedure again in the United States. (See Chapter 4 for reasons to re-finalize an intercountry adoption.)

Legally speaking

The court procedure consists of the filing of a petition and a court hearing. The petition filed by you will include:

- Your name(s), age(s), and address
- Your relationship to the child to be adopted

Watch Out!
It is a violation of the ICPC to travel across state lines with an unrelated child for the purpose of adoption without approval of the sending state and the receiving state.

Bright Idea
It's estimated that only 1 percent of adoptions are contested legally. Thousands of adoptions are completed successfully because people make the effort to practice good adoption procedures.

- The legal reason that the birthparents' rights are being terminated

- A statement that you are the appropriate people to adopt the child

- A statement that the adoption is in the child's best interests

Along with the petition, you must file either a written consent from the birthparents or the court order terminating their rights along with a request for the official name change of the child.

After you have filed the petition, you may have to notify the following people depending on your state's laws:

- The biological parents

- The adoption agency

- The child's legal representative if the court has appointed one

- The child, if the child is old enough (12 to 14 years in most states)

At the hearing, the court will determine that the adoption is in the child's best interests and will issue the final decree of adoption.

How to make it personal

Many people choose to make their day in court a special day for the immediate and extended family. They invite other family members to join them in court for the finalization, followed by a formal or informal celebration.

Many families also choose to celebrate this day as a special day each year. The parents of two adoptive and two biological children explained, "We celebrate the finalization day of each of our adoptive children as family anniversaries. In this way, we all have one more day to celebrate; our biological kids don't become jealous because they are also included in the celebrations." (See Chapter 11 for more celebration ideas.)

The truth about the lawbreakers

While most adoptions are arranged by law-abiding individuals or agencies and are completed legally, there are exceptions. In both international and domestic adoptions, you can fall prey to an adoption scam. You can avoid losing time and money if you make yourself aware of adoption scams and how they work.

The modern scams

The profile of adoption has changed with the times, and so have the types of scams that are practiced by unscrupulous individuals and agencies.

In all types of adoption, certain red flags should cause you to think twice and possibly find another attorney or agency to arrange your adoption. If the agency or attorney cannot justify the expenses, the following should be considered red flags:

- The agency, attorney, or birthmother asks for a lot of money up front.

- As time goes on, you are required to provide more money for special or unexpected expenses.

- The agency or attorney asks you to pay a "finder's fee."

Reputable agencies and attorneys will provide itemized expenses in writing and will offer payment plans that don't require all the money to be paid at the beginning.

Most adoption agencies are reputable agencies that have no motive other than to place children for

Moneysaver
Even if the law in your state does not require you to have a lawyer, it could save you thousands of dollars and much heartache if you hire a lawyer to finalize the adoption.

adoption. Unfortunately, there are those who portray themselves as representatives of licensed agencies, but in truth are individuals only interested in making a profit from your desire to adopt a child. In the summer of 1997, a couple in St. Louis lost $11,500 trying to adopt a child. The couple began working with a man who said he was a contact for a Pennsylvania-based agency that was endorsed by the United Methodist Church. After the couple paid the man $11,500, the contact disappeared. This incident emphasizes the need for the careful selection of the adoption agency or attorney. If you have followed the guidelines in Chapter 2 on how to choose a good agency or attorney and have made your choice, the following should alert you to a potential problem with that choice:

- You are promised the placement of a child in an unreasonably short period of time. (See the chapters on the types of adoption for reasonable time frames.)

- The agency cannot promise you reasonable and available medical records for your child.

- You are offered child after child who do not meet your requirements.

- You feel you are being pressured into adopting a child who may not be right for you.

- Your wait for the correct child exceeds a reasonable time frame as discussed in the various types of adoption.

- The agency or attorney suggests an easier way to adopt that would avoid certain laws and requirements, which would result in your breaking the law.

Timesaver
While it might seem to be taking extra time and effort to choose the right agency or attorney, it will pay off in the end. Do your homework up front by thoroughly checking references (see Chapter 2).

- The agency or attorney suggests anything that does not sound legal to you.

It's possible for a potential birthmother to scam a couple, and it happens. The scam is simple. A woman will answer an advertisement placed by a couple wanting to adopt. She will take money from the couple and then disappear. She will do this over and over, making a great deal of money for herself. Often, she is not even pregnant. Recently, a warning was posted on the Internet by the mother of a girl who was involved in a scam: "Please warn potential parents about placing adoption ads in newspapers. I have a grown daughter who has responded to these ads for the past 10 months, [and] when she started she was not even pregnant. Throughout this time she has contacted and met with several families. She has also received a great deal of cash as well as trips to meet the prospective parents. I have tried to stop this by contacting local authorities, the attorney general, and even the postal inspector, but all to no avail. She is currently in contact with a new family using stories of no food and the need for assistance to obtain cash. She has used different names each time so there is no way to identify her. She also changes her phone number frequently and uses addresses of friends. I am very concerned for these families who are so trusting."

Some countries outside of the United States have weak legislation and little control over their adoption practices. As a result, widespread corruption in the international adoption community is reported. Activists are calling for tighter international controls to prohibit illegal adoptions. They urge the ratification of the Hague Convention on Inter-Country Adoption (see Chapter 4).

Unofficially...
There are no reliable statistics concerning how many successful adoption scams are completed each year because couples who have been scammed are reluctant to report the scam to the appropriate authority.

Bright Idea
Contact the Office of Children's Issues, Bureau of Consular Affairs, of the U.S. State Department for addresses of the embassy and consulate in the country in which you are adopting. Write to these agencies to inquire about any complaints they have received concerning adoption scams.

Other countries are attempting to solve the problem domestically. For example, Russia recently introduced a controversial bill into its parliament that would tighten regulations on the intercountry adoption of children from orphanages throughout Russia. Opponents of the bill are afraid that it will result in more children remaining in Russian orphanages with no hope of being adopted.

What to do if you are scammed

Often, people do not report scams to the authorities because they are embarrassed, feel it's useless because they will not get their money back, and are too burned out to do anything about it.

The best thing to do is report the scam to the proper authorities. You may not be able to recover your own expenses, but you may be able to prevent the same thing from happening to another unsuspecting victim.

You should report any irregularities to your state licensing bureau, the Attorney General's office, the Better Business Bureau, and your local parent support groups.

A word about wrongful adoption

In the last 10 or 20 years, some couples who have adopted "healthy" infants or older children have subsequently brought damage suits (called wrongful adoption cases) against the agencies that arranged the adoptions. The adoptive parents have alleged that the agencies did not provide complete and accurate health records to them before the adoption was arranged. While many of these agencies, both public and private, may not have intended to scam the prospective adoptive parents, the courts determined that they did withhold information that was necessary to making an informed and appropriate decision regarding the adoption. Also, many parents feel that the knowledge of a physical or emotional disability would have allowed them to find the appropriate services and early intervention, which would have been of help to both the parents and children.

As more and more of these actions are brought to court, new laws are being passed in state legislatures, and agencies are changing their procedures. This has resulted in agencies providing more disclosure of pertinent medical and psychiatric information to prospective adoptive parents. (See Chapter 16 for a discussion of the controversy over open records.)

Just the facts

- ASFA was passed by the federal government to protect children first and find a permanent home second.

- The Interstate Compact is an agreement among states to make interstate adoptions possible.

- Adoption laws vary from state to state and change often.

- Reforming adoption laws is a highly controversial issue debated by many in the adoption business.

GET THE SCOOP ON...

Budgeting for all your adoption expenses ▪ How to raise money ▪ Getting your employer to help ▪ Tax credits you can use ▪ Tapping into subsidies for your child

More Dollar Signs

Chapter 7

The cost of adopting a child goes up each year. It's not unusual for an individual or couple to spend thousands of dollars in the adoption process. Adoption advocates fear that the high price of adoption is preventing many prospective parents from realizing their dreams of adopting a child.

The high price of adoption can be overwhelming. Few individuals or families have $20,000 to $30,000 immediately available for their adoption expenses. In response to this problem, the federal government, some state governments, adoption agencies that offer sliding-scale fees, and major companies in the United States are providing some answers to help take the financial sting out of the adoption process.

In defense of agency fees

"Adoption agency fees are often a source of hidden tension between clients and their adoption agencies, particularly when social workers do not explain them and adoptive parents are (understandably) afraid to ask for an explanation," says Deborah

McCurdy, the adoption supervisor at Beacon Adoption Center in Great Barrington, Massachusetts. When McCurdy and her husband started their own agency after adopting their own children, they realized the hidden costs of running an adoption agency. They learned how one home study translates into many hours of labor-intensive paper work, assistance with documents, phone calls, bookkeeping, supervision, and travel. Counseling a birthmother in a domestic adoption and doing business overseas add to the expenses. Of course, there are the normal expenses of running a business as well, such as insurance, salaries, accountants, attorneys, licensing studies, office equipment, advertising, other recruitment efforts, supplies, rent, utilities, continuing education, and mandated donations to other nonprofit organizations.

McCurdy suggests that adoptive parents might appreciate knowing that "most of the people employed by adoption agencies are sharing in their financial sacrifice. A social worker specializing in intercountry adoption typically earns far less than he or she would in private practice or another agency setting, and his or her hours tend to be longer."

Reviewing the high cost of adoption

In Chapters 3 and 4 I broke down the estimated costs of both domestic and international adoptions. The following is a quick review of those costs:

- Domestic and international agency fees range from $1,285 to $5,050.
- Attorney fees start at $3,000 and can go as high as $14,000.
- Advertising for a birthmother can cost as little as $500 or as much as $5,000.

- The birthparent expenses range from $1,500 to $35,000 in some cases.

- The filing fees for the required paperwork in an international adoption add up to an estimated $850.

- Travel expenses for an international adoption typically range from $2,000 to $3,000.

Patricia Irwin Johnston, an adoption educator and adoptive parent, advises prospective adoptive parents to also prepare for unanticipated adoption expenses such as the following:

- A newborn's illness, or a birthmother's complications

- Higher fees for foster care if a delay occurs in the birthparents' decision to place the child

- Counseling for the birthparents

- Lost money if a birthmother changes her mind

- Difficulties with the local bureaucracies in an international adoption, which will necessitate a longer stay in a foreign country

Reviewing the price of parenthood

Johnston also encourages adoptive parents to be realistically prepared for the financial impact of raising a child. She says, "For the infertile, family building is an expensive business! After several years of supplementing patchy health insurance coverage for medical treatments and then exploring options and finding loans or working the extra hours needed to finance adoption, many adopters have not given much thought to the financial realities of parenting. For those unprepared, money matters in raising a child contribute to the stress of adjusting to a new family configuration."

Get out your pencil, paper, and calculator and do some realistic financial planning for your future. The following issues should be considered and added to your budget prior to the arrival of your child:

- How you are going to finance the adoption expenses.

- A possible increase in your health insurance with a new child in the family who will need coverage.

- A possible change in your living situation based on the needs of your child. Determine if it will be necessary to move within the next few years. If so, do it now before the child arrives. (See Chapters 8 and 9 for more information on how and why to make the decision to move.)

- A possible change in the transportation you are using. Will you be able to transport your child comfortably and safely? If not, this may be the time to reevaluate your transportation needs.

- The benefits, if any, that will be available to you from your employer. (I will be discussing these benefits in detail later in the chapter.)

- How you will be adjusting your budget for the added costs of a child. Begin saving now for unexpected expenses in the future. What you don't use immediately can always be put into the post-high school fund.

- The possibility of you (or your partner) taking time off when your child first arrives. Experts recommend at least a year for the child to be in the full-time care of her new parent. If you are single, determine if you can arrange extended leave or vacation, work at home, or change to part-time for the recommended adjustment period.

- How you will provide daycare for your child. Investigate the possibilities and determine how much it will cost you. Start saving for daycare expenses now.

- The possibility of you or your partner not working in order to raise your child.

- Having a will drafted to protect your child's inheritance and provide for your child's future.

- Purchasing life or disability insurance if you don't have it already, in order to protect your child's future should you become disabled or die.

Preparing financially for the risk

As I've said before, adoption is a risky business. All the different types of adoption pose some financial risk for you. (See the chapters on the types of adoption.) While there isn't much you can do to prepare for the emotional impact of an unsuccessful adoption attempt, consider establishing an emergency fund to reduce the financial impact.

How to finance your adoption expenses

Your adoption expenses can be one of the largest expenses you will have after the cost of your home and an expensive car. For many, the amount of money needed to arrange an adoption can be overwhelming, especially when adopting a second or third child. If you begin now, you can creatively put together the amount of money needed for the adoption. Remember, you may have a year or two before a child is placed with you.

Borrowing from yourself

If you can take the entire amount of money for your adoption from your savings, you can skip the rest of

Bright Idea
Many daycare facilities have waiting lists. Even though you may not know exactly when your child will be needing daycare, it's never too early to add your child's name to the waiting list.

this section. If not, you may be able to borrow your own money from stocks, bonds, or 401(K) plans if your employer offers a plan that will let you do so. These loans are usually low-interest and may be enough to finance some or all of your expenses.

Borrowing from a bank

Most banks do not offer loans specifically for adoption. Banks do finance adoptions, but they do not classify the loans as adoption loans. In 1996, First Union in Rockville, Maryland, the sixth-largest U.S. banking company, started a pilot program offering adoption loans. The program was extended to cover all of Maryland, Virginia, and Washington, D.C. Check to see if your local bank offers adoption loans; if not, you have other options. If you own your home, you may be eligible to borrow on the equity, or you may be able to refinance your home.

A home equity loan has the following advantages:

- It is usually a low-interest loan.

- Payments on the loan may be tax-deductible.

- Most banks offer a home equity line of credit and will provide you with a checkbook. You can use these checks to pay the adoption expenses as they occur.

- You pay interest on the loan balance. As the balance goes down, so does the interest.

Borrowing from your credit card

Many adoption advisers suggest borrowing the money from your credit card. Some even suggest obtaining a new card which offers a low rate for the first six months and using the tax credits you will be receiving in order to pay off the balance before the significantly higher rate goes into effect. Use caution when using your credit card!

Borrowing from family members

Parents and other relatives may wish to be very supportive of your quest to adopt a child and be willing to help you finance all or some of the expenses. Be sure to work out your financial agreement in writing.

Raising the money

Some employers offer adoption benefits, which average around $2,000 per child. Check to see if your employer offers these benefits. If your employer does not already offer them, advocate for it to start offering adoption benefits in the future. Later in the chapter I'll discuss how to convince your employer to offer benefits. If you're lucky, by the time you will need the money, adoption benefits will be part of your company's benefits package.

Angie Taake of International Adoption Resource suggests other creative ways to raise money:

- Sell something you own. Check to see if you have any collections or possessions that would be of value to someone else.

- Ask your church to sponsor your child. Perhaps your church will sponsor a fundraiser for your child.

- Ask your extended family to sponsor your child. Suggest that they donate money instead of buying gifts for you and your family.

- Make craft items and sell them at local bazaars or flea markets.

- Hold a variety show with volunteer performers.

Saving the money

One financially wise way to "find" the money you need for your adoption expenses is to begin living today as if you already have your child living with

Unofficially...
According to *Working Mother* magazine, October, 1966, Eli Lilly offered a maximum of $10,000, making it the company with the most generous adoption benefits.

Bright Idea
If you own your own business, you may be able to offer yourself up to $5,000 in adoption benefits, and your business won't have to pay taxes on that revenue. Check with a tax consultant.

you. Put aside all the money that you would spend on food, clothes, toys, and other necessities for your child on a daily basis. This will give you a true idea of how much money it will cost to raise your child and may also provide a substantial amount of money toward your adoption expenses. Once you have determined the cost of daycare, start putting that amount into your adoption account.

Saving the money ahead of time has the following benefits:

- You will not be adding the stress of a large loan repayment to the stress of adjusting to a new child in your home.

- You will be accustomed to paying for many of the expenses involved in raising a child.

- You will have adjusted to living with less "disposable" money.

What your employer has to offer

In 1990, a survey by Hewitt Associates reported that approximately 12 percent of companies offered employee assistance in adoption. In 1996, another Hewitt Associates survey found that the number had almost doubled, with 23 percent of companies offering adoption benefits. While this is still not a significant number of companies supporting adoption, it's encouraging to note that the trend is going in the right direction.

In 1993, unpaid leave for adoption was mandated under the Federal Family and Medical Leave Act. This act allows individuals in companies with 50 or more employees to take up to 12 unpaid weeks off after adopting a child without jeopardizing their employment with the company. The company is also required to continue health benefits during the 12-week leave. Some states also require employers to offer their workers a minimum amount of parental leave.

As adoption has become more and more accepted as a viable method of building a family, more companies are becoming aware of the need to offer support to those employees who are considering adoption.

Company plans vary considerably in eligibility, amount of coverage, support services, and types of adoption leave. In 1996, *Working Mother* magazine noted that other benefits were offered by the 100 companies surveyed, including $20,000 for infertility treatments at TIAA-CREF, and a five-week paid leave for new adoptive mothers at Merrill Lynch. You'll need to research your own company to see what it will offer you. Contact your human resources department to find out the answers to these questions:

- Do I have to be a full-time employee to be eligible?

- Is there a requirement for length of service?

- Do I need to be enrolled in the company insurance plan?

- How much will you reimburse me for my adoption expenses?

- Do you reimburse for specific expenses and do you do that as a lump sum payment or as expenses accrue, or do you reimburse only for medical expenses through the company's medical plan?

- If you pay for specific expenses, what expenses will you cover?

Moneysaver
If you are insured by group health insurance through your work, check to see if your maternity benefits cover the medical expenses of the child's birthmother.

- Do you have a company legal plan that would cover my legal expenses?

- When do you pay the benefits?

- What kinds of adoption does the plan cover?

- Is there an age limit for the adopted child?

- Can I take a paid leave for the purpose of adoption?

- How many weeks of leave am I entitled to?

- Can I accrue my vacation time toward a leave?

Some companies have no set time limit for leaves but negotiate them on an individual basis. Other companies offer a combination of paid and unpaid leave.

Some companies offer support services to their employees who are considering adoption. Find out if your company offers access to the following information:

- Adoption information such as referrals to support groups and licensed adoption agencies and organizations

- Support in arranging adoptions such as stepparent, relative, or legal risk adoptions

Negotiating with your employer

If you work for one of the 75 percent of companies that do not offer any adoption-related benefits, it may be possible to negotiate with your company to begin offering them in the future.

According to Debra G. Smith of the NAIC, employers are finding many positive reasons to offer adoption benefits. She says, "More and more companies are offering benefits packages and many want to keep pace with their colleagues. In addition, legal actions have consistently supported the equity

> ❝
> When you discuss your plans, you may find that your employer has some difficulty dealing with the timing of an adoption leave. Your employer may be stymied by a statement like 'We don't know when the agency will contact us.'
> —Lois Gilman, *The Adoption Resource Book*
> ❞

consideration." She gives the following reasons for a company to sponsor such plans:

- *Equity.* It's only fair that employees who adopt should receive the same benefits as those who have children biologically.

- *Goodwill.* The company receives goodwill, positive publicity for its sensitivity, and workers feel greater loyalty to the company.

- *Social benefit.* Children and families benefit from the company support.

- *Low cost.* Since fewer than 2 percent of the employees use the benefit, it is very cost-effective.

Military benefits

The military will reimburse its personnel on active duty up to $2,000 per child with a maximum of $5,000 for one family in a single year, even if both parents are in the military. The benefit is paid after the adoption is finalized, but only if the adoption was arranged through a state adoption agency or a nonprofit private agency. Fees that can be reimbursed are the following:

- Agency fees

- Placement fees, including birthparent counseling

- Legal fees and court costs

- Medical expenses, including hospital and other medical expenses of the birthmother and the child

People in the military are eligible for leaves similar to those offered by civilian companies.

The truth about the tax breaks

The Adoption Tax Credit bill was passed as part of the small business/minimum wage bill in August of

Timesaver
Find other employees in your company who might be considering adoption and who would be willing to help you advocate for adoption benefits. If you all do your research, it may take only one meeting with a representative to convince the company.

Unofficially...
After finalizing the adoption of a child with special needs from the public welfare system, parents may apply for reimbursement of their expenses related to the adoption up to $2,000. This is a one-time payment of non-recurring adoption expenses.

1996. It allows adoptive parents to claim a tax credit on their federal income tax returns for qualified adoption expenses. The provisions of this tax credit are as follows:

- The credit can be claimed for an adoption that was never finalized, but that amount must be applied to the maximum amount on a second adoption.

- The tax credit limit is for expenses for each adopted child rather than an annual limit.

- The tax credit is for all types of adoption, but after 2001 it will apply to only domestic special needs children.

- The amount of the credit is up to $5,000 for each child, or up to $6,000 for a domestic special needs child.

- The tax credit is progressively phased out for high-income families. The phase-out begins with those who have an adjusted gross income of $75,001 and is phased out completely when the adjusted gross income reaches $115,000.

- The tax credit actually reduces your dollar-for-dollar tax liability. If your tax bill is smaller than the credit due, the credit may be carried forward for five years.

The tax credit covers qualified expenses including adoption fees, attorney fees, and travel costs such as transportation, meals, and lodging.

The lowdown on the Hope for Children Act

On February 4, 1999, U.S. Representative Tom Bliley (R-VA) and Senator Larry Craig (R-ID) introduced the Hope for Children Act in the U.S. House of Representatives. Along with increasing the tax credit to $10,000 for all adoptions, this bill improves the existing tax credit bill by providing the following:

- The Hope for Children Act is indexed for inflation so that the credit rises along with the cost of living.

- This act will be in effect for all adoptions, not only domestic special needs beyond 2001.

- Full credit can be claimed up to an adjusted gross income of $150,000, gradually phased out for adjusted gross incomes of $150,000 to $190,000 and does not apply for incomes over $190,000.

As of this writing, the bill is in the Ways and Means Committee in the House and the Finance Committee in the Senate. Representative Bliley is an adoptive parent who feels that more should done to promote adoption. "Today, thousands of children are without permanent families. It is time we all work together to fix this problem. We owe it to these children to put aside political differences and pass pro-adoption legislation this year," said Bliley.

If passed, the act will go into effect immediately and cover adoptions finalized in 1999.

Still more tax breaks

Adoptive parents can take the same dependency exemptions and child tax credits on their income taxes for their adopted children as they would for biological children. They can also take exemptions and credits on children who have been placed in their home for adoption but have not been finalized.

Be careful. You must prove to the IRS that you provide for more than half of your child's expenses,

Watch Out!
There are expenses that the tax credit will not cover. Review IRS Publication 968 to clarify what expenses qualify. Contact the IRS at (800) 829-1040 or on the Internet at www.irs.ustreas.gov.

especially if you are receiving a subsidy for your child. For example, if you are receiving $6,000 a year, you must be able to prove that your expenses are at least $6,001 a year for your child. Check with your tax adviser.

Several states will allow tax credits for families adopting children from the public child welfare system in that state. Check with your state social service agency to see if tax credits are offered in your state.

The facts about subsidies

Subsidies are provided by both state and federal governments to ensure that the adoptive parents of special needs or waiting children have the necessary services and financial resources to meet their children's needs. The two major sources of adoption assistance are the Federal Title IV-E Program, which falls under the Social Security Act, and individual state programs, which vary from state to state.

The Federal IV-E Adoption Assistance Program

Moneysaver
In 1999, the child tax credit for each qualifying child under 17 is $500. A qualifying child is a dependent child, descendant, stepchild, or foster child for whom you can claim a dependency. Check with your tax adviser to see if you can benefit.

In 1980, Congress enacted the Title IV-E Program to make it more financially feasible for prospective adoptive parents to adopt children with special needs. While this is a federally funded program, the states actually decide who will receive subsidies and how much they will receive on a case-by-case basis.

According to the North American Council on Adoptable Children, in order to qualify for the program the children must meet several criteria. All of the following are necessary:

▪ The court must have ordered that the child not be returned to the birth family.

▪ The child meets the state definition of a special needs child.

- The child could not be placed for adoption without a subsidy.

- The child was eligible for TANF or SSI before adoption. (TANF, Temporary Aid to Needy Families, replaced Aid to Families with Dependent Children in 1996. SSI, Supplemental Security Income, is a program for low-income persons with disabilities.)

Your income has no bearing on determining your child's eligibility to receive Title IV-E assistance, but some states do take family income, along with your child's needs, into account when determining the amount of subsidy you would receive.

Children who qualify for Title IV-E also automatically qualify for Medicaid benefits and Title XX of the Social Security Act, which provides for services to meet the special needs of children. These services could include specialized daycare, respite care, in-house support such as housekeeping and personal care for the child, and counseling. Title XX funds are limited and may not be available when you apply. You can apply again when funds are available.

Arrange your Medicaid benefits before you finalize the adoption. Don't assume that because you don't need the benefits now, you will not need them in the future. Even if you have your own health plan, Medicaid may cover expenses that are not covered by your plan.

Most states will send you an annual application to renew your Medicaid benefits. The application asks for pertinent financial information. You are not required to fill in the application. Simply sign the application and make a note of the fact that this is

Watch Out!
When you are negotiating the amount of your subsidy, remember to take your child's future needs into consideration. Often, problems do not surface immediately. Research potential future problems. Ask if your state will negotiate increases in the future.

for a Federal IV-E adopted child and your financial records are not relevant.

The amount of money that you will receive as subsidy payments cannot be more than the amount of money the state would pay a foster parent to care for your child. Most states make payments to foster care providers in varying amounts depending on the child's special needs. In some states, therapeutic foster parents receive considerably more money than the average foster care provider. Before you negotiate, check to see what the foster care payment scale is in your state.

You can receive subsidy payments for your child until your child is 18 or 21 if the state determines that there is just cause for continuing payments. The state in which you originally arranged subsidy payments will continue to make payments to you if you move to another state.

State Adoption Subsidy Programs

If your special needs child does not qualify for the Federal IV-E program, he or she may be eligible for a state adoption subsidy program. State programs usually offer three subsidies:

- Medical subsidies or Medicaid. Each will cover all the medical costs that are not covered by your own health plan.

- Maintenance or support subsidies paid to the adopting parents for the purpose of covering living expenses.

- Special service subsidies, which are usually one-time payments to cover a child's emergency needs. It's necessary to negotiate with the state on a need basis in order to receive this subsidy.

Who can apply for adoption assistance?

First, it must be determined that the child you are adopting is a child with a special need who is free for adoption. Each state defines a child with special needs differently, but in general, a child is considered special needs if one or more of the following is true:

- The child is an older child.

- The child is a member of a minority.

- The child has a medical condition, a physical or mental disability.

- The child is a member of a sibling group that cannot be separated.

What they don't tell you

Usually, the children in foster care have been abused, neglected, or abandoned; therefore, most children in foster care have already been designated as special needs. In some cases, it may be necessary for you to appeal a state agency's decision to change the type or amount of a Federal IV-E subsidy. You may find that the subsidy is not enough to handle all the expenses that your child is incurring. One mother in a challenging adopted child support group reports, "When we adopted our two boys, my husband and I were both working. We felt that we truly did not need the subsidy money; we were almost embarrassed to take it. At first we put it into the bank thinking that we would have a substantial college fund available when it came time for the boys to go to college. After a year or so, it became necessary for me to stop working as it became obvious that the boys needed me to be a stay-at-home mother. Then, there were the doctor and therapist

Timesaver
You don't have to declare the money you receive as adoption assistance on your income tax. Adoption assistance is exempt from taxes.

bills that were not covered by insurance. Needless to say, we could not save the subsidy money anymore. Finally, it got so bad we had to re-negotiate with the state agency for more help."

If the state will not change your subsidy payment, you can notify your state agency that you wish to appeal the agency's decision through the state's fair hearing and appeals process. You can also contact the Program Operations Division, U.S. Children's Bureau, Administration on Children and Families, P.O. Box 1182, Washington, D.C. 20201.

The Adoption Resource Center recommends making a checklist of questions to discuss with your agency in regard to subsidies. Your checklist should include the following questions:

- Have I had an extensive discussion with the agency adoption professionals about the present and future needs of the child and about the information and services that will be required to meet those needs?

- Have I been encouraged to view adoption assistance/subsidy programs and post-adoption services as essential parts of the post-adoption plan for a child who either has or is at risk to develop some special needs?

- Have I been encouraged to see the negotiation of subsidy benefits as analogous to securing a comprehensive health insurance plan for my child?

- Have I been encouraged to explore the child's eligibility for all adoption assistance and state-funded adoption subsidy programs?

- Have I or has the agency explored eligibility for the Federal SSI program?

- Do I understand that, according to federal law, agencies cannot refuse to act on an application

Unofficially...
Recent studies have shown that the vast majority of adoptive parents are happy with the subsidy program that is assisting them. The study also showed that neither parents nor children attached a stigma to receiving adoption assistance. (NAIC)

for Federal Title IV-E adoption assistance or reimbursement of non-recurring adoption expenses? The agency must respond in writing to each application.

- Do I understand that the amount of adoption assistance is determined by an individual written agreement with the agency?

- Do I understand that if an agreement for IV-E adoption assistance or reimbursement of non-recurring expenses is not signed prior to finalization, the subsidy can only be awarded by appeal through an administrative hearing?

- Do I understand that my child may be eligible for both Title IV-E adoption assistance and a state-funded service subsidy?

- In negotiating a service subsidy, have the agency and I considered my child's anticipated needs as well as his or her current needs?

- Do I understand that some states have post-adoption service subsidies that I can apply for after my adoption is finalized?

- Do I understand that existing Title IV-E adoption assistance agreements and state-funded adoption subsidy agreements may be amended at any time by mutual agreement between the adoptive parents and the agency?

The lowdown on SSI benefits

SSI, Supplemental Security Income, is welfare for poor, disabled people who have either not worked at all or not worked enough to qualify for disability social security.

If the SSI payments are for a child under the age of 18 and the child is living with the parents, the income and resources of the parents are taken into consideration.

The following are the requirements for eligibility:

- If blind, a person must have corrected vision of 20/20 or less in the better eye, or have a field of vision less than 20 degrees.

- If disabled, a person must have a physical or mental impairment that keeps him from performing any "substantial" work or result in "marked and severe limitations" that are expected to last for at least 12 months or result in death.

- Countable income must be below $500 for a single adult or child or below $751 for a couple.

- Resources are limited to $2,000 for a single adult or child and $3,000 for a couple but do not include the home a person lives in, a car, burial plots and funds, and life insurance with a face value of $1,500.

- The person must meet certain citizenship requirements.

Some states supplement the SSI benefits with either state-administered or federally administered benefits. The following states do not offer either of these supplements to SSI benefits: Arkansas, Georgia, Kansas, Mississippi, Tennessee, Texas, and West Virginia.

On February 23, 1999, the governors of all the states, along with Puerto Rico, U.S. Virgin Islands, and the District of Columbia, announced the launch of the "Insure Kids Now" hotline. Parents of children who are eligible for the State Children's Health Insurance Program and Medicaid can receive information and be referred to someone in their own state by calling (877) KIDS-NOW.

What you need to know about health insurance

Before you seriously consider adopting a child, you need to know what your own health insurance policy will cover with respect to the child you plan to adopt. In fact, some adoption agencies require you to provide a statement of your health insurance coverage with your application.

Most company-sponsored group insurance plans are mandated by federal law to pay medical expenses from the time you assume legal financial responsibility for the child. They are also required to pay the medical expenses for preexisting conditions.

Make sure your health insurance plan will verify in writing exactly what medical expenses are covered. Ask the following questions:

- Does the policy cover preexisting conditions in adopted children?

- When will coverage begin, with placement or finalization?

- If the coverage begins when the adoption is finalized, can I purchase an interim policy that covers the child from time of placement?

- Is there a waiting period before the policy goes into effect?

- How do I change my present policy to cover my adopted child?

- Can I change my group plan that presently covers me and my spouse to a family plan?

- Does the plan cover foster children?

Bright Idea
You can download "A Desktop Guide to SSI Eligibility Requirements" from the Social Security Administration at www.ssa.gov/pubs/11001.ntml.

Just the facts

- Many adoption agencies are responding to the high cost of adoption by offering a sliding-scale fee for their clients.

- Adopting and raising a child can be very expensive, but you can find help from a number of sources, including your own investment and retirement plans, employer, home equity, relatives, special fundraisers, and subsidies.

- It's best to start your new life as an adoptive parent with as little debt as possible.

- Although more and more employers are helping with the cost of adoption, only a small percentage actually offer such programs.

- If the Hope for Children Act is not passed, tax breaks for adopting parents will be limited to those adopting domestic special needs children in the year after 2001.

- Subsidies and other benefits may be available to those adopting domestic special needs or waiting children.

PART IV

Ready, Set, Action

GET THE SCOOP ON...
Home study success secrets ▪ Filling out
your adoption agency application ▪ What to
include in your autobiography ▪ How to choose
your references ▪ How to prepare for your
interviews ▪ Getting your home study
documents ready

The Secrets to Passing the Home Study

Chapter 8

Most prospective adoptive parents dread the home study, fearing that they and their homes will be investigated and judged. But, in truth, the home study is far more than an inspection of you and your home. It is a process that includes visits to your home, interviews, educational workshops, the checking of your references and other medical and financial information, and the gathering of a lot of paperwork about you. The process itself can take as little as a few weeks or as long as several months depending on the type of adoption and the agency that does the home study.

Adoption social workers are in the business of putting families together, and they try to put families together as painlessly as possible. If you become nervous at any time during the process, remember that social workers use the home study to prepare and educate prospective parents like you for the job of parenting an adopted child.

It's true that you will be asked a series of tough questions. Some of the questions may seem too personal or intrusive, but they are necessary to convince the social worker, birthmother, and/or the judge that you have thought through your desire to adopt and are truly prepared to go forward.

The real secret to passing the home study is to be emotionally and intellectually prepared with the answers to many questions. In this way, you indicate your readiness to take on the difficult yet rewarding task of adopting your special child.

Applying for your child

Once you have identified the adoption agency that you want to use to help you arrange your adoption, contact the agency. The agency will want to screen you as soon as possible. Most agencies prefer to do the initial screening before accepting an application; this will save them time and you money. Some agencies will ask you to attend one or two group orientation sessions, while others will have a social worker speak with you either in their office or at your home.

The orientation sessions or interviews will give you an overview of what to expect in this particular agency's adoption or home study process and give the social worker an introductory impression of you. Because you will be working with this agency and most likely this social worker for as long as two or three years in some cases, it's very important to feel comfortable with both the agency and the social worker. (See Chapter 2 to review how to choose the right agency.)

If you are pursuing an independent adoption and your state requires a home study to be completed, you will need to find an agency or qualified independent social or case worker to do a home study for you. The home study process will be the same for you as it is for those who are pursuing an agency adoption.

Assuming that both you and the social worker agree to move forward, your home study will begin and you will be given an application to complete. Agencies and home study case workers have different applications, but a typical application would ask you to briefly respond to the following questions:

- What is your background including age, date and place of birth, citizenship, general health, occupation, education, religion, and financial status?

- Do you have a criminal record? Most minor offenses committed in the past will not affect your eligibility to adopt.

- Do you have or have you had a medical or mental problem?

- Do you have or have you had an alcohol or drug dependency?

- Have you had marital problems in the past?

- What are your preferences for a child? Age? Gender? Siblings?

- Would you consider a child with a medical problem?

- Would you consider a child with a handicap?

- What racial background would you consider?

- Do you already have children in your family? Ages, gender, biological or adopted?

You will have the opportunity to expand and explain your answers to these questions in your interviews and autobiographical statements.

Watch Out!
Be as candid as possible when completing the initial application. It's better to tell the truth at this point knowing you will have ample opportunity in the future to explain yourself than to attempt to explain or cover up a lie later in the process.

Unofficially...
It is worth saying again, adoption social workers are in the business of putting families together. Unless you have a felony conviction in your background, or a current drug addiction, mental illness, or life-threatening medical condition, you are more than likely to be approved by the social worker.

The write stuff!

Many agencies also ask you to write an autobiographical or personal statement. While this is meant to help you by giving you the opportunity to present a positive picture of yourself, many prospective adoptive parents find this statement to be the most difficult part of the home study. Some people find it very challenging to express their emotions openly, especially in writing, while others get carried away. Ask a friend to proofread your statement and offer suggestions, or ask your partner to write your biography to help get you started.

The agency will usually give you guidelines and ask you to write a paragraph or two under each of the guidelines. While the exact questions or guidelines will differ with each agency, a typical autobiographical statement might ask you to write about the following:

- Your description: physical, personality, and character traits

- Your family background: brothers and sisters, parents, methods of discipline, the closeness of your family then and now

- Your education: how well you did in high school, highest level of education completed, educational plans for the future, plans for your children's education

- Your employment: satisfaction with your job, number of hours you work per week, plans for your career in the future including daycare for your child if you plan to continue to work

- Your marriage: how you met, how long you dated before you married, how long you've been married, strengths and weaknesses in the marriage, your strengths and weaknesses and your partner's strengths and weaknesses, how you make decisions, solve problems, show feelings, and communicate

- If you are single, how you plan to integrate your social life and parenting life as well as how you plan to provide opposite-sex role models for your child

- Your children: their personalities, strengths, and interests; how they feel about adding a new child to the family

- Your home and community: the type of neighborhood in which you live, your home or apartment, community resources for children

- Your religion and values: the religion (if any) in which the child will be raised, the moral values that are important to you and your family

- Your finances: your financial situation, your assets, how you anticipate financing the adoption expenses and the expenses related to raising a child, how you would be able to finance the unexpected

- Your health: any present health issues and prior health problems, the name of a doctor or therapist who could now recommend you

- Your parenting skills: your experience with children, your perceived strengths and weaknesses with parenting children

- Adoption issues: why you have chosen to adopt, your vision of the future, the child you prefer, issues of infertility, how you plan to discuss adoption with the adopted child and your extended family, how you know you can bond with a child that is not biologically yours

66

For every hour spent face-to-face with the applicants, there may be 10 or more hours of paperwork and telephone time for the social worker and administrative staff.
—Jayne Davis, an adoption social worker

Bright Idea
It's not too early to begin gathering your documents, notifying your references, and making an appointment with your physician for a physical.

Documents you will need

Soon after your application has been accepted, you will be asked to submit relevant documents. These documents usually include:

- Your marriage certificate, if applicable.

- Your birth certificate(s).

- Your divorce decrees from previous marriages, if applicable.

- A death certificate for a previous spouse, if applicable.

- Insurance policies, including future provisions for health insurance for the child to be adopted (see Chapter 7).

- Health statements: Some home studies require you to have a physical and may have their own forms for the doctor to fill out. All home studies require a current tuberculosis test. Some home studies require that a doctor verify that you are infertile if you are adopting an infant. Usually, medical conditions such as high blood pressure or diabetes that are under control will not prevent you from being eligible to adopt a child. Usually, medical conditions aren't significant unless you are unable to perform specific parenting tasks. In an independent adoption, people with all types of medical conditions have been able to adopt.

- Financial statements: You will be asked to verify your income by providing a copy of your paycheck, a copy of a W-2 form, or an income tax form. You may also be asked to provide copies of your mortgage statement, other loans such as automobile loans, and charge accounts. You may also be asked for proof of your savings and assets.

The home study wants you to demonstrate that you can manage your money responsibly.

- A criminal record check: Many states require that a criminal record check be run on all prospective adoptive and foster parents. In some states, you will also be fingerprinted. (INS requires fingerprinting for international adoptions.) Again, misdemeanors from your past will probably not prevent you from being eligible to adopt. Always tell the social or case worker up front the circumstances surrounding the criminal charge. A felony conviction, conviction involving a child, or involvement in child abuse/neglect cases will probably prevent you from being considered a candidate for adoption.

- References: You will be asked to provide the names, addresses, and telephone numbers of several people who will serve as references for you.

For intercountry adoption, add the following to your list:

- A power of attorney
- Photographs
- Affidavit of Support
- An introductory letter.
- A statement of infertility may be necessary. Check with your adoption home study social or case worker.

Regarding your references: Choose your references carefully. They should be people who have known you for several years, have some knowledge of your moral character, your marriage, and your ability to raise a child with love and stability. These people might be close personal friends, your employer, a neighbor, or your pastor. Be sure to verify with these people ahead of time that they are willing to either speak with the social worker over the telephone or write a letter about you. Take the time to discuss your adoption plans with them. Let them know that you have carefully considered all the aspects of adoption and are prepared for the seriousness of the task you will be undertaking. Also, be sure that they understand and agree that adoption is the best option available for you. An experienced adopter advises, "When you speak with your references, be sure to ask if you can read the reference letters before they mail them to the agencies. Sometimes, even well-intentioned friends can say something that could be misunderstood by a social worker or judge."

The social worker will ask them questions about your marriage, stability, and motivation to adopt. Rarely would a negative reference alone be enough for the social worker to deny approval of your application. Only if you received several negative references, or the negative reference was one in a series of negative reports, would it affect your approval by the agency.

Preparing for the interviews

After your application has been accepted, the agency will schedule a series of interviews with you. These interviews may take place either in your social worker's office or in your home. The social worker will make at least one visit to your home. The interviews could be with you and your partner, with each of you alone, or with the immediate family if there are children already in the family.

Timesaver
References submitted to agencies in a foreign country may have to be notarized and authenticated. If all your references come from the same area, you can have all the references notarized and authenticated at the same time.

Your social worker will ask questions concerning every aspect of your life, including personal questions relating to your finances, marriage, and family life. If you are not prepared, you may find yourself temporarily overwhelmed by even the simplest question. As one mother explained, "It was near the end of one of her visits to our home when our social worker asked me to describe one really bad habit that my husband had, a habit that really got on my nerves. I thought and thought but could not come up with anything. Finally, my husband thought of how much I hated his hogging the channel changer and changing the channels incessantly."

Each agency's home study will vary, but the following are a sample of questions from various sources. They can serve as a guide for the type of questions you can expect in your own interviews.

Watch Out!
Don't expect to know the answer to every question you are asked. No matter how prepared you are for the questions in your interview, successful adoptive parents generally agree there are one or two questions that will throw you.

Your personal history

You do not have to create a perfect picture of your background and family life. As a matter of fact, most social workers understand that the struggles that you have had and the problems that you have overcome will make you a better candidate for parenting an adopted child. You may be asked to answer the following:

- Where did you go to high school? What clubs and activities were you involved in?

- If you attended college, what degrees did you earn? What was your major?

- What is your employment history? Are you satisfied with your present job? Are you planning to change jobs or careers in the future?

- What kinds of activities did your family engage in together when you were growing up? What family traditions do you plan to maintain with your child?

- Describe your family. What did your parents do for a living? How many brothers and sisters do you have? Was your family close when you were growing up? Is your family close now?

- What are the names, ages, and occupations of your siblings now? Are they supportive of your decision to adopt a child? If you are creating a transcultural or transracial family, are they supportive? Will your child's new grandparents, aunts, uncles, and cousins welcome your child into the family?

- With whom do you celebrate major holidays now? Do you plan to celebrate holidays differently when your child joins your family?

- What kinds of discipline did your parents use with you? Was it effective, and do you plan to use the same methods of discipline with your child?

Your marriage

The questions concerning your marriage can be very personal. Again, it is necessary to tell the truth. The social worker does not expect you to paint a picture of the perfect marriage and might be very suspect if you did. Your social worker is looking for stability and consistency in how you manage the everyday problems in the average marriage. Your social worker may ask:

- How long have you been married? Where did you meet? How long did you date?

- What attracted you to each other?

- How do you handle problems and disagreements in your marriage? How do you reach decisions? What do you see as the strengths and weaknesses in your spouse? In your marriage?

- Have you and your spouse discussed how your lifestyle will change after the arrival of your child? What are some of the changes you will have to make? Are you both willing to make the changes?

- In what ways will the changes affect your relationship with each other?

- Have you discussed how you will be sharing the responsibilities of raising your child? Have you solved the issue of childcare while you each work? Sick days? Discipline?

Unofficially...
Today, most adoption agencies use the home study as a method to prepare singles and couples for the challenges and joys of adoption rather than as a means to eliminate people from the process.

Your infertility

The infertility issue is particularly important in adoptions involving an infant. Your agency may require you to provide a doctor's statement indicating that you and your partner are unable to conceive a child. You will also be asked some extremely personal questions regarding your infertility. Statistics indicate that in almost one-half of the couples who are infertile, it is the male who is unable to father a child. If you are among the 50 percent of couples who seek infertility treatments and fail to conceive, you must be able to show your social worker that you have worked through your issues of infertility and are ready to adopt.

To prove that you have come to terms with your infertility you may be asked:

- How long have you been trying to have a baby?

- What physicians and specialists have you consulted concerning your infertility problems? What results were determined?

- Have you come to terms with the issue of infertility? How have you done this? Has your spouse come to terms with the issue of infertility?

- Are you ready to focus on adoption? Is your spouse ready to focus on adoption?

Your motivation for adoption

If you are seeking to adopt for reasons other than your or your spouse's inability to have children, you will need to be able to express your reasons for choosing this option. You will be asked questions such as:

- Why have you chosen adoption as a way of building a family? Why have you chosen not to give birth to a child?

- If you are choosing to adopt a child with special needs, what qualities do you feel you have that will make you a good parent for this child?

- If you are considering adopting a transracial or transcultural child, are you willing to change your lifestyle in order to make your child fit in and feel comfortable?

Your experience with children

Your social worker will expect you to have some experience with children; most people have. It does not have to be a significant amount of contact. As one prospective adoptive mother explained, "I could not remember having any notable contact with children as I was growing up. I had no siblings, and my parents would not let me baby-sit when I was a teenager. Finally, I remembered I had taught Sunday school in my church for one year when I was a freshman in high school. I had almost forgotten." Your social worker will ask:

Bright Idea
If you have not had a lot of experience with children, you might want to volunteer to work with an organization that involves children. You might volunteer to be a mentor, do some respite work, or even work with your local boys' or girls' clubs.

- If you had younger siblings, did you help your parents care for them? Change diapers? Baby-sit?
- Did you baby-sit any children when you were in high school?
- Does your job involve working with children in any way?
- Have you ever volunteered to work with any children's organizations?

Your previous marriage

You will be asked questions about any previous marriage that you may have had, including the reasons it failed and what you did to try to resolve your problems. You may be asked questions similar to the following:

- What was the date of your first marriage? The date of your divorce?
- What were the problems in the marriage that resulted in the divorce?
- How did you try to resolve the problems prior to the divorce? Did you seek counseling?
- Who filed for the divorce?
- Were there any children? Who got custody? Why?
- If you do not have custody, what kind of contact do you have with your children? How often do you participate in activities with them? Do you receive child support?
- Have you and your children discussed your decision to adopt another child? Are they supportive of that decision? How will your relationship

change and/or remain the same after your adoption is arranged?

Your religion

Unless you are arranging your adoption through a church-affiliated adoption agency, your religious preference is not an issue for the agency. Some birthmothers may require that you raise the child in her chosen religion. You may be asked the following questions about your religion:

▪ What is your religion? Are you a member of a church, mosque, or synagogue? How often do you attend services?

▪ Do you plan to raise your child in a particular religion?

▪ How do you plan to provide for your child's religious education?

Your lifestyle

The agency will want to know how you spend your time when you are not working. They might ask some of the following:

▪ What do you do for hobbies? What sports do you enjoy participating in or watching?

▪ What types of activities do you plan to do as a family?

▪ How will you spend your vacation time together?

▪ Who will care for the child when you are going out as a couple?

▪ If you both plan to continue to work, who will provide the daycare for the child?

▪ What activities and recreation that you presently enjoy do you see yourself giving up when you are a family?

Watch Out!
Don't forget to update your home study should something change, such as your employment or an address. Especially in an international adoption, your adoption could be held up due to inaccurate information on your home study documents.

■ Do you have pets? If yes, what would you do if you couldn't have pets around your child? If no, would you consider having pets for your child?

Your feelings about specific types of adoption

You will also be asked questions that directly relate to the type of adoption you are pursuing. Expect to be asked questions similar to the following:

■ How do you feel about a mother who would make an adoption plan for her child?

■ How do you feel about parents who have abused or neglected their child?

■ How do you know you could love a child who is different from you?

■ Have you thought about how you are going to deal with your child's past? Will you be able to teach your child about his or her heritage?

■ Have you thought about who your transcultural or transracial child will date and marry? Have you thought about the fact that your grandchildren will be multiracial?

■ How will you feel when your child wants to search for his or her birthparents?

■ How will you handle racial and negative comments about your child?

If you are single

The social worker will be particularly interested in how you are going to manage your life with added parenting responsibilities. You may be asked some of the following questions:

■ Why have you not married? What is your sexual orientation?

Timesaver
Don't spend more time than usual cleaning your house before the home study. If your house is too clean, the social worker might wonder if you will be able to handle the mess and clutter that accompany children. Remember, it's not a house study, it's a home study.

- Do you plan to marry in the future? How do you think being a single parent will affect your chances of marrying in the future?

- How will you handle the social life of a single person along with single parenting?

- Who can you provide as role models for your child?

- What kind of support system do you have? Who will care for your child if you are ill? If your child is ill, who will care for the child while you work?

- Who have you designated as the guardian of your child in the event of a serious illness or your death?

- How will you handle your finances? How will you work and raise a child at the same time?

The ins and outs of the home visit

The social worker will schedule at least one visit to your home. Experienced adopters and social workers alike stress that this is not an inspection of your home, but rather an opportunity for the worker to get an impression of you as a family in your own home and an opportunity to see where the child will live. They will want to see the bedroom in which the child will sleep, although the worker will not expect the room to be decorated and ready for the child to move in. Your social worker may also want to see the basement and backyard if you live in your own home.

It will not be difficult nor should it be necessary to read the social worker's mind. The worker simply wants reassurance that your child will be living in a safe and nurturing environment. If you have any questions about what the caseworker will be looking for during the visit, ask. If you are worried that the caseworker will be opening your kitchen cabinets or closet doors, ask if this is what will happen. A good caseworker will tell you exactly what he or she will be checking while visiting your home.

Creating a child-friendly environment

This is a good time to consider moving to another location in order to provide the right environment for the child you wish to adopt. It is usually not necessary to move before the home study is completed. You should point out in the home study your intention to move once a child is on the way. Several circumstances might cause you to consider moving to another location:

- You might need a larger home or apartment because you don't have enough bedrooms in your present home. You will be required to provide a separate bed and enough room to store your child's belongings as well as enough room for all family members in general.

- You may wish to move to another community that has a better school system, more convenient childcare, or a more child-friendly home or neighborhood. Remember that consistency is important for your child, especially for the older child who may have experienced many moves already.

- You may wish to move to an integrated neighborhood or community if you are pursuing a transracial or transcultural adoption.

How to childproof your home

The caseworker will be particularly interested in the safety measures you have taken to protect a child in your home. As long as you can show that you are aware of any needed changes and are willing to make them, you don't have to have all of the

Moneysaver
Call your local fire station and ask if it will do a fire safety inspection of your home before your scheduled home visit. For a small contribution to the cause, they can point out the fire hazards before your case worker does.

changes completed at the time of the home visit. If you have stated that you plan to move, the case worker will probably still check these things in your present home just in case a child is placed in your home before you have a chance to move. If the child is placed after you move, the case worker may check your new home at the time of the placement. In your home visit, the caseworker will be checking the following safety issues:

- Adequate lighting and ventilation throughout the house

- Working hot and cold water, heating, plumbing, and electricity

- Potable well water

- Safe woodstoves

- Smoke detectors in good working condition throughout the house

- Fire extinguishers throughout the house

- A plan of evacuation in case of fire

- Handrails on all the stairways

- Gating on the stairs to prevent toddlers and small children from falling down the stairs

- Provisions for locking up all dangerous objects such as guns and hazardous substances such as medicines and cleaning materials

- Means by which to install childproof locks on kitchen cabinets

- Fencing around pools or around the yard if near a street or highway

Your kids and the home visit

The adoption worker will need to know that the children already in your family are ready and willing to

Watch Out!
Experts caution that young children tend to misbehave during the home visit. Adoption caseworkers expect this to happen. Don't overreact and discipline your children too harshly!

have an addition to your family. Your worker will ask to meet all your children, including your biological or adopted children still living with you, older children who have left home, or children from another marriage who visit on weekends. Your worker will want to speak with your children at least once. She may ask them the following questions to determine if they are prepared to accept and love another child in the family:

- What are your interests and hobbies? What sports do you like to watch and participate in?

- How well do you do in school?

- How are you rewarded and disciplined for good or poor behavior?

- Have you discussed with your parents how you will share their time with your new sibling?

- Have you determined how you are going to share things with your new sibling, such as the television, the bathroom, your toys, or sports equipment?

The worker may ask your child to write a brief statement describing how they envision family life after the new sibling has arrived in the family. A younger child might be asked to draw a picture of the new family group.

If you are pursuing an intercountry adoption, your caseworker will want to know if you are planning to take your child along with you on the international adoption trip. The time to make that decision is before your caseworker asks. Make the decision based on the following considerations:

- Will you be able to afford the added expense of another person traveling with you?

- Will your child be able to handle missing two or three weeks of school?

- Will your child have trouble adjusting to new foods and new experiences?

- Will your child have trouble adjusting to long hours of travel in airplanes, cars, or busses and different time zones?

- Would your child be comfortable with strangers frequently staring at, touching, or generally making a fuss over him or her?

- Can your child entertain himself or herself for long periods of time?

- Does your child have a generally positive attitude about adding a sibling to the family?

- Is your adopted child's medical condition good?

For hints on what to do with your child if you decide to leave him or her at home, see Chapter 9.

Dealing with pets

For many people, pets are part of the family. When you write your autobiographical statement or answer questions on your application, include relevant information about your pets; one of your favorite pastimes, for example, might be walking your three dogs or riding one of your horses.

You also need to do some soul searching to determine if your pets are child-friendly. You may need to ask yourself some tough questions as to how your animals will work out with the child you are planning to adopt. Especially if you are adopting an older, special needs child, you need to factor in the possibility of the child being allergic to your animal, afraid of your animal, or, in some cases, abusive to your animal. You may also be asked to take a new animal into your home at the request of the child you are adopting. Be sure to discuss these issues thoroughly with your caseworker and with your entire family.

When your caseworker visits your home, your animals should be clean, healthy, and up to date on their shots. The way you care for your pets may indicate to the worker how you will care for your children.

How to impress the social worker

Most adoption social workers agree that the best way to impress the caseworker is to *not* try to impress the caseworker. You can waste a lot of time and energy trying to prove that you are something you are not. Instead, focus on learning as much as possible from the process and work on establishing a good, positive relationship with the person who is evaluating you by being sincere and honest. That said, here are a few tips that will expedite the home study and help make the home visit easier:

- Ask questions. This will show that you are serious and have done your homework. (See the chapters on each type of adoption for examples of questions to ask.)

- Try to be yourself, relaxed, and natural. Show your sense of humor.

- Show that you are a warm and natural person, couple, or family.

- Try to be flexible with requests of the agency or social worker as this will demonstrate the flexibility needed in parenting.

- Treat the worker as you would any other guest in your home. Offer a soft drink or coffee, etc.

> ❝
> Flexibility and a sense of humor are desperately needed when raising children in this day and age. It would be a good idea for you to demonstrate these in some way during the home study process.
> —Debra G. Smith, ACSW, former Director, NAIC
> ❞

Bright Idea
A picture is
worth a
thousand words.
Have framed
photographs of
you and your
extended family
around your
home when your
caseworker visits.
It says a great
deal about you
and your
family life.

What to do if you are not approved

"Our assigned adoption caseworker, the person who did our home study, was on vacation when the 'perfect child for us' became available. We were notified by the caseworker who did our training and group sessions that this could be our child. The more we heard about the child, the more we became very excited and equally convinced that this was the child for us. Right before we were to meet the child and begin the actual process of placement in our home, the caseworker who did our home study returned from vacation. She indicated that she did not think we were ready to adopt, especially my husband, who had said very little during the home study. After many meetings among the two caseworkers and us, the problem was straightened out. It seemed that my husband had let me do most of the talking in our home as he considered this my area of expertise. In the training sessions, we had both been open about our desire to adopt. We proceeded and successfully adopted our daughter." Stories such as this told by a newly adoptive mother are not unusual and make the point that most problems in the home study can be worked out by open communication among participants.

If you are working with an agency and the agency will not approve your application, you can formally appeal the decision. Ask them to tell you why they have decided not to approve you. In a written appeal, address the reasons and ways in which you can rectify their concerns.

If the agency still will not change its decision, you may take your appeal further according to the laws of your state. In some states there is a separate appeal process, while in other states the appeal is part of the adoption hearing.

Being actively involved

Get actively involved in the creation of the final copy of the home document. While writing an autobiographical statement is one way to get the adoption agency workers to hear your side of the story in your own words, the autobiographical statement is often not included in the final copy of the case study. It is this final copy that is sent out to others such as the birthparent representatives or the international officials. Ask to read the final copies before they are distributed to whomever needs to read them. Check the home study documents to be sure they:

- Are factually correct and have corrected circumstances that have changed since the initiation of the home study.

- Contain no misrepresentations of who you are or what you have said in an interview session.

- Contain all the information that is relevant to convince a child's adoption worker that you would be the best family for the child. For example, if you are adopting a transracial child, be sure that it's noted in your home study that you live in a multiracial neighborhood.

- Are clean, neat documents with no typographical errors or omissions.

- Are typed darkly enough to allow photocopying.

Just the facts

- The purpose of the autobiographical statement is to give you a chance to explain yourself in your own words.

- All your children will be part of the adoption home study, even children from another marriage or grown children who do not live with you.

Unofficially...
If one agency or case worker does not approve your application to adopt, don't assume that your adoption quest is over. Try another agency, because some agencies are more flexible than others.

- If you don't let your references know what is expected of them, they might inadvertently give you a negative recommendation.

- You need to prove to the worker that you and your partner have resolved issues of infertility.

- Pretending that you are perfect or live in a perfect home will send out immediate warning signals to the caseworker.

GET THE SCOOP ON...
How to creatively pass the time ▪ Naming your
adopted child ▪ Finding a pediatrician the right
way ▪ Preparing siblings for a new family
member ▪ Sympathetic pregnancy and
post-adoption depression

The Secrets to Passing the Time

Chapter 9

Your home study is complete, you've been approved, and you're waiting for your child. Now is the time to practice the art of positive thinking. Keep telling yourself that you are going to be a parent. Many adoptive parents report that even after the home study was completed, they were not convinced that they were truly going to become parents. Perhaps past experiences with infertility, or the lack of physical evidence of pending parenthood, or the feelings of helplessness that come from waiting while others determine the future lead to these doubts. No matter what the reason, many adopters find the waiting period to be a wasted period of time, a limbo in which nothing is accomplished.

But the period between the completion of the home study and the actual placement of a child in your home can actually be a very productive time for you. As it is for any parent to be, the time before the arrival of a child should be an exciting time, a time filled with anticipation and planning. You can do many things to prepare yourself, your family, and your home for the arrival of your new child. Remember all the adages about a watched pot never boiling and time flying when you are having fun? They may be old and overused, but they make sense. The secrets to passing the time are to keep busy and have a positive attitude.

Discover the fun side of paperwork

Just when you thought all the paperwork was completed, it's time to create some more! There are many small details to attend to and some fun projects to begin.

Watch Out!
Don't forget to let your employer know that you will be a parent sometime in the future. Arrange your leave now. This will give you ample time to negotiate with your employer if paid leave is not presently an option with your company.

Make lists

You will need to do many things while you are waiting for your child, and even more things once you hear when your child will be available for placement in your home. Experienced adopters agree that no matter how many times you adopt, once you know when your child will be available, chaos erupts. Be as prepared as possible for the chaos by making lists of things that need to be done over the next several months and during the different stages of the wait, such as the following:

- The things you can do now and what will have to wait until you know the gender and exact age of your child

- The paperwork to complete once you know the name, age, and arrival date of your child, such as additions to wills and insurance and notification of employer to increase payroll deductions

- The personal accomplishments you wish to complete during the waiting period

- The things that you will need to purchase in preparation for your child, such as clothes and toys for the child, or a car or new home for the family

- The addresses of relatives and friends you will notify of your child's arrival and how you will let them know

- The items to be packed to take on your trip if you are traveling to your new child's birth-country

- The things you need to tell the person who will be caring for the children who will not be accompanying you on your international trip if you are arranging for an intercountry adoption

- The questions to ask your child's caretaker about your child's eating and sleeping habits

Bright Idea
Consult with your tax adviser now to update yourself on the latest on adoption tax credits. Ask your tax adviser to let you know if there are any changes while you are waiting for your child.

Keep a journal

Writing your thoughts and emotions in a journal might help you to get through the daily frustrations and joys during this time of waiting. You may wish to create a journal of your own or purchase a journal that has been created specifically for the "adoption pregnancy." Journals that have been created for this purpose may have the insights of experienced adoptive parents and therapists to help you with each stage of the adoption process. Whether you create your own or purchase one, keep in mind that you may wish to share your journal with your child as he or she gets older.

Create a photo album

Go through all your photographs and put together a book that will tell your life story to your new child. Arrange your pictures in a scrapbook either sequentially or under categories such as major events, family gatherings, and favorite pastimes. Remember that you are telling your life story to your new child. Be creative—use water paints or magic markers to add a few details to the pictures. Include pictures of your pets and extended family. Often a social worker will ask you to create a picture history of you and your family to give to an older child before the child is placed in your home.

Begin a baby book

Begin a baby book of pictures and other memories that will become part of your child's history. Add pictures that will have special meaning to your child such as you waiting for the plane, the nurses in the hospital, the entrustment ceremony, or the arrival party of an older child. Many adoptive families use this book of memories to help them tell their children about adoption.

Make other decisions

During your home study process, you were encouraged to think about important issues such as disciplining your child, childcare, and lifestyle changes. Take this time to make some practical decisions regarding how you (and your partner) want to raise your child.

Solve the name dilemma

One of the first decisions you will need to make will be what to do about your child's first name. Many adoptive parents struggle with this decision. Naming a child is one way of saying that the child belongs to you, but an adopted child may already have a name that is part of that child's heritage and past.

In each type of adoption, parents have tried various solutions to the name dilemma. If you are arranging an open adoption with birthparents, you and the birthparents might discuss the naming of the child and one of the following could be determined:

"
Some children may want to change their names when they are adopted as a way of trying to get rid of their past. This wish may indicate that a child has unrealistic expectations about adoption.
—Lois Ruskai Melina in *Raising Adopted Children*
"

- The birthparents may not wish to name the child and will leave the choice of name to the adoptive parents.

- The birthparents may wish to name the child and will ask the adoptive parents to use the name in the future.

- The adoptive parents and birthparents agree on both the first and middle names of the child.

- The adoptive parents choose the first name and the birthparents chose the middle name, or vice versa.

- The birthparents name the child on its first birth certificate, and the adopting parents give the child its forever name as part of the adoption procedure.

If you are adopting a child from another country, you need to consider all the implications of changing the child's first name. If the child is older, you may want to discuss the name change with the child. Children may prefer being teased about their names or having their names mispronounced rather than losing names that have traveled with them over the years. On the other hand, children may prefer new names to help them assimilate into their new lives without ridicule from their peers. Sometimes, as teenagers or adults, adoptees choose to use their original names.

There are several possible solutions:

- Keep the child's given or orphanage name as a middle name, especially if it is difficult to pronounce and may cause problems later.

- Choose a name that is very similar to the original name.

❝
In contrast to
the offhand way
that children are
sometimes
placed with
adoptive
parents—in a
hospital parking
lot or attorney's
office—an
entrustment
ritual helps the
adoptive parents
take on their
new role and
helps the birth
parents let go.
—Lois Melina,
*Raising Adopted
Children*,
HarperPerennial,
1998
❞

- Give your child a nickname that could be used informally.

Most experts do advise using your child's new surname as soon as the child is placed in your home even though the adoption has not been finalized. On the other hand, don't assume that older children will be eager to give up their surnames. Most older children have traveled around the system with only their names traveling with them. An older child might resent giving up this one tie with the past. This is something that needs to be discussed with each child on an individual basis.

Resurrect or create family traditions

If this is your first child, consider the family traditions that you want to incorporate into your new family life. If you have a partner, discuss the traditions that your families had which made the holidays special for each of you.

You also might want to research the traditions and holidays of the country from which you are adopting a child in an international adoption or the culture from which your child comes in an interracial adoption. Your child will appreciate celebrating special days that are part of the culture into which he or she was born.

There are also some special days that are unique to adoptive families. One that is gaining in popularity is the "entrustment ceremony," in which the birthparents or someone representing the birthparents formally entrusts the child being adopted to the adoptive parents, and the adoptive parents formally accept the responsibility. Many believe that this ceremony alleviates some of the role confusion that is present in many open adoptions today by defining these roles clearly. Usually, adoptive parents arrange the ceremonies and ask the person of their choice, such as a minister, Imam, or rabbi, to officiate at the ceremony.

Another way some adoptive families celebrate their adoptions is to commemorate the day their child was placed in their home or the adoption was legalized. Some call this day "gotcha day" and they celebrate the day as they would a birthday or anniversary. Others actually celebrate this as a "family anniversary." One mother of two adopted biological siblings proudly displays the framed family unification certificate on her wall, which states that the four members of the family "shall be united in love and respect forever and shall be hereafter known as the Smith family." They celebrate their family anniversary as a special day every year.

Find a good pediatrician

If this is your first child, you need to find a good pediatrician. You will be looking for a doctor who is a board-certified pediatrician and a fellow of the American Academy of Pediatrics. Your pediatrician will manage your child's total health care needs including growth and development, illnesses, nutrition, immunizations, injuries and physical fitness, as well as behavior, emotional or family problems, learning and other school problems, preventing and dealing with drug abuse, puberty, and other teen issues. Your pediatrician will work with your child from infancy through the teen years, so take the time to find the right one.

Begin your search by asking your physician, friends, and coworkers who they recommend as a good pediatrician. Also, check with your local adoption support group to find out who other adoptive parents recommend. It's important that your pedia-

Timesaver
When adopting a child, make an appointment with your child's pediatrician for a complete physical for your child. This will allow your pediatrician to know your child as soon as possible and give you a realistic assessment of your child's physical condition.

trician is experienced in working with adopted children, especially if they are children from other countries or different racial backgrounds. Your pediatrician needs to know that you will not have all the answers to questions about your child's history. Also, your pediatrician needs to be experienced in dealing with children of all races and ethnic groups. As one mother of two adopted Hispanic children pointed out, "There were no other Hispanic children in the small town in which we lived, therefore, our pediatrician either did not know or did not think to warn us that both our boys were at high risk for diabetes. Unfortunately, we did not find this out until it was too late. Both our children were diagnosed with diabetes in their teens."

Don't wait until your child has arrived, or worse, is sick, before you look for a good pediatrician. Once you have a list of names, set up meetings with the doctor as soon as you can. Some pediatricians charge for a consultation, others don't. Be sure to ask about the charges before scheduling the appointment. Here are some of the questions you should ask:

- What are the office hours?
- How does the office handle billing?
- How are insurance claims handled?
- Do you have an area of expertise or specialty?
- Do you have experience working with adopted children?
- How do I reach you after hours or in an emergency?
- To what hospital do you admit patients? (It's best to choose a doctor who works with a hospital close to you.)

- If I have a minor question, when is the best time to call?

- If I cannot speak with you, who will handle my questions?

- Is there a separate waiting room for children who are contagious?

- What is the typical waiting time in the waiting room?

- How long do you spend with each child?

You need to determine from your interview if this pediatrician is the right doctor for you. You are looking for a doctor who listens, encourages you to ask questions, and is concerned about the welfare of your child and family. You might ask some direct questions about the doctor's philosophy about pediatrics and how he or she tries to support the family.

If you are adopting a child from abroad, be sure your pediatrician does the following tests:

- Updated vaccinations

- Complete Hepatitis B profile

- Mantoux (intradermal PPD) skin test with Candida control and chest X-ray for tuberculosis.

- Complete blood count with erythrocyte indices for a variety of possible conditions.

- Stool examination to check for ova and parasites.

- Stool culture for bacterial causes for diarrhea.

- Blood test for syphilis.

- Urinalysis and urine culture.

- HIV-1 and HIV-2 testing by ELISA.

- Vision and hearing screening.

- Developmental assessment. (It's a fairly good rule of thumb that for every three months your

Unofficially...
Some health insurance plans require you to choose a pediatrician from their approved network of doctors. This does not mean that they are recommending these doctors as the best available. Be sure to check them out according to the same guidelines.

child has been in an orphanage, your child will be one month behind in development.)

Find a good therapist

Not all adopted children will need to see a therapist. Not all adopted children who need to see a therapist will need to because of issues related to adoption. But all therapists who treat adopted children should have training specific to working with adopted children and have knowledge of all the issues related to the adoption experience for both the adopted child and the adoptive family.

If you are adopting an older child either internationally or through the domestic foster care system, you might need to find an adoption competent therapist who has specific knowledge of attachment issues for your child. (For more information on attachment issues, see Chapter 12.) This means you will need to start looking for a therapist who has had experience with adopted children and issues of attachment. It's not too early to begin your search. Be aware that providing the wrong therapy for your child can do worse damage than providing no therapy at all. Again, start by asking your local adoption support group for recommendations. Questions you will need to have answered by the therapist include the following:

- How much experience have you had working with adopted (or foster) children with attachment issues?

- Do you include parents in your therapy sessions? A good attachment therapist will be aware of the need to have parents included in sessions.

- What kind of therapy do you provide? Some therapists do a type of therapy called "holding" therapy. This therapy is controversial and will be discussed in Chapter 12.

Find good childcare providers

Now is the time to determine if you are going to continue to work, and, if so, who is going to care for your child while you are working. Research all the possibilities and start lining up your resources. Remember to have childcare backup for the days your child is ill and cannot go to the customary childcare situation.

Prepare your home

Complete all the projects you told your home study worker you were going to do:

- Trade in the sports car for a family car or van.

- Move into a larger home or apartment.

- Fence in the yard. Put on the addition or add the extra bathroom.

- Do all the fun projects that reinforce the fact that you are adding a child to your family.

What about decorating the child's room? Most adopters report that this seems to be the most difficult decision to make during the waiting period. Some prospective adoptive parents find it very difficult to decorate a nursery when they are not sure when, and even if, the baby will be arriving. Some adopters of older children find that it's best to prepare the room with new paint, but to let the children decorate the room themselves. It seems to be a matter of personal preference, and you should do what makes you feel comfortable and happy.

Prepare your children

If you already have children, continue the education you started in preparation for your home study.

Watch Out!
Some therapists believe that every problem an adopted child has is related to the lack of bond between the adoptive parents and the adopted child. They erroneously believe attachment problems mean a child cannot attach. Make sure your therapist has a clear understanding of attachment issues in adopted children.

Moneysaver
Choose the furniture for the nursery ahead of time, save the money needed, and purchase the furniture with cash as soon as you know when your infant will be arriving. In that way, you can furnish the room in a few days without paying interest on the furniture.

As time goes by, your children will continue to have concerns and issues relating to the addition of a sibling in their lives. Some of these concerns may include the following:

- The new child may threaten the child already in the home and raise fears of abandonment.

- The existing child may worry that you will be too busy to spend much time with him or her.

- The existing child may worry that he or she will have to share everything, including you, with the new child.

- Older children already in the family may worry about what their friends will think about the adoption of another child.

Make sure you include the children already in the family in all the preparations surrounding the arrival of the new child, including decorating, choosing names, and discussions of the changes that will occur after the arrival of the new child. You can help the children sort out their feelings about the arrival of the new child by directing them in play with dolls or other toys. You can ease your children into their older sibling roles by throwing them a "new big sister" or "new big brother" party or giving them small gifts that celebrate their new status.

The important factors in preparing the children in the family are individual time and special attention to each child in order to ensure them that they are still special people in your life. Later in this chapter, I'll discuss how to include your existing child in the trip for an international adoption.

Prepare your extended family

Most of your relatives will be immediately supportive of your decision to adopt a child, but a few in your extended family may need some time to adjust to your decision to adopt a child. Often, prospective adoptive parents forget that other family members need to go through the same processes of acceptance that they have gone through concerning issues of infertility and the continuation of the family's bloodline. Don't be surprised if someone reacts to the initial announcement of your intention to adopt with "Don't expect me to love this child the same as I do my own flesh and blood." Additionally, most family members may not be as informed as you are about the new types of adoption such as interracial, international, and open domestic independent adoption.

If extended family members are not informed and educated, an extremely important support for both you and your adopted child will be missing. Be prepared to be patient and understanding. It's your job to educate your family, especially the prospective adoptive grandparents, in the following ways:

- Make them part of the process right from the beginning. Be ready for their questions and concerns.

- Recognize that their concerns are legitimate, and they need to be reassured. If you are confident, they will accept your decision much more readily.

- Tell them the facts of adoption as you have learned them.

- Educate them with books, magazines, and workshops as much as possible. Some adoption agencies include extended family in their workshops.

- Be prepared to forgive the family members who express misgivings in the beginning. Chances are they will have a change of heart once they meet your child.

Watch Out!
Be very careful how much and who you tell concerning the history of your child and your child's birth family. It is usually not necessary information and could be hurtful to you and your child in the future. Determine what should be kept private early on.

■ Ask for their help, especially when your child first arrives. Often, feeling needed is all that it takes to change the mind of a reluctant relative.

■ If you are single, it might be wise to share with your parents and extended family the plans that you have carefully considered and shared with the social worker doing your home study. Once they know that you have thought out all the complications of raising a child on your own, they will be more likely to accept your decision.

■ Offer a little information at a time. It often takes time to accept the decision to adopt. More often than not, the decision is not only accepted in the end, it is accepted with love and anticipation.

Prepare yourself

Prospective adoptive parents can do very little to ensure the health of the child for whom they are waiting, but they can do a lot to ensure that they are in the best possible physical and emotional condition to raise that child. The waiting period is a good time to give up bad habits and introduce good habits into your life.

Practice healthy living

Not only do you need to take good care of yourself during this stressful period of waiting, you will also want to adopt new habits that will model healthy living for your child. Consider doing the following:

■ Give up smoking. It will be easier now than it will be when you are dealing with the stress of a new child in your life.

■ Incorporate healthy foods into your daily life. Eat meals on a regular schedule. Include five servings of fruits and vegetables a day.

- Slow down. If you have been a workaholic, now is the time to cut back on your hours on the job. Schedule fewer social engagements.

- Exercise daily. No matter what your age, you will learn very quickly how heavy an infant or toddler can be. Do strength-building as well as aerobic exercises.

Educate yourself

Take this time to find out everything you can about adoption and raising children:

- Read everything you can find on adoption and child rearing.

- Take a course at your local college. If you are adopting an infant, you might find some courses on infant care at your local hospital or community center. You can also find courses on first aid and infant CPR through the American Red Cross and the American Heart Association.

- Join an adoption support group in your area.

- Volunteer to be a respite worker, Big Brother or Sister, or mentor.

- If you are adopting internationally, take a course to learn the language of the country you will be visiting. It will be helpful to know some of the language while you are there, and it will help you communicate with an older child for the first few months.

If you're lucky, there's an adoption agency or group in your area that offers one or two basic courses on caring for a baby. After attending a course given by The Open Door Society of Massachusetts, Jamie Katz, a prospective adoptive parent, reported, "The value in the workshop, in

Bright Idea
If you would like to breast-feed an adopted infant, contact the La Leche League in your area for more information.

the end, was threefold. First, we saw we were not alone in our anxieties about so many tasks so seemingly mundane and routine. Second, we received some very practical, useful advice that has demystified some of what we will face. And finally, we know now that there is no single, prescribed way to do many of the things we need to do."

Nurture yourself and your partner

You will also need to get away from it all and nurture the relationship between you and your partner, or simply rejuvenate yourself. If you can afford it, take the vacation you have been planning. If you cannot afford a vacation, take long walks, go on a picnic, or find a new hobby that will allow you to take your mind off the wait.

Don't put your life on hold while you wait for your child to arrive. Don't quit your job and find yourself with nothing to do for a year or two. Find a balance that will allow you to plan for and anticipate the arrival of your child, but not spill over into an obsessive preoccupation with waiting.

Expect a sympathetic pregnancy?

Pat Johnston, an infertility and adoption educator, describes a condition that she and others have noticed in both prospective adoptive mothers and fathers. She calls this condition a "sympathetic pregnancy" and describes symptoms that sound very much like the symptoms reported by over 60 percent of the spouses of physiologically pregnant women. Symptoms include nausea, food cravings, and weight gain along with sleep disturbances and emotional peaks and valleys. Johnston goes on to explain that there could be logical reasons for this, such as the tension of the wait, or increased weight gain due to tension-induced snacking or craving for "comfort foods" that lead to sleep disturbances and discomfort. Whatever the reason, it's possible that these symptoms could occur during your waiting period.

Prepare for the trip

If you are adopting a child through an international adoption, you need to start planning your trip and making decisions. First, decide who is going to actually go abroad to do the necessary paperwork and bring your adopted child home. You must decide whether your children will accompany you on the trip or whether they will stay home while you are traveling. In either case, it will be necessary to prepare your children in advance.

Prepare your child for the trip

For the most part, experienced adopters advise adopting parents to leave children at home when traveling abroad to adopt another child, but this is a decision each family must make on an individual basis.(See Chapter 8 for a list of questions to help you make the decision.) Susan Hall and her husband made the decision to take their two children along to Vietnam to adopt their eight-year-old son and described it as an "emotional decision that we will be paying off financially for years. Had we adopted an infant, I'm positive we would have taken the financially sound route and just sent one parent to Vietnam. However, it became extremely important to us that Ari (age 12) and Mia (age 10) know where their brother had spent the first eight years of his life. We now know that our decision made our unique journey much easier for everyone. ALL of my children can relate to the emotions, stress,

Unofficially...
Sometimes, adoptive parents report feeling depressed after the arrival of the child similar to the postpartum depression experienced by biological mothers. Post-adoption depression can be caused by the complexity of the adoption process and can be worked through with the help of a support group and/or competent therapist.

difficulty, and love that we feel individually and as a family."

If you decide to take your children along with you on your trip, experienced adopters suggest preparing children in advance by doing such things as:

- Making sure that each child is willing to have the medical exams, vaccinations, medications, and to follow the health and safety precautions of international travel.

- Practicing what you will do on the long trips on airplanes, buses, cars, and other forms of transportation. Stock up on books and games that will keep children occupied.

- Learning as much as possible about the country you will be visiting in advance. Read as many books as you can find and study maps.

- Speaking with people who have visited the country.

- Preparing children as much as possible for the poverty they might see and extreme differences in culture and lifestyles they will encounter.

- Preparing children for the different types of food they will be eating by serving typical meals to them at least once a week, such as rice for breakfast.

Steven Brown explains why he and his wife left their two pre-teenage sons home after months of preparing them to accompany them on the trip. He recalls, "In the beginning the boys were eager to make the trip to Vietnam with us. We all started to learn a few words of the language, read as many books as we could find, and even visited restaurants which served the native food. Slowly, over the months, we noticed that the boys were more and more reluctant to join us in our cultural education. In the end, we arranged for their grandparents to stay with them while my wife and I made the trip. We were glad that the boys lost interest before rather than in the middle of the trip."

Prepare children to stay home

Many adopters see the wisdom in leaving children at home while traveling internationally. When JoAnne Baker and her husband traveled to Russia in September 1997 to adopt their eight-month-old son James, they chose not to take along their four-year-old daughter Susan. "We were very concerned about the medical conditions in the country and felt that Susan would find the trip very stressful and confusing. We also worried that we would not be able to give our new child all the attention he needed if we had Susan with us. She can be very demanding at times. We knew she would be better off waiting for us at home." They arranged to have Susan's aunt stay with her.

Adopters experienced in international adoption point out that the secret to leaving your child at home without unnecessary trauma for all involved is careful planning and preparation from the very beginning. Some hints they have discovered include:

- Find a competent, trustworthy person to care for your child, preferably someone your child already knows.

- If possible, arrange to have the person caring for your child move into your home for the duration of the trip rather than care for your child in his or her home. This will allow your child to continue with normal schoolwork, activities, and routines.

Moneysaver
Videotape a different message to your child or children for every day you plan to be gone. In this way, they will see and hear you daily, but you will not have to place an expensive international call every day.

- Involve your child in the planning of the trip as much as possible. Show your child on a map where you will be traveling.

- Give your child a schedule of where you will be each day so your child can follow your trip on the map.

- Explain the differences in time, food, culture, and climate.

- Give the caregiver all the necessary information needed for a medical emergency, such as insurance information, pediatrician's phone number, and written permission to seek medical help.

- Leave notes and gifts that the caregiver can give to your child daily.

- Arrange all appointments and play dates before you leave.

- Talk with your child often about the trip, the adoption, and the feelings of sadness that your child might feel when you are gone.

- Encourage your child and the caregiver to plan a homecoming celebration while you are gone.

- If possible, send faxes daily to let your child know that all is going well and to help your child feel part of the process.

Prepare for the worst

Even in the most carefully planned adoption, something could go wrong. A miscarriage or stillbirth can happen. A birthparent might have a last-minute change of heart before placing the baby for adoption, or even worse, after allowing the child to be placed in your home. A once-cooperative government or orphanage might suddenly have a change of policy.

In each of these scenarios, prospective adopters suffer a singly painful loss that is often neither recognized nor understood by society in general. People who have experienced this particular loss stress that well-meaning friends and family often say things that are more hurtful than helpful.

In their article in the January/February issue of *Adoptive Families* magazine, "Losing an Adoption: Practical Advice for Moving on after a Uniquely Painful Experience," Pat Johnston and Wendy Williams offer advice on coping with adoption reversal or losing a child you have actually parented for a period of time. Their advice is relevant to anyone who experiences any significant loss related to adoption. Some of their advice includes:

- Have someone else make the initial calls to employers and friends and field the initial questions.

- If possible, arrange for a bereavement leave from work.

- Nurture yourself (and your partner) as much as possible. If you have a partner, understand that your partner may need to grieve differently than you.

- Find support, preferably someone who has been through this particular experience.

- Keep a journal and/or write letters.

- Consider some kind of service or ritual to acknowledge your loss.

- After the shock is over, consider taking a vacation.

- If or when it feels right, become an advocate to explain this type of loss and help others to deal with it.

> **"**
> Miscarriage, stillbirth, and other pre-placement deaths of a hoped-for baby happen in adoption at rates nearly identical to the pregnancy loss and neonatal death rates for the general population.
> —Pat Johnston and Wendy Williams in "Losing an Adoption"
> **"**

If you experience grief in the adoption process, allow yourself to grieve. Then move on. If you choose to pursue another adoption, you will eventually succeed.

Just the facts

- Stay healthy and active during the waiting period and reduce stress by making lists, keeping a journal, and getting household projects done.

- Whether or not to decorate the child's room or the nursery before the arrival of the child is a personal decision based on comfort levels.

- Children already in the family must be totally prepared for all aspects of the adoption, including any travel connected with the process.

- Consider all the pros and cons carefully when changing your child's given name. Whenever possible consult the child, keeping in mind that your child may have a change of mind later.

- Even in the most carefully planned adoptions, something can go wrong. Allow yourself to grieve, and then if you choose to, try again.

How to Construct a Solid Family

GET THE SCOOP ON...
How genetics influences your child's
development ▪ Your influence on your child's
development ▪ Getting to know your child
▪ Parenting according to your child's personality
▪ Dealing with disabilities and disorders

PART V

Is It Nature or Nurture?

Chapter 10

R aising a child today is difficult at best. Adoption experts agree that raising an adopted child is not only difficult, it is different. As the parent of an adopted child, you will need to be an expert on child rearing in general and adopted child rearing specifically.

The truth about the role of genetics

Certainly one of the issues that concerns adoptive parents is the role of genetics in the development of children. With the emergence of open adoption and the growing emphasis on genetic influences, many adoption experts fear that fewer people will be willing to adopt a child with a "history" of any type of disease, illness, or disorder. But all children, including adopted children, are a combination of genetic influences, parental and environmental influences, and peer pressure. Some adoptive parents might be tempted to take credit for the successes in their children and blame genetics for their less desirable attributes, but a good parenting goal is to accept adopted children as individuals. Parents need to be able to communicate that acceptance in unconditional love.

Just how much do genes influence the development of a child? Researchers have been seeking the answer to this question for many years. While there are no definitive answers, researchers have found that genetic factors make an important contribution to the development of a child. But, the good news for adopters is that researchers have also found that the environment plays a major role in that development. A warm and loving environment provides a secure place in which a child can develop abilities and talents which might otherwise have gone unrealized.

How strong is peer pressure?

According to Judith Rich Harris, who reignited the nature/nurture debate with her book *The Nurture Assumption* (see Appendix C), it doesn't really matter very much what parents do in the home because it is outside the home in the company of their peers that children become the people they are.

Several of her conclusions relate to the adopted child. In response to a study done which indicated that adoption can raise a child's IQ, for example, she responds that a child raised in a middle class home has peers who are also raised in middle class homes where reading and computers are considered important. It is therefore as much the influence of peers as it is the influence of parents.

Penelope Leach, an authority on childcare and author of many books, disagrees with Harris. According to Leach, both genetic and parental

Unofficially...
One of the benefits of open adoption is the ability to maintain contact with the birthparents, who can update you on medical conditions that may not surface until later in both the birthparents' and adoptees' lives.

influences are very important in raising children, since they teach children their earliest lessons and help them evaluate peer-inspired ideas. She stresses the importance of not giving up on a child through the teen years, but continuing to balance the values for them.

Whether the experts agree or not, whether the research substantiates the assumptions or not, most parents want to believe they are a major factor in how their children turn out. However, there are certain factors and influences that make parenting an adopted child different and challenging.

Getting to know your child

As with any kind of relationship, the relationship between an adopted child and the adoptive parents needs to develop and grow. One of the most surprising facts for new adopters is that they may not instantly love their child. As one parent explained years after she adopted her infant in China, "We had traveled for days on airplanes, trains, and finally for hours in a small car traveling much too fast. We finally arrived at the orphanage, completed the paperwork, and I was handed my baby. I looked into the face of a stranger. I almost panicked and returned the baby to the kind Chinese woman who had given me my daughter. The infant needed to have her diaper changed and was crying hysterically. I remember nothing of the return trip home. It was several days before I lost this horribly sinking feeling in my stomach, and several weeks before I realized that I loved my new daughter."

For some, like Diana Nichols, a single adoptive mother, the panic set in the minute she heard that she had been assigned a baby in China. She

> **"**
> Each (adopted child) is a unique individual, and we must be sure we communicate to our children that we love each one as an individual and as a whole human being—not just the parts we influenced.
> —Lois Ruskai Melina in Raising Adopted Children (see Appendix C)
> **"**

Watch Out!
The first three
years are very
important in the
development of
an infant. It is
during this time
that the infant
learns to trust
the caregiver and
learns how to
have healthy
attachments. See
Chapter 12 for
more on
attachment.

describes her feelings at that moment: "What thoughts raced through my head. I'll be responsible for this child for the rest of my life. I'm too old. I'm single—what happens to her if I die? Who will care for her? What if she isn't healthy? (I'd heard horror stories of babies adopted from Russia and Romania.) What if I don't love her? What if she turns into a hellion? What if I don't like being a mother? What if...what if...After a while I didn't even know what if. Just, what if?" She almost made the decision to back out, but changed her mind when she was reassured by her psychiatrist, the adoption agency, and other mothers who had experienced this same feeling. She was having normal feelings of anxiety.

The truth about loving your child

Parents who have adopted children of all ages could tell similar stories. It is not unusual for a person to feel anxious soon after the arrival of a new child. Experienced adopters advise new adoptive parents to give themselves time to adjust. Most adoptive parents experience doubts and misgivings at some point in the first few weeks or months. For the vast majority, these feelings are soon forgotten.

Often, the adoption process has been extremely difficult with a great deal of stress immediately prior to and following the arrival of the child. Your adoption support group can be especially helpful in advising you how to avoid some of the more common stresses you will encounter during the weeks preceding and following the arrival of your child. Try to surround yourself with people who can give you positive advice; avoid those, including relatives if necessary, who are negative or ill-informed. Some of these stresses include:

- The constant waiting for the unknown

- A lack of support from family or friends

- A long and arduous trip overseas, including a difficult return with an infant or an older child who does not speak English, if you are doing an international adoption

- The shock of seeing your child, if your child is unhealthy or unclean

- The feeling that your child is not responding to your care giving

- The changes in routine and the resulting chaos in your home and lifestyle

- The testing that an older child will do to see how you will react

- The inevitable changes in all the relationships within the family, both positive and negative

Well-meaning friends and family may wish to visit your newly adopted baby or child, failing to recognize that you may be exhausted—not from the birth of a child, but from the lack of sleep and adaptation to the incredible change in your lives. To minimize your exhaustion:

- Buy frozen dinners or prepare and freeze microwavable main dishes. Collect restaurant take-out menus and set aside budgeted money for help with meals.

- Consider budgeting for professional house-cleaning during the first weeks (you might suggest this as a welcome-baby gift).

- If you are adopting an infant, don't try to get too many things done while the baby is sleeping—you sleep, too!

■ Speak to your child's prospective grandparents, aunts and uncles, and family friends about your needs for arrival week, finding ways to include them that will not deplete your energies.

You need to plan the first few weeks after your child's arrival very carefully. It will be up to you to find the balance between celebration of the new arrival and the private family times that will be necessary for you to get to know and love your new child.

Who is this child?

Some people wonder how adoptive parents can raise children who have personalities so unlike their own. As a matter of fact, many people considering adoption list this as one of their strongest fears. These are the people who make the false supposition that biological children are born with personalities just like both of their biological parents. Experienced parents realize that all children are born with their own distinct personalities.

Knowing a child's personality type can help parents raise children with better understanding and compassion. In *Nurture by Nature: Understanding Your Child's Personality Type—And Become a Better Parent,* Little Brown & Co., 1997, Paul D. Tieger and Barbara Barron-Tieger explain the 16 Myers-Briggs personality types and give advice on how to parent and nurture each type of personality. The point is to parent children in a way that will work with their natures rather than against their natures.

The Myers-Briggs personality assessment describes 16 different types of personalities, which are characterized by the following:

- Preferences in interpersonal interaction
- Types of information noticed and remembered
- Methods of decision making
- Degrees of desirable structure

In Chapter 11, I'll discuss how successful adoptive families not only adjust to the differences among the members of their family, but also celebrate the uniqueness and individuality of each member.

Surviving the stages

All biological and adoptive parents need to learn about the different stages in a child's development. There are additional considerations when learning about the stages of an adopted child's development. Some adopted children have had complex histories and may be behind in development. There are also specific issues that adoptees need to deal with, and it will help both you and your child if you know how they will express these needs at their different stages of development. Some of the issues unique to the adoption experience are loss, grief, anger, separation, and questions of identity. Remember that each child is an individual; not every child will have difficulties in each stage nor will the intensity of the problems be the same for each child.

The first two years

During the first two years of life, your child is learning to trust. Your child is learning that you are providing a world that is predictable and reliable. You and your child are interacting in a way that establishes a secure parent-child bond and gives the child a solid basis for trust. If this bond and sense of trust is not established, serious attachment problems can result (see Chapter 12).

Bright Idea
Read books and gather information on raising children in general as well as books specific to raising adopted children. In this way, you'll be able to tell when your child is simply being a child.

Timesaver
If you have adopted internationally, be sure to learn how babies attach in the culture of birth. Learn if there is a special way to hold your child or a word that soothes his crying. Knowing how to comfort and nurture your baby can save you hours, days, and months of anguish.

Especially during the second year, your child begins to separate from you and venture out into the world. At this time, your child may express anger and aggressiveness. This is normal toddler behavior and not a manifestation of an undesirable genetic trait. Despite the fact that your child may be able to state, "I am adopted," the words will not mean anything special to your child at this age.

The "how and why" years

As soon as children have learned to speak and continuing through their pre-school years, they have a seemingly never-ending list of questions that need answering: Why do birds fly? How do fish swim? Why do...? How does...? Often there are so many questions, parents are unable to answer them all. Often, too, parents are reluctant to answer questions because they feel their child is too young to know or would not understand. It's important for parents to answer their child's questions as truthfully as possible. This includes the inevitable question, "Where did I come from?" In Chapter 15, I'll discuss the issue of when and how to discuss adoption with your child.

At this age it's normal for all children to do the following:

- Have fears about being abandoned and not loved by their parents
- Have difficulty distinguishing between reality and fantasy and fear monsters or witches, etc.
- Become argumentative, often with the same-sex parent
- Have bad dreams or nightmares that awaken them

A word of caution: If the occurrence of sleep disorders is accompanied by sadness during the day or other unusual events, a parent should contact the child's pediatrician. This might be related to a trauma experienced by the child prior to adoption.

The elementary-school years

This is the period in which children spend much of their time out of the home and begin to view themselves in relation to the world. All children are working on issues of self-esteem and security, which they sometimes express in troubling ways, such as aggression, defiance, and stubbornness. Often, children do poorly in school for short periods of time and have difficulty with relationships, including relationships with their parents.

It's in this stage, between ages 7 and 10, that the full emotional reality of the loss is realized by an adoptee. By this age, the adopted child is able to understand the concept of being adopted. The adoptee begins to perceive himself or herself as different from other children, a view often reinforced by the teasing and name calling of other children in the school or awkward questions by insensitive adults. Questions asked in front of the child, such as "Who is his real mother?" or "Is she your real child?" do nothing to bolster the security and self-esteem of a young child.

It's not unusual during this stage of development for an adopted child to create a fantasy to explain the past. Children who are not adopted also often create fantasy parents or parents who let them do what they want or never embarrass them. Adopted children, however, create parents to help them deal with the grief process. If they create a parent who dies of cancer or is killed in an automobile accident, then they have created a parent who loved them and did not have a choice in placing a child in

Unofficially...
Adoption experts agree that loss is an issue for adoptees throughout their lives. They need to work through and express this loss at each stage of development in childhood as well as through their adult lives.

an adoptive situation. Sometimes, adoptive children's fantasies embarrass the adoptive parents. One adoptive father said, "My daughter told all the children in her class as well as the teacher that we stole her from her birthparents when they were not looking. She is a very good storyteller, and we got some very strange looks at the next parent/teacher meeting."

While this can be an embarrassing and challenging time, the best thing you can do is wait for this phase to pass. If it persists beyond the age of 10, contact a therapist to evaluate the situation. In the meantime, try the following:

- Listen, and don't argue with your child.

- Play along, letting your child know that you know it is pretend.

- Say, "That would be nice" or "That would be scary."

- If it happens in front of another adult, say "Sometimes we don't want things to be the way they were so we pretend they're something else."

- Encourage your child to accept the truth by reminding him or her of the positive things in the past.

Fitting in—the middle-school years

By age 9 or 10, children are entering middle school and facing a unique set of challenges. The schools are usually larger with different teachers for each subject. There may be far more students and each one has a desperate need to feel that he or she fits in. It can be devastating for a pre-teen to feel left out of the crowd.

Often, adopted children stand out simply because they are adopted. Many, along with being adopted, are of a different racial or ethnic background than most of their classmates. During this period, adoptees may be angry at their adoptive parents and critical of what their adoptive parents have or have not done to help them understand adoption.

Adolescents indicate they are having trouble not by words but by their behavior:

- Reluctance to go to school; oversleeping, lethargy, or frequent illnesses

- Falling grades

- Blaming failures on not being liked by the teachers

- Withdrawal from family and/or frequent outbursts of anger

- Withdrawal from friends and activities

- Suddenly becoming destructive or self-abusive.

- Finally and most seriously, just giving up

If you notice these behaviors in your child, seek the help of a professional who is experienced working with adopted children and attachment issues. Check with your support group for recommendations for therapists and other professionals who are adoption competent.

Who am I, anyway?

In high school, adopted teens are still grappling with the normal adolescent problems of self-identity and self-esteem. But, as Frank Kunstal, a licensed psychologist and author of *Troubled Transplants*, University of Southern Maine, 1993, says, adopted teens have the added burden of loss. He emphasizes that young teens need support and validation from

> 66
> Remember, your middle-school child is growing up. Children this age move in and out of childish behavior. One day she carries a doll to school. The next day— her purse. Children want to be treated with an increasing degree of maturity and understanding.
> —Jayne Schooler, author of *The Whole Life Adoption Book*
> 99

Bright Idea
Adoptive parents can become advocates for their children and help avoid some of these problems by working with the schools to prevent children from feeling left out because they are "different." (See Chapter 13 for a discussion of how to educate the schools.)

people they trust to initiate issues of mourning and grieve appropriately. Kunstal suggests helping them work through their grief by:

- Encouraging and validating their everyday feelings

- Helping them to identify, understand, and share hurt feelings

- Establishing family acceptance for expression of negative and painful emotions

- Using positive discipline, reassurance, and encouragement

- Staying emotionally connected to them, especially in the face of normal, expected crises, and particularly when told they need us the least

As one mother in a support group for challenging children said, "We were simply not prepared for our adopted daughter's rebellion in her pre-teens. She raged and told us she hated us. Because we had the support of people who understood the stage she was going through, we were able to hang in and be there for her. It has been a tough few years, but we can now see how important we are for her. The best part is that she can see it, too."

Adopted girls also tend to struggle with the concepts of motherhood and sexuality. The adopted female has two distinct role models in this area: her biological mother, who chose adoption for her child; and her adoptive mother, who chose for a variety of reasons to raise a child who was not her biological child. This can be very confusing to a young adolescent. Because adolescents have difficulty talking with parents about sexual issues, it might be necessary to provide someone outside the family to offer support and understanding for an adolescent girl who has inconsistent views of motherhood and sexuality.

Parenting the special needs child

There has long been a battle raging in the mental health arena as to whether or not adoptees have more mental health problems than people who were not adopted. Various research studies have been unable to prove or disprove the basic premise that the adoption experience itself leads to psychological problems. There are too many variables and too many unanswerable questions.

On the other hand, it probably can be concluded that there are several issues that all adoptees deal with at some point and to some degree throughout their lives. These issues would include:

- Attachment: feelings of ambiguity or not belonging in the family

- Self-esteem: feeling rejected by birthparents

- Shame and guilt: shame about being bad enough to be rejected, anger at adoptive parents, and guilt about being angry

- Identity: difficulty finding true self

- Lack of control: feelings of lack of choice in life

- Loss and unresolved grief

- Learning disabilities and other emotional/behavior problems due to genetics, poor prenatal care, and birth trauma

While experts stress that the vast majority of adoptees do not have serious problems, adopted children are at a higher risk for some behavioral and psychological problems. It's possible that adoptive parents are aware of problems such as learning disabilities and mental or physical illness before they adopt the child, but sometimes they learn of these conditions after adopting.

Moneysaver
Sometimes, the best psychiatric support can come from parents who have "been through it." Find a support group for parents of challenging adopted children. It can be invaluable.

Unofficially...
The Adopted Child Syndrome became well known when psychologist David Kirschner used the term in testimony to defend a young man who was accused of murdering his adoptive parents in 1984.

What is Adopted Child Syndrome?

In the early 1980s, David Kirschner, a psychologist in private practice in New York, developed the theory that adopted children and adolescents exhibit proportionally more extreme antisocial behavior and behavior disorders. Kirschner felt that genetics could only partially account for this pattern and that problems unique to being adopted—primarily resulting from minimizing or ignoring the child's efforts to understand his or her origins—were the real cause of such problems. He called this condition the Adopted Child Syndrome and suggested that by dealing more honestly with the child's need to understand his or her origins, the condition might, in part, be remedied. Since then, new theories have come into favor, including Reactive Attachment Disorder discussed in Chapter 12.

Children who have been sexually abused

The most recent statistics estimate that in the general population one in every three girls and one in eight boys has been sexually abused. According to the National Adoption Information Clearinghouse, experts estimate that nearly 75 percent of the children in foster care have been sexually abused. You should consider the possibility that your child has been sexually abused if one or more of these signs or behaviors is present:

- Scratches, bruises, itching, rashes, cuts or injuries, especially in the genital area
- Venereal disease, pregnancy
- Aggressive behavior toward younger children
- Advanced sexual knowledge or "sexy" behavior, excessive masturbation
- Eating disorders

- Fear of a particular person, sudden changes in behavior

- Poor relationships with peers

- Self-mutilation, threats of suicide

- Use of drugs and alcohol

- Promiscuity or prostitution

- Fire-setting, lying, stealing, running away

- Preoccupation with death

Watch Out!
Many of the signs of sexual abuse mimic the signs of other problems. Find the support of an expert who is aware of all the aspects of the adoption experience. For more on this topic, see Chapter 12.

Parents can help a child who has been sexually abused by setting clear guidelines that will provide the structure, comfort, and security that will help the child both inside and outside the home. Some of the issues parents need to be aware of if their child has been sexually abused are:

- Privacy. A child should be taught to knock on closed doors.

- Bedrooms and bathrooms. Caution should be used when children are sharing bedrooms and bath times. Parents should not take an older child into their bed; instead, leave the cuddling for the living room.

- Touching. A child should be taught the difference between good and bad touching.

- Clothing. Appropriate clothing should be worn.

- Saying "no." Help your child learn to say "no" to unwanted touching.

- Sex education. Make sure your child is appropriately educated.

- Secrets. Don't allow games involving secrets.

- Being alone. Try not to allow your child to be alone with an adult or other child.

- Wrestling and tickling. These may have sexual overtones for your child.

- Behaviors and feelings. Help your child differentiate between feelings and behaviors. Emphasize that a person does not always act on all feelings.

Children who have been physically abused or neglected

Often, children who have been physically abused or neglected have been diagnosed with post-traumatic stress disorder or "PTSD." Most people associate post-traumatic stress with war veterans who returned from war with psychological symptoms due to the terrible traumas they experienced. Children who have also experienced trauma have symptoms such as:

- Nightmares

- Intrusive thoughts

- Flashbacks

- Apathy, lack of responsiveness

- Sleep disturbances

- Poor concentration

- Terror reaction when reminded of the original trauma

Children with these symptoms need to be treated by a competent therapist or other expert. Again, check with your support group for recommendations for adoption/trauma competent professionals.

The baby with HIV

Fortunately, most of the babies who are born to HIV-infected mothers are false-positive and will convert to negative before the age of two. It is predicted that with the better prenatal treatment of women infected with HIV, the number of babies infected will decline. Nevertheless, there are babies testing positive for HIV available for adoption at this time. Prospective parents must consider the following before they decide to adopt an HIV-infected baby:

- It's possible that your child will die young.

- You will be dealing with the loss and grief of a child who was placed for adoption by a birth-parent and rejected by society because the child had AIDS.

- As the parent of this child, you may lose members of your support system who may not understand your desire to parent this child.

- You will have to become a strong advocate for your child because you will need to learn as much as possible about the disease and you will need to educate society about HIV.

Timesaver
Get as much medical and genetic history about your child as possible at the time of adoption. This will not only provide you with the information you need to raise your child, it will also provide your child with invaluable information to take into adulthood.

Children born to drug and alcohol abusers

Children who are born to mothers who used and abused either (or both) drugs and alcohol during pregnancy are at risk for having birth defects and life-long implications.

It's possible that infants born to mothers who used drugs during pregnancy will exhibit developmental difficulties and delays throughout their lives. In the past, experts were not optimistic about the future of these infants, but early intervention has been effective in changing the negative prognosis.

Children whose mothers drank prenatally are at risk of having alcohol-related birth defects. Along with low birth weight and learning disabilities, they may have the more serious complications of Fetal Alcohol Syndrome (FAS) or Fetal Alcohol Effects (FAE). Some children with FAS have facial abnormalities, are very small, and have varying levels of mental retardation in three or more of the following areas:

- Self-care and hygiene
- Expressive language
- Comprehension
- Learning
- Motor skills
- Judgment and understanding of cause and effect
- In adulthood, keeping a job or budgeting money

Children with FAE have somewhat less serious complications. These children are very active and may find it difficult to concentrate on specific tasks.

The facts about ADHD

Depending on the type of ADHD your child has, your child may have problems listening to directions, working alone without being distracted, or finishing assignments. Your child may lose things, forget things, or regularly make mistakes. Your child may find it difficult to sit still in class. Your child may fidget and squirm. Your child might blurt out answers, interrupt, or have problems waiting his turn.

More adopted children than non-adopted children are diagnosed with Attention Deficit Hyperactivity Disorder. The reasons for this are not clear, but could be due to poor prenatal health or genetic factors. The most common risk factors for ADHD are:

- Family history of ADHD
- History of alcoholism in the family

- Living in poverty
- Being male
- Child abuse or neglect
- Mental retardation
- Conduct disorders
- Low birth weight

It's also quite likely that adopted children are being misdiagnosed, as there are other conditions with similar symptoms:

- Conduct disorders
- Mood disorders
- Anxiety
- Developmental disorders
- Medical disorders
- Seizures
- Side effects of drugs (including medicines used to treat seizures or asthma)
- Chronic illness, especially thyroid problems
- Sensory problems, especially hearing loss

Parents who suspect their child may be showing symptoms of ADHD should have him or her evaluated by a competent psychologist who has experience working with both ADHD and adopted children. Parents should also consult the learning disability specialist at the child's school.

Accentuating the positive

There is no way to determine why some children overcome immense adversity in their lives and grow to be strong and competent adults, while others do not. But many famous educators, scientists, politicians, and leaders in numerous other fields of

> 66
> Sometimes, the things that drive parents and teachers crazy, like risk-taking, perseverance, or marching to your own music, are the same qualities that can bring light to the world.
> —Joan McNamara, M.S., associate director of Family Resources
> 99

Unofficially...
The following are
a few well-known
and successful
adoptees: Edward
Albee,
playwright; John
J. Audubon,
naturalist; Gerald
Ford, U.S.
president; Newt
Gingrich; Steven
Paul Jobs, co-
founder of Apple
Computer; Art
Linkletter; James
Michener, author;
and Moses.

endeavor have managed to translate their seemingly negative "disabilities" into positive attributes that have helped them live successful lives.

Experts stress the importance of encouraging children and young adults to concentrate on their attributes rather than their shortcomings. In this way, they not only learn to compensate, but also to acquire a sense of identity that will carry them through life. It's particularly important to help young adoptees work through their struggles with self-esteem and self-concept by encouraging them to see their uniqueness and value.

Just the facts

- Good parenting, peer pressure, and genetics all influence how your child turns out.

- Each stage of normal child development has some ramifications for the adopted child.

- Adoptees struggle with identity and self-concept throughout all stages of development.

- Adoptees are at risk for a variety of disabilities and disorders at an average slightly above the general population.

GET THE SCOOP ON...
Becoming a healthy adoptive family
• Maintaining your commitment to succeed
• How to discipline effectively • Handling
prejudice and racism • Signs that
your adoption is in trouble

The Truth About Adoptive Families

The most obvious truth about the typical adopted family in the United States today is that there's no such thing as a typical adopted family in the United States today. Therefore, when it comes to parenting and building a successful family, there are no hard and fast rules, no gems of wisdom that will fit all families.

How do today's adoptive families, with children adopted at all ages from all corners of the world with incredibly diverse backgrounds, make it work? What do they all have in common despite the fact that they are all so different?

In this chapter, I'll show you how to avoid some of the pitfalls and give you some successful strategies that other adoptive parents have found useful in parenting their children. I'll also discuss how and why some families decide it cannot work.

When it works

When researchers study adoptive families, they look at several factors that may predict the adopted family's success, which I discuss below.

Being prepared

One of the most important factors is how well the prospective adoptive parents are prepared to adopt. Experts and experienced adopters stress over and over again the importance of preparation. I've already covered many of the issues that will help you prepare for adoption, among the more important of which are:

- Doing all your homework and understanding exactly what is required of you (and your partner) as adoptive parent(s)

- If you have a partner, both of you agreeing to the adoption and working through any emotions related to previous loss

- Involving the rest of the family, especially other children, in the preparation, and helping them to understand the role each will play

Making a commitment

The vast majority of adopters begin parenting their children with the firm conviction that they will be a family forever. It would be difficult to believe that anyone would form a family thinking, "Well, if this works, great. If not, we can always back out anytime." Yet adoptions do disrupt. Why?

Some experts contend that it is the attitude of the parents themselves that results in the failure of adoptions. These experts feel that adoptive parents are not prepared to commit to a relationship with their child "for better or worse." When things become difficult for the parent, the parent questions whether he or she can continue to parent the child.

Adopters whose adoptions disrupted or dissolved have countered the commitment argument by stating that they were not given the complete and necessary history of the child; therefore, they could not make an informed decision about adopting and raising a child with problems revealed after the placement was made.

Social workers in the field of adoption complain that prospective adopters often close their ears and hearts to the truth concerning a certain child, believing that love and a warm, nurturing home will be enough. "No matter what we tell adopters who are adopting special needs children, no matter how much information we give them concerning their child, the history, [and] the background, prospective adopters are convinced that all they need to do is take this child home, feed him good food, and love him; all will be fine in a few weeks," a social worker who works for a state agency told me. "Adoptive parents need to realize that their child will go through stages in which they will do anything to hurt their parents. It isn't simply a matter of good food and love."

Often, too, the professionals working with the family to help it stay together don't have the education and experience to offer the appropriate help to the family and actually facilitate the disruption. For more on this subject, see Chapter 14.

To help you make a commitment that will last forever, make sure you:

- Have a realistic view of adoption and a clear picture of the child you are willing to adopt.

Unofficially...
In the past, much necessary information was withheld from prospective parents for a variety of reasons. Today, the trend is toward informing adopters so they can make better decisions. In some states, laws have been passed that mandate disclosure of information.

- Are aware that it takes more than just love to parent any child, especially the adopted child.

- Are willing to wait for the "rewards" of parenting. They may not come for a long time.

- Become an informed adopter. Learn all you can about the experience through books and dialogue with people who have been there.

What good discipline means

Good parenting means good discipline. Children need clear limits in order to build trust and security. Even though they'll test these limits, sometimes to the point that you are ready to scream, setting them shows them you love them and take their well-being seriously. This is especially true for an adopted child, who has a unique set of loss and grief issues I've already discussed.

You can find many excellent parenting manuals, some specifically for adoptive parents. Barbara Tremitiere, an author and mother of 12 adopted children, travels the country giving workshops and speeches concerning a variety of adoption subjects. In one of her workshops on effective parenting and discipline techniques for adopted children, she advised parents to choose which behaviors of their children they'll put up with, and which behaviors they won't. She also suggested the following:

- *Decide who owns the problem.* It's the child's problem if it concerns such things as how the child dresses or keeps his bedroom clean. It's the parent's problem if it's the kitchen or another part of the shared house that is not kept clean.

- *Learn to detach.* Children become worse the more the parent becomes emotionally involved and excited. To help to learn to detach, Tremitiere tells parents to list 10 things they value most in life, then shorten the list to 5. These five things become non-negotiable in the family, and everything else is negotiable. Tremitiere's five family values are:

1. Education—children are required to finish high school.
2. Religion—children are required to attend church.
3. Jobs—children are required to do work around the house.
4. Smoking—no smoking is allowed in the house.
5. Hitting—children are not allowed to hit their parents.

Adoptive families are different. Parents will need to determine what they consider to be the most important non-negotiables in their family, thereby setting standards that are attainable for the children they are raising.

■ *Choose logical consequences that make children think.* Time out does not have much meaning if children are sent to their rooms where they have exciting toys, a TV, and a computer. It's better to have a consequence that will allow children to see what they did wrong and how they can do better the next time.

A method of discipline called logical consequences encourages children to develop a sense of responsibility. The goals of logical consequences are to acknowledge mutual respect and rights while allowing the child to make choices. It should be

You have to teach them discipline. You have to show them who's in charge. If you give in to them every time, they're going to run your life.
—Madonna, on raising her daughter, Lourdes

Watch Out!
Stanford University researchers tracked the habits of more than 1,500 ninth-graders and found that just two hours of music-video viewing per day leads to a 31 percent increase in the risk of drinking over the next 18 months. (Don Knapp, *CNN San Francisco*)

directly related to the misbehavior and stated in a calm manner by the parent. Always follow through on the consequence you've described. For example:

- A father to his son with a loud TV: "I understand that you want to watch TV this morning, but it's very early and the rest of us want to sleep. Either turn down the TV or go outside to play."

- A mother to a daughter with a dirty room: "I'm going to vacuum the house today, including your room. There are things all over the floor that you'll need to put in a bag, which you will put in the basement. I will be vacuuming your room in an hour."

- A father to a son who refuses to do an assigned job around the house: "You want to play baseball this afternoon. If you don't rake the leaves as you were told this morning, you will have to stay home and do it this afternoon."

Sometimes, parents who follow the theory of logical consequences find that those in authority outside of their home don't agree with the theory. The baseball coach in the situation above might have tried to intervene, for example. You may need to take other people into account when you are choosing your child's logical consequence; in other words, remember that a situation can have more than one logical consequence, and you can discipline your child without punishing an entire team.

Tips for unique situations

As an adoptive parent, you will face issues that biological parents will never have to face. I am including only a few of those issues here, but these should serve as an example of what types of things you may encounter.

Same-age siblings

One of the unique situations resulting from adoption is the occurrence of same-age, unrelated siblings in the home. These pairs can create some challenges, particularly in the area of competition, which parents can handle by doing the following:

- Parents can respond effectively, not necessarily equally, to the talents and interests of each child.

- Encourage each child to develop his own special strength. Avoid comparisons as much as possible.

- Celebrate birthdays separately.

- Consider separating them in classes at school.

Summer problems

For some adopted children, summer can trigger memories of summers past. If your child was born in a country with a warm, humid climate, the warm weather of summer may evoke feelings of time past. Holly van Gulden and Lisa Bartels-Rabb, co-authors of *Real Parents, Real Children: Parenting the Adopted Child* (see Appendix C), suggest that you discuss the issue with your child and explain what is happening. They also suggest that you try the following:

- Keep a predictable schedule to minimize anxiety.

- Provide structured activities.

- Let your child know that it's OK to feel sad once in awhile. Offer lots of support.

Other issues of the past

When you adopt a child who is older than an infant, be prepared for issues that are rooted in past experiences. Some of the issues will be around food.

Children whose early life experiences included food deprivation can continue to exhibit problems later in life. Food problems are also an indication of Reactive Attachment Disorder, which I'll discuss in Chapter 12.

Your child may also display behaviors such as unusual fears or nightmares resulting from an unknown incident in the past. Discuss these fears with a competent therapist.

You're not my parent!

I can almost guarantee you that you will hear this at least once while you are raising an adopted child, probably when your child is a pre-teen or in adolescence. Try to remember that your child will probably say it in anger when he's not getting something that he wants. It's a ploy to get your attention, and most adopters report that it does what it's intended to do. While many adoptive parents expect a comment like this, no one is ever really ready for it. Experts agree that this comment is best ignored when said in anger.

Some coping strategies

I strongly urge you to find the support of others who are in similar situations. By telling your story to other people with similar experiences, you will probably feel connected and able to validate your own feelings. For more on the importance of finding support, see Chapter 14.

Successful parents have learned that it's OK to be angry with their children; they have also learned ways to vent their anger and frustration without harming their children either physically or emotionally. Experienced adoptive parents offer some tips for dealing with frustrations:

- Get away from it all, even for just a few minutes. A drive in the car, a walk, or a peaceful period of reading can help.

- Turn up the music, dance and sing, let the energy escape.

- Take a shower and cry—a lot if it helps.

- Clean the house.

- Call a friend, talk, and cry.

- Joke about the situation afterwards. Somehow seeing it in a funny light makes it easier the next time.

Honoring differences

Another trait that successful adoptive parents have in common is the ability to accept the adopted child as a unique individual and the ability to meet the needs of each individual child. Adopted children are a bundle of differences, not the least of which can be appearance, race, and/or culture. Successful adoptive parents value all the differences in their children and do not impose their own dreams and expectations on them.

The "rainbow" generation

The make-up of the general population in the United States is changing dramatically. According to the following statistics, the next generation will truly be the "rainbow" generation:

- By the year 2000, less than half the students in California will be of European origin.

- By the year 2050, 75 percent of the work force will be people of color.

- By the year 2025, only 63 percent of the country will be Caucasian.

Bright Idea
The kindest thing you can do for your children is accept them for who they are, and prepare them for the fact that the rest of the world may not do the same.

Many Americans are becoming more tolerant of differences, accepting people more easily, and learning to celebrate cultural and racial differences. Unfortunately, we are far from being a tolerant society. People who are different still have a problem fitting in, although the irony is that everyone is different in some way. If you are short, tall, white, black, red, heterosexual, homosexual, skinny, fat, male, female, young, old, or any combination of the above, you are different. Learn to celebrate it, and you will be able to help your child celebrate his or her differences, too.

Helping your child fit in

To further help your child, experts and experienced adopters recommend the following:

- Provide your child with role models from a variety of ethnic groups, but especially those of the same group as your child.

- Model friendships with people of all social, ethnic, and economic groups.

- Consider adopting siblings or children of the same race or ethnic group. Children who can relate to another child in the family or even continue to use their native language may adjust better than those who have no one to whom they can relate.

- Remain firm in your belief that you are the best parent for your child.

- Don't tolerate any racially or ethnically biased remarks. This includes remarks made to, about, or by your child. Make it clear that it's unacceptable to make offensive or biased remarks about any aspect of a person's gender, religion, age, physical appearance, disability, race, or ethnicity.

Attempt to keep your remarks gracious and polite, thus modeling appropriate responses to prejudice.

- Surround your family with diversity. Teach your child about all cultures. Celebrate many holidays and special occasions. Invite your friends to your celebrations and attend theirs.

- Teach your child the differences between people, but also point out the similarities. It's important that your child feel like part of the family. For example, you might tell your child who is feeling sad because she does not have the same color hair as you, "You might not have the same color hair as I do, but you sound just like I do on the phone, and you like to dance as much as I do."

- Take your child to places where people of your child's ethnicity or color predominate. This can be an enriching experience for your child and for your family.

- If your child is from another country, take a "roots" trip to that country. Be sure to visit your child's home town or surrounding areas so that your child can get a true picture of what life is like in that area.

- Teach your child as much as possible about his or her heritage through books, films, and the Internet.

Establish a continuing dialogue about your child's race and culture; you need to acknowledge that not all people from all cultures and races are accepted and treated the same. Discuss issues with your child as they arise, such as the following:

- How life and opportunities are different and the same for people of different races and cultures

Unofficially...
Not all adoption professionals agree that transracial adoption is positive. The National Association of Black Social Workers continues to believe that only African-American parents can teach African-American children how to handle racism.

- How people of ethnic groups might be treated differently by police officers, social organizations, government agencies, and others

- Your views on interracial dating and marriage, as well as the views of the general public

You might not hear about all the issues of race or culture that your child encounters on a daily basis. I suggest that you use television programs or news articles as starting points for discussions about prejudice and racism, even when the subjects seem difficult.

Along the way, someone may be unkind to your child simply because of your child's ethnic background. You can prepare your child for that experience by giving her the tools to handle such situations and by letting her know that you will be there to provide support through the rough spots.

Parents who have experience in raising children of different ethnic backgrounds or races advise parents in the same situation to teach their children how to handle difficult situations themselves by teaching and modeling problem solving skills. They caution against solving the problems for the child, which can result in more problems. Finally, take the time to prepare your child for what might happen—don't assume it could never happen.

Preventing identity crisis

In Chapter 10 I outlined the stages that all children go through in a normal, healthy development. Children of color and differing ethnicity growing up in a predominantly white culture go through other stages before finally reaching a level of security with who they are. In her article in the January/February, 1998, issue of *Adopted Families* magazine, "Racial/Ethnic Identity: How Is It Formed?", Jane

Schooler quotes Dan Houston and Denise Good-man, experts in cultural diversity and writers for the Institute for Human Services in Columbus, Ohio. According to Houston and Goodman, parents and families of children of color need to be aware of the struggles young people face. According to Houston and Goodman, the stages of development are:

Bright Idea
One of the strongest tools you can give your child is self-esteem. Do whatever you can to help your child develop natural talents. Praise your child's strengths.

- *Stage One: Pre-Encounter.* In this stage, the pre-teen sees little relevance of race to his or her life.

- *Stage Two: Awareness.* The older pre-teen to young teen begins to experience confusion about his or her racial/ethnic group, often as a result of a racist experience.

- *Stage Three: Awakening/Immersion.* The older teen to young adult endorses the values and norms of his or her own racial/ethnic group, often rejecting values of other groups.

- *Stage Four: Incorporation.* The adult has a positive self-identity that allows him or her to value other groups.

I want to emphasize that every child is an indi-vidual with different experiences; therefore, the ages associated with each stage will vary.

Celebrating diversity

Help your child learn to celebrate diversity. Ask your local adoption group or multicultural family group if it sponsors celebrations, picnics, and other events that bring children of different cultures and races together.

In anticipation of attending a Diversity Day orga-nized by a group called Multicultural Families of Vermont and New Hampshire, an eight-year-old girl wrote, "Last year I loved Diversity Day. I had my name written in many languages. I thought that was neat. I liked making kites and playing instruments from different parts of the world. This year I want to go early and help my mom set up. I am looking forward to wearing a lahnga and meeting people just like me."

Groups such as these, along with many adoption agencies, also offer workshops and classes dealing with specific issues adoptive parents have, such as hair care for children of different races and health-related issues. Some adoption groups offer culture camps, which can help a child by exposing the child to ethnic-related activities.

Experts encourage adoptive parents to look beyond adoption groups to find others who represent the cultural or racial background of your child. You might look into groups formed around civic, ethnic, recreational, sports, arts, music, cultural, educational, religious, political, or anti-bias issues. If your child is reluctant to attend these groups and activities, attend them without your child even if it means venturing a little beyond your own comfort level. In this way, you will send a message to your child that you value diversity.

Moneysaver
If you take your child on a roots trip, forget staying in the beautiful tourist hotel compound. Not only could this cost a great deal, it doesn't give your child a true picture of the country. Stay at a small hotel where the locals are more likely to stay.

What if you are "different"?

If you are older, single, gay or lesbian, or disabled, you may be considered a non-traditional parent by society in general, and more importantly, you may be considered different by your own child, especially when he or she reaches adolescence. You, too, will have the responsibility to help your kids deal with prejudice. Some of the ways to help your child include the following:

- Be prepared for the time when your child is "embarrassed" by you. Understand that this feeling stems from your child's struggle to fit in.

- Discuss the issue before it becomes a problem. Prepare your child for the negative comments he may hear on the outside. Help your child with answers to the negative comments.

- Help your child to develop self-esteem.

- Help your child understand that most children are embarrassed by their parents at one time or another. It's a stage that will pass.

When it doesn't work

This is real life; all adoption stories don't end with the family living happily ever after. Some adoptions fail. A failed adoption is most commonly referred to as a disrupted adoption, although technically this term refers to an adoption that fails before the adoption is finalized. The technical term for an adoption that is reversed after finalization is dissolution. Dissolutions can occur years after the placement and are more difficult to obtain and may involve large legal bills.

Preventing failure

Statistically, people who adopt older children are at greater risk of experiencing a failed adoption, but disruption can be prevented by taking some precautions:

- Adoption experts should match the child with parents who have a thorough understanding of what the child has experienced in the past and will need in the future.

- Prospective adoptive parents should seek the advice and expertise of professionals such as adoption social workers and therapists who have experience working with the types of children they plan to adopt.

Unofficially...
Disruptions can run as high as 10 to 20 percent in older child adoptions (Barth and Berry, 1988). This is 10 to 20 times higher than with infant placements, and doesn't count children living out of the home but still legally part of the adoptive family.

▪ Prospective adoptive parents should be aware that all types of adoption and parenthood present risks. They should make themselves aware of the possible risks.

▪ All the professionals involved in the adoption, as well as the adoptive parents, should plan for possible problems in the future and make sure the proper support is available for the adoptive family. I'll discuss the type of support in Chapter 14.

Many advocates encourage a "safety net" or clause to be inserted into an adoption assistance contract between the adoptive family and the state agency making a placement. This clause states that in the event residential care is needed, the state placing the child will locate the facility and pay any expenses not covered by other agencies or insurances. Some states have agreed to add similar clauses, while others have refused to do so. Be sure to check your state's policy if you are adopting a child who is at risk. Your child would be at risk if one or more of the following pertains to your child:

▪ A biological family history of mental illness, behavioral and emotional problems, or drug or alcohol abuse

▪ Has had multiple caregivers

▪ Has experienced any type of abuse or neglect

▪ Was hospitalized or institutionalized frequently and for many consecutive days during the first 18 months of life

▪ Has a drug or alcohol abuse problem

▪ Engages in high-risk or illegal behaviors

▪ Has a history of emotional or behavioral problems in foster care or at school

- Has been seen by mental health professionals on a regular basis

- Exhibits moderate to severe emotional or behavioral problems with you or with other caregivers prior to finalization of the adoption

Terminating the placement

Despite careful preparation and precautions, you may find that your adoption is not working. It's important to contact the social worker or other professional as soon as possible. With the help of a qualified professional, you will need to decide if the adoption can go forward. Professionals stress the importance of asking for help as soon as possible to prevent trauma for both the child and the parents.

Research has found that some of the signs of a failing placement are:

- The mother and father are divided about the placement.

- One parent, usually the mother, is the target for the bad behavior, and the other parent sees the good behavior.

- There are constant behavior problems wherever the child goes.

- Parents start setting time limits; if things aren't better in a certain amount of time, then... There seems to be no solution.

- Other children in the family are targets for physical or sexual abuse.

- Family, friends, and finally adoption workers suggest disruption.

- Parents begin to feel like psychiatrists rather than parents.

Watch Out!
Children who
have been
abused by birth
or foster parents
or other adults,
particularly
children who
have been
sexually abused,
sometimes
make false
accusations
against
subsequent
parents or
caregivers.
For more
information,
see Chapter 12;
also check
"False Abuse
Allegations" at
www.homes4kids.
org.

- The marriage begins to founder.

- There is no joy in the home.

- The child asks to be removed.

- Parents feel hatred and rage toward the child.

- The adoptee alleges physical or sexual abuse by one of the parents.

Each state handles adoption disruptions differently. Be sure to discuss how disruptions are handled in your state with your adoption worker before a child is placed in your home.

Just the facts

- One attribute most well-adjusted adoptive parents share is a sense of humor, which allows them to be flexible and not take themselves or their children *too* seriously.

- An adoption is more likely to succeed when all, including partners and other children in the home, agree to the adoption and are thoroughly prepared.

- Raising special needs or "at risk" children can be very rewarding, but parents need the positive and informed support of professionals.

- In the real world, a small percentage of adoptions do disrupt or dissolve as a result of many factors.

First Things First

PART VI

GET THE SCOOP ON...
Who is at risk for RAD? ▪ How children develop
attachment problems ▪ The behaviors RAD
children exhibit ▪ How to parent RAD children
effectively ▪ Why some people choose
to parent RAD children

The Facts About Reactive Attachment Disorder

Chapter 12

Reactive attachment Disorder is more common than you might think: approximately one million children have RAD in New York City alone, according to Keith Reber of the Phillips Graduate Institute (Karen, 1990). The National Adoption Center reports that fifty-two percent of adoptable children have attachment disorder symptoms. Twenty percent of the children under five who visit Kaiser-Permanente in Southern California show RAD symptoms (Brill-Downey, 1994). Although these statistics are somewhat dated, more current statistics are not available, and many experts believe that the reported incidence of attachment disorder symptoms will rise as knowledge and understanding of this disorder increase.

The child with Reactive Attachment Disorder is a very complex child. Often superficially engaging and charming with strangers and others who don't threaten his or her need to control every aspect of his or her life, the RAD child is often misunderstood and misdiagnosed by teachers, therapists, and other professionals. The RAD child is often delayed in emotional development. He or she lacks the foundation of basic trust that underlies a sense of self, acceptance of adult authority, empathy for others, the capacity to regulate emotions, and cause and effect thinking.

Scientific evidence

Despite strong evidence that maternal activity before birth actually changes fetal brain development, researchers have only recently had tools sophisticated enough to study these changes. In the past few years, these researchers have compared the brain development of children whose mothers did not practice proper prenatal care with the brain development of children whose mothers did. The researchers have been able to note differences in brain size and other areas of development. Their research has scientifically proven the importance of not only the first three years of life but also the nine months before birth.

As a result of the new scientific research, the importance of the entire prenatal period and the first three years of life has become headline news. The implications for all parents have become obvious, especially to a generation raising children depending on daycare providers to be partners in parenting their children.

The implications for the adoptive family are also significant. In the past, prospective adoptive parents were not made aware of potential attachment problems when adopting a child, or they were led to believe that attachment problems could be solved simply by providing a loving home for a child. Experience has shown that this is not true.

Today, as researchers discover more information about attachment issues and Reactive Attachment Disorder (RAD), more adoption workers are making parents aware of potential problems and providing post-adoption support. Many are not. It's up to you to become educated so that you can ask the right questions and make informed decisions.

The history of attachment

Attachment theory is not new. In 1969, British psychiatrist John Bowlby defined attachment as a "lasting psychological connectedness between human beings." Bowlby was a leading researcher and teacher in the field of personality development and president of the International Association of Child Psychiatry. Today, his work is considered the foundation of attachment theory in child development.

Along with Bowlby, other researchers expanded on his original work in the '70s and '80s, but it was not until the '90s that the importance of this disorder fully came to the public's attention. Because the number of children seriously injured by maltreatment accompanied by disruptions in attachment quadrupled from 1986 to 1993, more and more people have become convinced that Reactive Attachment Disorder is a very serious issue in the United States today.

The definition of Reactive Attachment Disorder

Reactive Attachment Disorder is, simply stated, the inability to form *normal* and *trusting* relationships, with accompanying developmental delays. The medical books say that RAD appears before the age of five and that children with RAD exhibit disturbed

> **66**
> When the child with a weak attachment interacts with a caring adult, the child assumes that it is his own successful manipulation. . . rather than any nurturing quality of the adult or any intrinsic worth of the child.
> —Daniel A. Hughes Ph.D., author of *Facilitating Developmental Attachment*
> **99**

and developmentally inappropriate behavior when relating to others.

Off to a bad start

Attachment between mother and child begins before birth. With the aid of new scientific tools, researchers have shown that the attunement between mother and child begins *in utero* when the infant is able to tune in to the melody of its mother's voice. Therefore, the emotional and neurological development of the baby can be greatly affected by the attitude of the mother and whether or not she abuses drugs and alcohol during pregnancy.

The risk of developing attachment problems continues through the first three years of a child's life. Most child development experts agree that a child who is neglected and/or abused during this time frame could be physically and emotionally scarred for life. Geraldine Dawson, a psychologist at the University of Washington, monitored the brain-wave patterns of children born to mothers who were diagnosed with depression and concluded that the children's brain-wave activities closely followed the ups and downs of their mother's depression. She also found that as the children grew older, their ability to rebound became less and less apparent.

How children develop RAD

In order to help you understand how a child develops attachment problems, let's first look at how infants and young children normally develop trust and therefore attach to caregivers:

- *Infant cycle:* The infant expresses a *need* (for food or comfort) by crying; the parent responds with food and comfort such as rocking, holding, eye contact, and warmth; the infant receives

Unofficially...
Most children might not like limits set by adults, but children with RAD consider limits as a matter of life and death. They believe if they do not stay in control, they will die.

gratification; the infant repeats this cycle over and over and learns to *trust* the caregiver.

■ *Toddler cycle:* The toddler expresses a need (for example, to touch a hot stove) and takes it upon himself to fulfill the need; the caregiver stops the toddler before harm is done; the toddler is upset; the caregiver comforts the toddler. The toddler *trusts* the caregiver and learns that he is valued even when limits are set.

If either of these cycles is upset, the child runs the risk of not attaching to the caregiver. During the infant cycle, if the needs of the infant are not met, or are met inconsistently, the infant does not learn to trust.

When the toddler learns that no limits will be set, or that the responses to limit testing are erratic or abusive, he or she learns to believe that needs will never be met by others. The toddler must attempt to meet his or her own needs and, over a period of time, tries to control everything. The toddler's inevitable failures result in extreme fear and rage that begin with temper tantrums and escalate into destructive and self-destructive behavior.

Who is at risk?

Children who are at risk for developing Reactive Attachment Disorder may have experienced some sort of interruption in the prenatal bonding cycle and/or have experienced trauma in the first three years of life. They may have experienced some sort of interruption in the prenatal bonding cycle due to any of the following:

■ Birthmother's denial of pregnancy

■ Birthmother's dislike of the father

■ Substance abuse by birthmother

Bright Idea
Ask your adoption social worker for a suggested reading list on Reactive Attachment Disorder. If he or she cannot offer you some suggestions or avoids the issue, you may need to find another worker.

■ Poor diet or self-care during pregnancy

■ Birthmother's resentment of others

■ Premature birth

■ Lack of family support

After the birth of the infant, the following factors can put a child at risk:

■ Physical problems resulting in a long hospitalization of the child

■ Lack of parenting skills by the birthparents

■ Ongoing substance abuse of the caregiver

■ Undetected and therefore untreated pain in the child

■ Emotional detachment of the caregiver

■ Living in an orphanage or institution

■ Uncontrollable environmental factors, such as war

■ Abuse and/or neglect

■ Multiple caregivers; multiple placements in foster homes

■ Protein malnutrition or other organic problems that affect brain functioning

As you can see from the risk factors, it is not only children adopted from orphanages overseas or children traveling in the domestic foster care system who are at risk for developing RAD. All infants run the risk of early development problems due to a variety of circumstances. Remember that in many cases, except for the most severe, children can overcome these problems if they are addressed early in the child's life. Early intervention is the best prevention.

Identifiable behaviors of kids with RAD

Children can have just a few symptoms of RAD, or they can have almost all of them. The number of symptoms a child has indicates the severity of the disorder. Symptoms include learning lags, lack of cause and effect thinking, and a lack of conscience. Of course, children under the age of six might have some of these symptoms without having RAD, but other symptoms, like nonsensical lying or cruelty to animals, do indicate that a child has had some arrested development. Another area of concern would be obsession with fire and gore.

The list goes on and on

Many of the behaviors presented by children with Reactive Attachment Disorder are symptoms of other diagnoses such as Post Traumatic Stress and ADHD. It is necessary to factor in the history of bonding disruption during the prenatal period or first three years of life to determine that it is RAD. The following are symptoms that may indicate that your child has RAD:

- Cruelty: Often teases and abuses animals and other children.

- Firesetting: Sets fires that are usually controlled. This proves to your child how well he can control his world.

- Food issues: Steals food in the middle of the night, hoards food, agrees to eat only a few chosen types of food (often sweets), or refuses to eat food. Your child might also eat odd foods such as paper, raw flour, raw oatmeal, or uncooked package mixes.

- Superficially engaging: Is indiscriminately affectionate toward strangers and distant acquaintances.

- Affection: Is unable to give and receive affection unless it is on the child's terms, which is

Watch Out!
It's not always possible to obtain all the necessary information about the child you are adopting to determine if your child is at risk for RAD. Be on the safe side—watch carefully for signs of attachment problems.

usually for the purpose of manipulating an adult.

▪ Nonsensical lying: Tells lies about everything, even when she is caught in the act, or it results in people thinking badly of her. She also lies about her family and her situation to manipulate people into thinking she is still a victim.

▪ Violence: Has a preoccupation with fire, gore, or blood.

▪ Eye contact: Has poor eye contact except when *not* telling the truth.

▪ Lack of guilt: Displays no remorse for misdeeds.

▪ Lack of cause-and-effect thinking: Is unable to see how he may have caused something to happen. Interestingly, the child is able to see how others cause problems.

▪ Lack of impulse control: Often acts "hyper" and acts without thinking.

▪ Peer relationships: Is unable to maintain relationships with children in the same age group.

▪ Relationships with adults: Often clings inappropriately to a parent or other adult and prefers adults to peers.

▪ Speech patterns: Has abnormal speech patterns or arrested speech development.

▪ Fun or rewarding experiences: Often sabotages fun and rewards.

▪ Emotions: Is often unable to verbalize emotions.

▪ Tasks or homework: Often does not finish tasks or complete homework.

▪ Intellect and education: Often has learning lags despite capabilities.

Timesaver
Don't assume that your child will outgrow the behaviors associated with attachment issues. Experts agree that the earlier RAD is diagnosed, the easier it is to treat.

- Control: Shows an extreme need to exert control over self and others

- Blame: Blames others and sets others up to be blamed. Watches from the side while others get in trouble.

- Overreaction: Uses theatrical displays of emotion, overreacts to small bumps and bruises.

- Bladder problems: Has problems with wetting or soiling.

- Petty criminal behavior: Engages in theft, vandalism, or destructive behavior.

This is an ominous list of behaviors, but most of the children with these behaviors can be helped with the proper therapeutic treatment by professionals and by informed parents. The answer lies in treating the cause of the behavior, the inability to form secure attachments, rather than randomly stabbing at the symptoms. For more on this subject see Chapter 14.

Complex children

On average, RAD children are developmentally delayed at least three years. They believe that they must control every aspect of their lives, especially adults, who they have learned cannot be trusted. Although they present themselves as victims, internally they believe they are responsible for everything that has happened to them, causing them to feel an overwhelming shame for what they feel they have caused. If they are disciplined, they feel shame and guilt, which proves to them that adults wish to hurt them. Because they see themselves as victims, they believe that they do not have to accept any responsibility. When adults treat them with caring, they believe they have manipulated the adult to do

> **"**
> Too often, no matter how much pre-adoption information is given, parents don't want to hear it. They persist in believing that if they take the child home and love him or her, everything will be OK.
> —Gregory C. Keck, Ph.D., founder of the Attachment and Bonding Center of Ohio
> **"**

so. RAD children usually have difficulty distinguishing one feeling from another, and they cannot determine what triggered their feelings.

The truth about relationships

"I would like to change the name of this disorder," complains the mother of two adopted RAD children. "Because it is called an attachment disorder, people immediately believe that our two children do not love us or have not bonded. That leads most people, professionals included, to assume that we are meaningless to our children. Nothing could be further from the truth. We are a very connected family, but our two children struggle with trust. At times, it is very difficult for all of us; nevertheless, we are a family secure in our love for each other."

Children with RAD do struggle with relationships, and when left untreated may exhibit many of the following problems with interpersonal relationships:

- Adults in authority are viewed as incompetent and easy to manipulate. The more an adult gives, the more vulnerable he appears to RAD children.

- RAD children's need to control includes controlling the emotions and behaviors of those close to them, including adults and other children. Their methods of control include oppositional behavior, passive/aggressive behavior, avoidant behavior, and withdrawal and withholding.

- Their attempt to control peers and siblings leaves them without relationships of any duration. They often set up peers and siblings to get them in trouble without being aware of consequences to the relationship.

Children with RAD often use charm with adults to secure gratification rather than have a meaningful engagement with the adult. Often RAD children use charm with strangers, casual friends of the family, extended family members, mental health professionals, and school personnel for the purpose of getting what they want. As soon as the charmed adult sets too many limits, the "honeymoon" is over, and the child may use other methods in an attempt to control the adult. On the other hand, if no limits are set by the adult, the child sees himself as successfully manipulating the adult. If this goes on for any period of time, the adult feels that he is "managing" the child, often better than the parents have been able to do.

This splitting (setting one adult up against another) is further complicated by the need of RAD children to avoid the truth at all costs. They feel that if they tell the truth, they are giving adults power over them. RAD children actually believe that they can create their own reality when they tell a lie. They are not only attempting to deceive the listener; they are also attempting to make it real. Therefore, their lies appear to be senseless to the adult or another child. The father of a RAD son told me, "I could not understand how my 10-year-old son thought I could possibly believe that he had not hit his brother when he knew that I actually saw him do it. He continued to maintain that he had not hit him. It was not until I understood that he was truly trying to change reality that I could begin to help him understand that he could not do what he was trying to do."

How to parent a child with RAD

Certainly, the RAD child can have a devastating effect on unprepared parents and families. Their frequent rages, controlling and splitting, and sabotaging of

Watch Out!
The mother commonly receives the child's worst acting-out behavior for many reasons, usually relating to issues around the biological mother abandoning the child. The child is usually better when the father is home. Thus the child is able to "split" the family and create conflict within it.

planned activities can destroy even the best of families. Yet, many parents have successfully raised and helped children who have attachment issues.

Preparing for the hard times

It takes a special type of person to raise a child with Reactive Attachment Disorder; not everyone should volunteer. It takes certain characteristics to parent a child with RAD. These characteristics are:

- An ability to have a sense of humor when the going gets rough

- A willingness to learn and accept alternate methods of managing a child's behavior

- A willingness to be flexible

- A willingness to be totally committed with time and effort

- An ability to have one's own personal needs met through other interests and relationships

- An ability to advocate for the child in a positive manner

- The ability to support and trust one another in the marital relationship or partnership, if you have a partner

- An ability to model control of emotions and attitudes in front of the child

- An ability to not take the child's behavior personally as well as the ability to tolerate those who suggest you should take it personally

Experienced adopters would add one more characteristic to the list: commitment. You need the ability to commit to the child no matter what happens and no matter how difficult it seems at the time.

And difficult it can be! You may go down some roads with your child that you never imagined you

Bright Idea
No one can parent a special needs child without pre-adoptive education, professional post-adoption support, and a strong personal support system. Make sure you have all three before knowingly adopting a special needs child. (See Chapter 14.)

would travel. Courts, jails, police—the stuff of a fictionalized world may become your reality. It's not an easy journey, yet those who choose to parent needy children reap a reward that no other parent could possibly understand. To see a child healed and on the way to having a normal, productive life is an experience like no other.

Some strategies to try

If you are bringing home an infant, you can do several things to help him or her adjust to a new environment. For an infant, the sensory world is very important. Babies are very much aware of tastes, smells, sounds, and how things feel and look. It might be a good idea to re-create the world from which your baby came and gradually ease the baby into your world.

Adoption expert Patricia Irwin Johnston offers suggestions of ways to re-create the sensory environment for your infant who is less than one year old:

- Determine the colognes, soaps, powders, deodorants, detergents, fabric softeners, cleaning products, and cooking odors your infant would recognize. When traveling to another country, purchase local products.

- Trade new blankets, sheets, and other items for ones that your infant has already used.

- Ask the birthmother or foster mother for an unwashed tee shirt that she has worn. Wear the tee shirt several times without washing it.

The more you know about the short history of your infant, the more you can do to reproduce that environment for your child in order to make the transition easier and begin the attachment process.

Moneysaver
As soon as your baby has been identified, send ahead some inexpensive toys and blankets that you can bring back with your infant. This allows you to choose what is familiar to your infant. Even if for some reason you do not complete this adoption, you have spent very little money.

The main job of parents adopting a toddler is to re-create the attachment process by reinforcing trust and security in the toddler. In her book *Toddler Adoption: The Weaver's Craft* (see Appendix C), Mary Hopkins Best offers some strategies to foster attachment in the toddler. Some of those strategies include the following:

- Differentiate between needs and wants. Toddlers should have their needs met as quickly as possible. Wants can be met on an individual basis.

- Provide food as a comfort. Food is a need; so is comforting. The toddler may have trouble distinguishing between needs. Providing food during physical comforting and gradually providing comfort before offering food may help the child distinguish between the two.

- Comfort you child. Parents must get up in the night and comfort a toddler when he or she cries to help build attachment.

- Teach independence gradually. An overly clinging toddler can be taught to deal with separation gradually.

- Consistently meet your baby's needs. The toddler will learn to delay gratification gradually after needs have been met consistently.

- Provide tactile awareness. Help toddlers who have shut down sensory receptors by providing tactile awareness—bubble bath, soft towels, flannel pajamas, etc.

- Encourage spontaneous laughing. Play with your child often.

- Provide motion. Walk, rock, gently bounce, and swing your baby.

- Establish routines and rituals with structure and consistency. Don't leave when a toddler is sleeping and will wake up with a stranger. Keep the toddler's environment consistent and predictable.

- Provide predictable family rituals. Do predictable things such as read to your child before he or she goes to bed.

The first few weeks and even months that your new toddler is in your home should be spent focusing on the family and establishing attachment. Keep the outside stimuli at a minimum during this period.

The older child who is still struggling with attachment issues needs parenting strategies that are focused on managing behavior as well as strategies that encourage attachment. Many of the experts on attachment issues have offered suggestions and strategies for parenting children with RAD. These strategies include the following:

- Be unpredictable: Have a variety of responses to inappropriate behavior available.

- Try to be unemotional in response to negative behavior and show conviction that the child will change negative behavior.

- Actively teach the child how to respond appropriately to situations. Children with RAD cannot discriminate between different situations and feelings.

- Teach the RAD child cause and affect by pointing out how poor choices have negative consequences.

- Always offer the RAD child the choice of two behaviors, both of which are agreeable to the

Bright Idea
Do something a little different and special each night of the week, like having pizza on Friday or watching a special TV program on Saturday. This will provide a routine and a predictable event each day. Children with attachment issues find a great deal of security in patterns.

parent. Example: "Do you want to wear your mittens out into the snow, or put them into your pocket?" Avoid confrontational battles at all cost. The RAD child will battle until he or she wins, no matter how long it takes or what the cost.

▪ Practice the one-minute scolding: Parent confronts the child, maintaining direct eye contact, and scolds the child briefly, expressing concern over the child's welfare. No further consequences.

▪ Overpractice: After breaking a rule, the child must practice following the rule three times.

▪ Take away any item that the child misuses. Once the child has demonstrated the ability to use the item correctly and promises to use it correctly in the future, return the item.

▪ Allow planned times when the child can revert back to a younger age. Hold and rock the child and allow the child to do what would be appropriate for a child of that age to do.

Remember that RAD children have not learned to trust. It does not mean that they cannot learn to trust. In order for them to be able to trust an adoptive parent, the parent must show strength and unflappability. Once the child has learned that he can manipulate or intimidate the parent, it will be very difficult for the child to trust the parent.

Experts also agree that some strategies don't work with RAD children. Among those are physical punishment, rescuing the child from consequences or solving problems for the child, emotionally reacting to negative behaviors, being predictable, and using behavior modification.

The role of residential schools

Sometimes, it's necessary for a child with more severe symptoms of RAD to be placed in a residential school for a period of time. Adolescence is a difficult period for many teenagers and their parents, especially for the teenager struggling with issues of attachment and trust. Some children don't display major symptoms of RAD until they reach early adolescence. Whatever the circumstance, residential school may be the appropriate place for the child for a period of time.

Many people, including professionals who should know better, view the placement as a disruption in the adoption. But parents who maintain commitment to the child and have learned to parent from afar realize that their children still need to know that there is a place for them called home. Those parents who hang in realize that children need a family for a lifetime, not just until they are 18.

Many parents and professionals do not realize that the federal government has recognized the importance of the adoptive family during the time a child is in residential school. The federal government requires states to continue to pay federally funded adoption subsidies while a child is in foster care or residential placement as long as the adoptive family remains involved in the treatment.

This is a stressful period for every member of the family, and each will be struggling with conflicting emotions. The family needs time to accept the fact that the child has been removed from the home, perhaps for an indefinite period of time, and to learn to adjust to the new situation. Often professionals, friends, and extended family may not understand the

Unofficially...
Uninformed professionals sometimes suggest placing a child with a foster family instead of in a residential school. Experienced professionals realize that introducing yet another "family" into a RAD child's life can be very confusing for a child who is already conflicted by relationships.

grieving process that the family is experiencing. Some of the normal emotions might be:

- Relief that a disruptive influence has been removed from the home

- Grief at the loss of a child or sibling

- Fear, especially for other adopted siblings who wonder if they might have to leave next, or that when the sibling returns the home will be disrupted again

Fortunately, many RAD children are able to work through their attachment issues with the help of the therapeutic environment provided in the residential placement. They are able to maintain a relationship with their family and return home in a relatively short period of time. The mother of a child who was placed in a residential setting said, "I am convinced that our daughter grew closer to us over the two years she spent away from us. She was angry at first and even refused to talk with us on the phone. Eventually, she was calling three times a week. We visited her at school, then she spent weekends at home. Finally, she was spending two-week vacations with us. I think she needed a little distance from us to realize that we were her family and would be there for her no matter what."

Choice or chance?

Why would anyone want to parent a child with RAD? The truth is that in the past, most prospective adoptive parents didn't actually make the choice to do it. Little was known about attachment issues and little was told to prospective adopters. Today, a great deal of information is available, and both adoption workers and prospective adoptive parents should be

> **"**
> No one but the parent of a RAD child can understand the joy I felt when my child asked for my *help* in making a decision. I knew that day that I had succeeded.
> —Sheila, mother of a child with RAD
> **"**

aware of the risks and the difficulties in parenting these children.

Why then would anyone choose to parent children who are at risk for having such serious problems? Attachment Disordered children have a sense of survival and an adaptability that other children do not have. They have a great potential for success based on these abilities. To parent one of these children, while difficult and requiring a great deal of emotional commitment and energy, can be one of the most rewarding experiences a person can have.

Just the facts

- Recent scientific research has proven the importance of proper prenatal care to begin the life of a mentally healthy child.

- RAD represents a continuum varying in intensity from child to child, and children vary in their ability to overcome attachment issues.

- There are strategies to help parents manage behaviors associated with RAD.

- It takes a strong, committed individual to parent a RAD child, but the rewards are great.

GET THE SCOOP ON...
What people think about adoptive families
■ Telling people about your adopted child ■ How
you can educate the educators ■ Meeting
with your child's teachers ■ The right words
for talking about adoption

In the Public Eye

Chapter 13

If you are like the vast majority of adopters today, you don't intend to keep your adoption plans a secret. As you've learned, you should at least share this information with your extended family members, who can offer support. You probably also intend to confide in friends and coworkers, if you have not already done so. Like many other excited new parents, you may even plan to send announcements of the arrival of your new child. This is a joyful time, and you'll want to share the joy with friends and family.

But, as time goes by, you'll need to decide just who should know what about the way you built your family, and, most importantly, your adopted child's history. This might be a good time to slow down and carefully consider how much information you'll make public concerning your adoption.

You might also use this time to prepare yourself for the thoughtless comments and questions that can do a great deal of damage to the psyche of everyone in the adoptive family. In this chapter, I'll discuss some of the difficulties that experienced adoptive families have had in social and educational situations and some of the solutions they have found.

What will the neighbors think?

Everyone will have an opinion about the decision that you have made to adopt a child. Many will choose not to share that opinion, and some will express it whether you ask for it or not. In some cases, you will elicit the opinions of those around you as you wrestle with the many decisions that you have to make in the adoption process. What may surprise you, though, are the people who feel they can continue to intrude in your life even after your child has been placed in your home. Experienced adopters find that even casual acquaintances sometimes feel free to offer opinions about many aspects of the adoptive family's life, including the level of parenting expertise.

You're a saint!

At one time or another, most adoptive parents hear that they are doing something incredibly wonderful by adopting a child that "no one else wants." In *Shared Fate: A Theory and Method of Adoptive Relationships* (see Appendix C), David H. Kirk reports that 92 percent of adopters have heard the statement, "Isn't it wonderful of you to have taken this child."

The mother of two girls adopted in China said, "It began on the plane coming home from China. People would stop as they walked to the back of the plane and comment on what a great thing we were doing. The flight attendants made a big fuss over the girls and gave them extra treats. We assumed that this would end with the plane trip, but the 'fuss' continued wherever we went in the first few months. People continuously pointed out how good we were to adopt our girls. People in our community don't comment as much today, but I wonder what would happen if we were to go outside our small environment. I don't think people realize that by saying how good we were to adopt the girls, they were also saying there must be something 'bad' about our girls. We knew we would stand out as a family; we just didn't realize people would feel free to comment about it."

You can't possibly be a good parent

Of course, the opposite opinion can also be expressed. Adopters additionally report that if there are some problems with their child, especially behavioral problems, many people automatically assume that poor parenting must be the cause. According to experienced adopters, some people, especially professionals who are supposed to be helping, often feel that adoptive parents are somehow lacking in good parenting skills or had an existing pathology (problem) in the family before they adopted the child.

Fortunately, informed professionals are helping people understand that often a child with attachment or other issues creates problems for parents with good parenting skills. For more on this subject, see Chapter 14.

Your child is our child

Some experienced adopters also report an odd and generally annoying attitude that some adults have toward adopted children. They seem to feel that they need to be overly nice, kind, or solicitous to adopted children, sometimes to the point of being

Unofficially...
In 1997, the *New York Times* reported on a study done in the United States in which half of the people responding felt that adopting was "better than being childless, but is not as good as having one's own child."

intrusive in the adoptive family's life. At a recent round-table discussion I attended concerning the subject, a group of adoptive parents compiled the following list of ways in which adults intruded into their children's and families' lives:

- Asking the child thoughtless questions about the adoption experience. One parent said that her daughter had recently been asked by a teacher "how it felt to be adopted."

- Asking the child questions about his or her life prior to being placed in his present adoptive home. "Where did you live before you were adopted? Who were your parents?"

- Giving the child special attention beyond what is given other children. One parent described how a teacher invited her son to spend weekends with the teacher's family. No other child ever received the same invitation.

- Subtly, or not so subtly, telling the adoptive parent(s) how to parent in another way.

All the parents attending the round table agreed that, as adoptive parents, they were sometimes treated differently than "other" parents were treated.

What you should tell your neighbors

How do you handle the intrusion into your family? How much should you reveal about the history of your child? While adoptive parents are generally more direct with information about their adoptions than they were in the past, many professionals and experienced adoptive parents caution adoptive parents not to reveal too much about the history of their child. There is a balance between telling people what they need to know to help your child and

> 66
> Parents do need to tell the teacher that the child is adopted, because it allows the teacher to support the child if they are dealing with adoption issues in their play, or with other children in the classroom.
> —Ann Elyacher, an educational consultant
> 99

telling them the details that might cause harm to your child later in life.

When it is none of their business

You must determine who needs to know what on a case-by-case basis. You will probably want to tell people close to you that your child is adopted and give a little information concerning your child's history. You need to weigh the pros and cons of who to tell and how much to tell. If you feel that the person needs to know the information in order to help your child, then you should share the information.

Often without thinking, prospective adoptive parents give away information prior to the placement of their child that will come back to haunt them later in their child's life. Leslie Elstein, an adoptive parent and social worker, cautions parents not to make the same mistake she made, saying, "During the intensity of awaiting my child, I turned to family and friends for support and shared with them bits of information about my child's history. It was a perfectly natural reaction to the stress of such an emotional time, but one that backfired for me and is likely to for others, too." This backfired because her child learned information about her past from other people rather than from her.

She and other professionals stress that the history of your adopted child belongs to your adopted child, therefore:

- Your child is the one who should determine with whom that history is shared.

- Your child has the right to hear that information from you, not inadvertently from other members of the family.

- Your child has the right to hear the information from someone who can sensitively discuss it.

Well-intentioned people will sometimes ask probing questions or make rude statements concerning your adopted child. You need to be prepared for these with the appropriate vocabulary and some good answers discussed later in the chapter.

Who needs to know?

Adoptive parents are not in agreement about telling teachers and the schools that their children are adopted. Obviously, it's not a decision that parents of transracial or transcultural children will have to make, as it will be apparent to school personnel that their children are adopted, but other parents will need to make this decision.

Many parents have found that it makes the school experience easier for their children if the teacher is at least made aware that their children are adopted without giving them unnecessary information. I would recommend this as well, for the following reasons:

- It makes it easier for the teacher to help a child if the teacher knows that the child is adopted.

- It makes it easier for the teacher to give adoption-sensitive assignments.

- Since a child knows that he or she is adopted, it's likely that the child will tell this information to other students. If the teacher also knows, the teacher can prevent teasing, bullying, and other problems before they start.

On the other hand, other professionals and adopted parents reject the idea of sharing information with teachers because the teachers may do one or more of the following:

Watch Out!
Don't give your child's teachers any more information than they absolutely need to know. Usually, the knowledge that your child was adopted and at what age is enough.

- Single out their children in either a positive or negative way
- Make their children feel different
- Cause their children to be teased or called names

Whether to share information—and how much—is a personal decision that each family has to make based on what they feel is right for the child at the time. If you decide not to share the information at one point, you may choose to revisit that decision at another time.

Educating the educators

The vast majority of adoptive parents do share the fact that their child is adopted with the child's teacher. Often, they make the decision to tell the teacher because their child has had a challenging adoption-related experience either with a difficult assignment from the teacher or teasing on the playground.

Some teachers are not aware of the difficulties adopted children can have both in and out of the classroom. This is most likely not a prejudice on the part of the teacher or a desire to embarrass a child; instead, it's usually because the teacher has not been exposed to much information concerning adoption. A teacher may not realize how difficult it can be for an adopted child to have to bring a photo as an infant, write an autobiography, or do a family tree.

As an informed parent, you are in a position to educate the educators. You can teach the teacher by simply meeting with him or her frequently to make a suggestion, to suggest reading material, or to schedule a time when you could go into the classroom to speak to the students about adoption. Whatever method you use, you will be helping your child to have a happier and more positive experience.

Pointing out potential problems

Parents of adopted children should be able to point out to teachers events and dates that might be difficult for their children, such as the following:

- Birthdays
- Holidays
- Mother's and Father's Days
- World events in the news
- Certain classroom discussions dealing with relationships, sexuality, birth control, and parenting

If these are issues that affect your child, it's important to have a close working relationship with your child's teacher. Let your school know that you are a resource to help them work with your child. Also, remind teachers that all children have good and bad days; not every problem is related to adoption.

Introducing adoption in the classroom

A teacher can use several methods to introduce the concept of adoption in the classroom by including families with adopted children in discussions about families. Teachers can avoid insensitive adoption language (see information later in this chapter) and use the following ways to introduce adoption in the classroom:

- Recognize that November is National Adoption Month. Read an adoption book, discuss adoption, or invite the parent of a child who was adopted to the classroom to share their adoption story.

- Be aware of teasing in the class; handle it as you would any teasing. Use it as a way to introduce a discussion of the many different ways families are formed.

- Allow children who are adopted to tell their stories in a non-threatening environment.

- Reflect family diversity in literature, posters, and playthings.

Modifying classroom assignments

Some assignments can be particularly difficult not only for adopted children, but for all children in non-traditional families. Teachers can modify many of these assignments.

Family tree——The usual printed tree does not accommodate all the diverse family configurations. Here are some other options:

- A family bush, family forest, family poplar tree (which has many, many branches), loving tree, or caring tree

- The Self Wheel, with the child at the center and relatives surrounding the child

- My Home, with people inside

- The Chart, with the child and lines drawn to family members

All of these can be used to initiate a discussion of the various forms of the modern family, both traditional and non-traditional.

Baby photos—This excludes many children who do not have pictures of themselves as babies. Some options include:

- Have the child bring in a photo of himself or herself at a younger age.

- Have the child bring in a book, a pet, or a treasured object.

Timesaver
Do some of the research for the teacher: take some informative literature on adoption with you on your first trip to speak with your child's teacher. Include some age-appropriate literature that the teacher can read to the class. Chances are the teacher will use the information.

Bright Idea
Cheri Register, author of *Are Those Kids Yours?* (see Appendix C), helped her daughters draw a peony bush with roots that intertwined to illustrate their family. They marked each family member's roots with their ancestors' country of origin. She marked her Korean daughters' roots with the word "birthparents" and a South Korean flag.

Family history—A child with a traumatic or unknown history may find it difficult to write an autobiographical statement. Here are two other options:

- Have the child write the story of a significant event in his or her life.

- Have the child write the story of a favorite experience in school.

Mother's Day/Father's Day—These days can be difficult for children with single or divorced parents. Here are some options:

- Expand the subject to any man or woman a child admires.

- Change it to Family Day.

- Change it to Caring Day.

- Thank someone who cares for the child.

- Conduct a lesson on how to express concern for others.

If a teacher is made aware of the need to broaden the definition of family to include all the different ways of building a family today, all the students in the class will benefit.

How to prepare for the individualized education program

A great deal has been written over the years concerning the theory that adopted children have more learning disabilities than other children. There could be many reasons for this phenomenon, including genetic considerations, environmental influences, or simply because adoptive parents are more watchful and tend to seek professional help sooner. Whatever the reason, your child may need special education services from the school. If so, you will need to meet at least once a year with representatives of the school to prepare your child's individualized education program (IEP). For many parents, this can be a stressful meeting. To avoid much of the stress, you need to be prepared. Some things to do before the meeting include:

- Ask for the special education statutes, regulations, and policies, which your school is required by law to give you. Read them carefully.

- Remember that you are an equal member of the decision-making team.

- Request a copy of the IEP form before the meeting and study each section of the form.

- Think about and develop your child's ideal IEP ahead of time.

- Become an expert about your child's educational performance.

- Keep in close contact with your child's teacher and other professionals at the school.

- Have an independent assessment of your child at your expense if necessary.

- Find out who will also be at the meeting. Determine if you and your child's teacher agree about the issues on the IEP before the actual meeting.

- Invite whatever allies you feel you will need to attend the meeting with you.

- Remember that if you don't like the findings of the IEP, you may appeal the process.

Good words/bad words

Experts maintain that adopted children are usually aware of the fact that they are adopted during their

Moneysaver
If you'll be required to pay for an expert to attend an IEP meeting on your child's behalf, ask the expert to state his opinion in writing instead. Often, an expert will write the report for no additional charge.

preschool years, but at that age it has little meaning to them. While they may tell others that they are adopted, they have little understanding of what this means in terms of family relationships. By the time they enter elementary school, they can better understand many of the implications of being adopted and tend to question much of the information that was given to them earlier in life. This is the beginning of a time of great confusion for them. As they mature, they have an increased understanding of the differences between an adoptive family and a biological family and are no longer willing to accept simple explanations for why their biological parents chose adoption. They have many questions concerning their past and their birthparents.

This is a vulnerable time in your child's life. You need to be able to answer your child's questions and discuss his or her situation in terms that are easy to understand. You will need to help your child cope with difficult feelings and develop a positive self-image. For more on talking about adoption with your child, see Chapter 15.

Timesaver
Organize all your papers and documents relevant to your child and school in a three-ring binder with labeled sections for easy access at school meetings. If the teacher needs to copy any information, you can easily remove the document from the binder.

The power of positive language

Many outside of your immediate family may inconsiderately make statements and use words that may further confuse, and, in some cases, cause unnecessary distress to your child. By using Positive Adoption Language (PAL) yourself, you are educating others about the adoption experience.

The following are examples of turning negative phrases into phrases with positive connotations:

- When referring to your child's *birthparent* or *biological parent*, don't use the terms *real* parent or *natural* parent. If there are real and natural parents, are there unreal and unnatural parents?

- An *adoptive parent* is a *parent*; there is no need to differentiate between the two unless there is a specific need to point out that your child is adopted.

- Instead of saying *my own child*, say *my birthchild* when it's necessary to distinguish between a birthchild and an adopted child.

- When referring to your child, simply say *my child* instead of *my adopted child*.

- Never say *a hard-to-place child*, but rather say *a special needs child*.

- *A foreign child* is *a child from abroad*; *foreign* has a negative connotation.

- Instead of saying that a birthparent decided *to give up* or *to give away* a child, say a birthparent decided *to make an adoption plan* or *chose adoption*.

- A birthparent may decide *to parent* a child, not to *keep* a child.

- Rather than use the term *illegitimate* to describe a child born out of wedlock, say that the child was *born to unmarried parents*.

- A *foreign* adoption is an *international* adoption or *intercountry* adoption.

- Members of the adoption *triangle* (birthparents, adoptive parents, and the child) are called the adoption *triad*.

- One does not *track down a birthparent*, but rather *searches for* or *locates* a birthparent.

- To *have a reunion* with a birthparent or another member of the birth family is *to make contact* with them.

- When a birthparent places the child for adoption, the birthparent is *terminating or surrendering their parental rights*, not *giving up the child*.

Unofficially
While it is not
accepted Positive
Adoption
Language to call
an international
or intercultural
adoption a
foreign adoption,
the term "foreign
country" is
commonly used
by the general
population to
indicate another
country.

- A child is not *taken away* from birthparents, the court is *terminating parental rights.*

- A child is *biracial,* not *mixed race* or *mulatto.*

- Ask, "Do you have any other children?" not, "Do you have any children of your own?"

Using positive adoption language helps others to show respect for all members of the adoption triad. The words people use are a reflection of what people think. If people learn to use PAL, they are learning to think positively about adoption.

"Your mother didn't want you"

Being different is not easy for young children. If other children tease the adopted child because that child is different, it can be very painful. Unfortunately, the teasing often seems to come at a time when the child is trying to understand the reasons and circumstances of the adoption and is very sensitive to issues of identity.

It is almost a certainty that at one time or another, an adopted child will hear more than one insulting remark concerning parentage. Adoptive parents are encouraged to prepare their children in advance. If the child is prepared for some hurtful remarks or teasing, he will feel in control of the situation rather than victimized by it.

Experts advise parents to practice responses with their children. It may be helpful to have them use puppets to practice what they will say the next time a child makes a comment or asks a question that is meant to hurt them.

You may also want to help them work out answers to the more common questions themselves. Some of the historically more common responses to the taunt, "Your real mother didn't want you" might include the following:

- My parents chose to adopt me, but yours had to keep you.

- My parents aren't fake, they are real.

- At least my parents are good parents. They taught me to respect people, something your parents haven't taught you.

Perhaps the best type of response for your child is a response that encourages a positive attitude about all types of families, such as "All moms and dads who love their kids are real."

Good answers to silly questions

Often, people make remarks that are unintentionally rude or hurtful to the adoptive family, or they make innocent remarks that an adoptive parent may misunderstand. "Where did you get those beautiful eyes?" is a question that people often pose to young children and to which they certainly don't expect a detailed answer.

Unintentionally rude and probing questions from strangers and casual acquaintances can undermine the foundations that parents are trying to develop. Often, children are getting the message at home that their birth cultures are something to celebrate, while the inadvertently rude questions posed by strangers give them the message that there is something wrong with being different. This can be very confusing for children.

What to do about rude people

You can't always avoid rude questions or comments, but you can respond to them in several ways, depending on the following:

- Does this person have a need or right to know the answer to the question? If not, don't offer

Bright Idea
One of the best responses to teasing and taunts is no response at all. Help your child to understand that walking away from someone who is saying hurtful things is demonstrating just as much control over the situation as acknowledging the taunt with a reply.

any answer at all or give one of the suggested answers below.

- If you feel that the person is genuinely interested and deserves an answer, determine if it's the correct setting to discuss the issue.

- Decide if it's the right time for a discussion. Will you have enough time to discuss it completely? Are you involved in another activity from which you do not want to take time?

- If the comment is made or the question is asked in front of an older child, determine if your child would like to answer the question.

Once you have concluded that you're going to respond to the rude question or comment, you must decide on what type of response you will give:

- You can simply tell the person he or she is being rude and intrusive in a variety of ways.

- You can answer with a "one-sentence" educational statement.

- You can use humor.

- You can give them a look accompanied by dead silence.

Sample questions and answers

The following are examples of typical questions and possible answers:

- *Where is your child from?*

  China.

  She was born in Korea and her brother was born in Boston.

  The United States.

66
Natural child: any child who is not artificial. Real parent: any parent who is not imaginary. Your own child: any child who is not someone else's child. Adopted child: a natural child, with a real parent, who is all my own.
—By Rita Laws, an adoptive parent
99

- *Isn't she lucky that you adopted her?*

  We are the lucky ones to have such a beautiful child.

- *How long have you had him?*

  We can't remember what life was like without him.

- *How much did it cost?*

  Oh, she is priceless.

  How much did your child cost?

  It's about the same as giving birth in a hospital.

- *What do you know about the real parents?*

  We *are* the real parents.

  We don't know much about the birthparents.

- *Are they real brother and sister?*

  They are now.

  Would they fight like that if they weren't real siblings?

- *Do you have any children of your own?*

  Just these two.

  These *are* my children.

- *Are you baby-sitting?*

  No time for that now that I have my own children.

- *Whose children are these?*

  Ours. One is from Colombia and the other is homemade.

Getting involved

Adoptive parents need to get the word out about positive adoption language and the value of families

Bright Idea
The NAIC can
help you educate
your school by
sending adoption
information to
your school
system. Contact
them at 330
C Street, SW,
Washington, DC
20447.

formed through adoption. Think about being an adoption advocate in your child's school by doing one or more of the following:

- Make sure that adoption is part of your school's curriculum. Lobby for age-appropriate lessons on adoption starting in kindergarten and continuing through high school.

- Donate a book on adoption to your library. If your child was adopted from another country, donate a book about that country.

- Make school personnel aware of adoption conferences in your area.

- Suggest that the school start a support group for adoptive parents.

- Make a presentation at a PTA meeting encouraging parents to teach their own children about adoption and positive adoption language.

Just the facts

- The majority of adoptive parents have to deal with the opinions expressed by relatives, friends, and strangers.

- The details of your child's life prior to placement in your home should remain private.

- Most teachers and school personnel are open to becoming more sensitive to issues surrounding adoption.

- Using the correct words when speaking about adoption encourages respect for families formed through adoption.

GET THE SCOOP ON...

How to get the help you need ▪ How to avoid unwanted help ▪ Finding the right support group ▪ The truth about mental health issues ▪ How to be your child's advocate

When You Can't/Shouldn't Do It Alone

The McCords adopted an infant two years ago in an open adoption. They worked with a lawyer who located a birthmother for them and finalized the adoption in a relatively short period of time. They felt that with the help of the lawyer they had covered all the possible pitfalls of open adoption and were totally prepared for the experience. Two years later, both the McCords were experiencing misgivings about the openness of their adoption. There were so many unanswered questions and no one to answer them.

Theresa spent three exhausting weeks in China and has just returned with her new baby. There is a welcoming committee at the airport consisting of friends and extended family, several of whom are planning to spend the next few weeks with her to help with the new baby. All of this sounded like a great idea before she left, but now Theresa would like to have her home to herself to relax and get to know her new baby.

The Smiths adopted a child from their state foster care system ten years ago when the child was four years old. From the beginning raising their child was challenging and no one, including therapists and other professionals, had been able to help them. After ten years, the Smiths felt that there was no help for them or their child.

Finding support in your family

One of the first places to turn for support is to your extended family. Relatives can do much to "glue" the family together and help both you and your child begin the bonding process. Involving the extended family also reinforces the bond they have with this child.

Teaching relatives how to help

Welcoming an adopted child into a family is usually a new experience for the entire family. Extended family members in particular may feel awkward about how to rally around the new parents to offer help for the newly adopted child. It can be especially perplexing if the child is older. Adoptive parents who have been through the process offer the following suggestions:

- Be prepared from the beginning to educate relatives and extended family about what you need. Don't expect them to know automatically.

- Encourage them to use positive adoption language (see Chapter 13) from the beginning. Rather than correct them when they use a negative phrase, give them a vocabulary lesson ahead of time. Forgive them when they slip.

- Encourage family members who do not live in the area to send cards, photographs, and small keepsakes to your child often. Keeping in touch with relatives establishes the sense of family.

- Try to arrange visits with relatives as soon as possible after the placement, but not so soon as to threaten the child's developing sense of security within the immediate family.

- Ask relatives for small bits of parenting advice to encourage them to feel part of the process.

How to handle unwanted help

Some children bring special challenges to their adopted family. Children who were adopted as older children, children who were abused and neglected, children adopted from another country, and other children at risk for attachment issues present problems that an uneducated adult may find very threatening. In many cases, the only advice extended family can offer is to "give the child back" to the agency.

Sally Richardson knows this situation well. An adoptive mother of three challenging children, she says, "When our son began to exhibit some behaviors common to children with attachment issues, my mother and father became very upset. They saw his anger and were afraid that nothing could ever help him. Almost every time we were with them, they advised us to take him back to the agency. It made things more difficult for us because they were not supporting us even though they felt they were telling us to do what was best. At the time, we didn't know how to tell them how they could help us."

Consider your personal needs when trying to tell relatives how they can help. Sometimes all you need is a few hours of respite or a shoulder to cry on for

Moneysaver
Encourage children who are able to write to send electronic mail (email) to relatives, whether they live across the street or across the country. Many people who use email claim that it helps keep families together. It also encourages children to use their writing skills.

a few minutes. Maybe you need someone to talk about something other than "your problem" and would like to go out to lunch and gossip for an hour or two. Your friends and relatives will only know how to help you if you find a way to tell them.

Supporting do's and don'ts

To help relatives and friends understand how they can be supportive before and after adoption, I have put together the following list of do's and don'ts from seasoned adopters:

- Our decision to adopt is a personal decision, do respect our decision.

- Don't tell us that if we adopt a child we will get pregnant and have a child of our own. Adoption does not cure infertility, and our adopted child will be our child.

- Don't feel sorry for us because we have made the choice to adopt.

- Don't tell us how wonderful we are to do such a noble thing as adopt a child.

- Don't question our capability or readiness to parent a child.

- Do accept our choice of a child regardless of his/her race, age, social background, and other characteristics.

- Do remain positive and enthusiastic during waiting periods even though we may have trouble remaining positive ourselves.

- Don't constantly ask for news while we are waiting to adopt. Do understand that we will share all relevant information as soon as possible.

- Don't offer us unsolicited advice, but do offer us practical help.

- Do share in the joy we feel for our new child and our family.

- Do understand that in the beginning we may want and need quiet time with our new child to bond and adjust.

- Do understand that we might not be able to fulfill your needs as quickly as we did before we became parents.

- Do understand that good parenting is a skill that one learns, often from good role models, and respect our style of parenting.

- Don't ask personal questions about the history of our child.

- Don't feel sorry for our adopted child or us.

- Do try to understand why we have chosen to have a level of openness with our child's birth family.

Bright Idea
Offer your home to a family who may be traveling from another area to adopt a child in your area. It will save them money and will offer you a wonderful opportunity to network with another adoptive family.

The lowdown on support groups

Many times, relatives, friends, and coworkers simply don't know enough about adoption to be of help in areas beyond basic parenting. The logical person to turn to next for support is someone who is experienced in adoption. Many different types of adoption groups exist for both adoptive parents and adopted children. If you can't find one in your area, consider starting one yourself.

Adoptive parent groups

Adoptive parent groups offer support for all types of adoption-related questions and problems. The right parent group can help you find advice on anything from the paperwork to take with you when picking up your child in an international adoption, to how to get your challenging teen into a residential school.

Parent groups can also help your child. While parents share and learn from each other, they gain a sense of empowerment which can be transferred to their children.

Parent groups can also be a place where you can go to let off steam or say something negative without the fear of judgment. Group participation helps reduce frustration and the sense of isolation for both parents and children. Consider the following benefits of a parent group:

- Parent groups provide a place where your children can meet other children who are adopted and perhaps from different cultures.

- Parent groups provide a place where you can meet other parents who are dealing with the same cultural issues. You can exchange ideas and share stories.

- If the parent group has a newsletter, you can stay current on workshops, cultural events, and other news concerning adoption.

- You can help other parents who are considering adoption by speaking with them at groups or by participating in a telephone or email network system.

- You can learn how other parents discussed the issues of adoption with their children, or how other parents reacted when their child informed them they wanted to search for birth relatives.

- You can participate in a variety of groups as many are made up of a particular type of adoptive parent, such as single parents, gay parents, parents who adopted internationally, or parents who adopted waiting children.

Unofficially...
The first formal adoptive parent group started in the New York City metropolitan area in 1955, according to the National Adoption Information Clearinghouse. The group was called the Adoptive Parents Committee, and it is still active today.

■ You can be instrumental in making positive changes in the issue of adoption. (See the section "Advocating for change" later in this chapter.)

Usually, groups offer more than just support for each member. They also provide a variety of other activities for both parents and children. Some of the activities are:

Bright Idea
Some parent groups encourage older children to share toys and clothes with younger children. Others provide a children's lending library with books about adoption.

■ Potluck dinners

■ Multicultural parties or picnics

■ Holiday celebrations

■ Discussion groups for older teens

■ Educating legislative groups on child welfare issues

■ Participating on parent panels for conferences and seminars

You need to find a group that meets your particular needs. You can participate in as many or as few activities as you and your family wish. Some parents attend only a few meetings to establish that a group is there for them when the need arises.

Groups for parents of challenging children

If you have adopted a child who is presenting challenging behaviors, a group of other parents in your situation can be your most valuable support. Often, professionals are not able to understand what you are experiencing, but other parents can understand and will be able to offer comfort as well as understanding.

Members of a support group can exchange the following information:

■ They can recommend therapists who are able to work well with adopted children and have knowledge of attachment issues.

- They can recommend other professionals for necessary testing for disabilities and for school purposes.

- They can recommend where to find services such as respite care. Sometimes, members provide respite for each other.

- They can give each other advice on what works and what doesn't.

- Some offer a "buddy system," in which a more experienced family shares information with a family experiencing a crisis.

- They can provide a place where parents can laugh and see the funny side of themselves and their situations.

Support groups for parents of challenging children can help the helpers by teaching and instructing them on the best ways to offer help. Social workers and mental health professionals can gain vital information from experienced parents.

Adolescent and children's groups

In some areas, groups for adopted children offer young people a place to discuss some of the issues that may affect them, such as attachment or a history of sexual abuse. Children can benefit from having a group of peers who have experienced some of the same issues and concerns. Other groups may have a less therapeutic focus, such as play groups for young children or activity groups for older children.

Teen groups, often just informal rap sessions, can be very effective in helping teens relate to others with histories and issues that are similar. Teens who are able to share with each other often feel less isolated and have a greater sense of self-esteem. They often acquire a sense of hope when they realize that they are not alone and others experience similar feelings and anxieties. Some of the issues covered in teen groups are:

- Peer pressure
- Sexuality and dating
- School issues

How to find a group

The first place to look for a support group referral in your area is with your local private adoption agency or state agency. If you are working with an attorney or facilitator in an independent adoption, ask him or her about a support group in your area. Some adoption attorneys have started their own support groups for adopting parents in all stages of the process. Also, check the newspaper and local magazines or the Yellow Pages of the phone book. On the national level, the following organizations may be able to help locate a group near you:

- The North American Council on Adoptable Children (NACAC), 970 Raymond Avenue, Suite 106, St. Paul, MN 55114-1149, (612) 644-3036. http://members.aol.com/nacac
- Adoptive Families of America (AFA), 2309 Como Avenue, St. Paul, MN 55108, (800) 372-3300 or (612) 535-4829. http://www.adoptivefam.org

Starting a group

If you live in a rural area, you may not find an existing parent group or one that meets your needs. In that case, think about establishing a parent group yourself. Groups don't need to be formal or have meetings every week. Terra Trevor describes a group that has been successfully gathering for 15 years: The secret to the success of this group is a

> 66
> Along the way in parenting teens, I could count on other adoptive parents, especially those whose children were older than mine. In many ways, we became a team, akin to the whole village needed to raise a child.
> —Joan McNamara, author of numerous books and mother of 13 children
> 99

commitment to a few traditional meetings a year, such as an annual camp-out at the beginning of each summer and a pizza night in mid-winter. Trevor suggests that a good way to start a support group is to hold a gathering at a pizza parlor. According to Trevor, the worst thing that could happen is that your family will end up eating pizza alone.

Contact the North American Council on Adoptable Children or Adoptive Families of America for more information on starting a group in your area. NACAC and AFA can also advise existing groups on how to sponsor an educational workshop or conference or help you find other local groups with which to form an association in order to sponsor such an event.

Timesaver
Call AARP's GIC to find out if there is a support group for grandparents near you. The telephone number is (202) 434-2296.

Support for grandparents

Grandparents (and other relatives) raising their grandchildren have a challenging responsibility. The American Association of Retired Persons (AARP) established the Grandparent Information Center (GIC) in 1993 to help grandparents by providing information about services and programs that can help them. For more information write: AARP GIC, 601 E Street, NW, Washington, DC 20049.

The GIC can help grandparents find help for the following:

- Legal issues
- Financial issues
- Medical care/insurance
- Childcare
- Education

- Psychological/emotional issues
- Their own health

You can also find help closer to home by looking for support and information in your local telephone directory or calling your local library to ask for help in locating services.

Getting needed support from the experts

Experienced adopters and some other adoption experts have long realized the need for post-adoption services for many adoptive families. These services should be provided by social workers and mental health professionals who understand adoption-related issues and who are able to support the adoptive family's importance in the child's life. Unfortunately, these services have not been available in the past and may still not be available in some areas.

Vera Fahlberg, M.D., author of *A Child's Journey Through Placement* (see Appendix C), stresses the importance of post-adoption services and the need for the professionals providing the service to understand the role of the adoptive family. She writes that although therapy will benefit the child, it is the daily interaction between the child and the family that determines if the child will heal or the adoption will disrupt.

Getting good support

Some private and public agencies provide supportive services after the child has been placed in the home. They are usually called post-adoption support services and are available to adoptees and adoptive parents until the adoptee is 18 or even older in some cases. They may provide educational

Watch Out!
Some caseworkers still view the placement of a child in a family as the solution to a problem rather than the beginning of a life-long healing process in which all members of the triad may need support at different stages.

groups for both parents and children. Some examples of these groups are:

- *New parents groups.* These groups help new parents adjust to the changes in their homes and lifestyles. Groups discuss a variety of topics, including the stages of adjustment, how to manage stress, and how to ask for help from family and friends.

- *Advocate groups.* These groups teach parents how to advocate for the social, emotional, and educational needs of their child.

- *Social skills groups.* These groups help adopted children overcome any trouble they may be experiencing with basic social skills, such as making and keeping friends or sharing. Social skills groups help children of all ages.

- *Fathers groups.* These groups help fathers gain some recognition and support in their new roles.

Many agencies also offer individual consultation with adoptive families to help both parents and children deal with topics specific to adoption, including behavioral problems, answers to difficult questions, and birth family issues. These services may be available to those who are involved in an independent adoption. Check with agencies and support groups in your area.

Crisis intervention

An adoptive family with a long history of problems may be threatened and need effective crisis intervention. A family that has been dealing with repeated self-destructive or violent behavior of a child needs the help of informed experts to learn how to manage the child's behavior and may need to receive a variety of services. The experts need to be flexible and able to offer a variety of services. Some of the services that threatened families might need include:

- Dependable respite by people who have been trained by agencies that are informed about adoption and attachment issues.

- Short- or long-term out-of-home placement

- Competent adoption and attachment therapeutic intervention

Agency-provided mental health services

Some adoption agencies have begun offering mental health services along with their other post-adoption services. They have hired and/or trained psychotherapists to provide short- and long-term therapy to adoptive parents. Families can obtain counseling for many reasons, including:

- Marital problems as a result of adoption

- Problems with extended family

- Sibling rivalry

- Identity issues in adoption

- Behavioral problems

- Interpersonal and/or family problems

The fees for mental health services provided through an agency are sometimes covered by the family's health insurance. Some agencies charge on a sliding-fee scale, while others don't charge a fee if the child was adopted as a special needs child. Check with your agency to see if the agency provides post-adoption services and how fees are paid.

Finding your own therapist

Most agencies don't have an affiliation with mental health services, leaving adoptive parents to find a therapist on their own. Experts and experienced

> 66
> Many times these are very competent parents who may have difficulty convincing others of the seriousness of the problem. They may be more skilled than the people they are turning to for help, who in turn may be intimidated by the parents.
> —Vera Fahlberg, M.D.
> 99

parents agree that it is extremely important to find a therapist who has had experience working with adoptive families. In the past, the general training of therapists did not include instruction about the unique dynamics specific to adoption.

Unfortunately, in the past some therapists did more damage than good. Many parents of children with complex histories complained that therapists didn't understand that their children had a tendency to lie or misrepresent, which made it difficult for the therapist to get a true picture of what was happening. Also, the therapist may not have been educated or had experience working with children who had attachment issues stemming from neglect and abuse prior to living in the adoptive home. Today, more and more therapists are becoming aware of attachment and adoption specific issues and are better prepared to work with adopted children with complex histories.

To make sure the therapist you hire to work with your child and family has experience working with adoption and attachment issues, ask for recommendations from the following:

- Other adoptive parents in your area
- Members of local or national adoptive parent support groups
- Reputable adoption agencies
- Mental health associations, universities, hospitals, or medical schools

Remember that you are hiring someone to assist you. You should interview several therapists before making the final decision. If you don't think that you and your family can establish a rapport with the therapist, find another one.

Looking for attachment therapy

There are many different types of therapy that can be used with children. The type of therapy you choose depends on the issues that need to be worked on and the severity of the problems.

One of the more controversial therapies over the years is a type called "holding therapy" or "rage-reduction" therapy. Holding therapy was first discovered to be effective by Martha Welch, M.D., while she was working with autistic children. It has since been accepted by professionals such as Foster Kline, M.D., Vera Falhberg, M.D., and Gregory C. Keck, PhD., and many others who work with children with Reactive Attachment Disorder. Holding is accomplished by having the child lie across the laps of two therapists and/or his parents. The child's right arm is behind the therapist who is sitting closest to his head. His left arm is free as long he does not attempt to harm himself or others. The child is required to maintain eye contact with the therapist or parent who is speaking to him. Often, the child will become angry during the session. The media has often reported on the negative aspects of holding therapy, showing bits and pieces of it out of context.

Proponents of holding therapy maintain that it's an effective type of therapy that has evolved over years of intensive study and research. Those therapists who actually use this method of therapy report a high degree of success with children who are struggling with attachment issues. The holding re-creates the bonding cycle that was never completed for children with RAD. The goal is for the child to release control in order to receive help in learning how to trust.

Bright Idea
Consider preventative therapy as a routine part of your post-adoption plan. At significant times in your child's development, it would be wise to check out how your child is doing with adoption issues.

The actual holding is only a small part of the therapeutic process, which involves many other interventions and strategies as part of the healing program. Other therapists who are not convinced that holding is the answer are adding these other strategies and interventions to their treatment practices.

Author Daniel Hughes, Ph.D., writes in *Facilitating Developmental Attachment: The Road to Emotional Recovery and Behavioral Change in Foster and Adopted Children* (see Appendix C), that he considers adoptive parents as co-therapists. He emphasizes the need for parental participation in the therapeutic process because he believes that adoptive parents can help the child in many ways, including the following:

- Give emotional support for the child.
- Experience mutual enjoyment.
- Share their thoughts and feelings with the child.
- Challenge lies, distortions, and excuses.
- Provide expert knowledge about their child.
- Reinforce parental authority.
- Receive support, ideas, and validation of their parenting.

Good therapists understand that the adoptive family is usually not the source of the child's problem, but is absolutely necessary for the healing process.

Advocating for change

Parents are the most eloquent and best advocates for their families and have been very instrumental in bringing about some of the most important changes in adoption over the last several decades. Parents have had a strong voice in making the public aware of the normal, everyday aspects of adoptive family life as well as obtaining funds from the federal government for subsidized adoptions and mental health issues.

A great deal of work must still be done by individuals and parent organizations. The most important change that is needed is funding and support for those adoptive families who need help after the adoption is completed. If you choose to become involved in any aspect of adoption advocacy, from simple awareness to major reforms, you can learn from experienced adoption advocates.

Enhancing adoption awareness

November is Adoption Awareness Month (AAM), and it's a good time to promote adoption awareness in your community. If you want to do something on your own to promote adoption in your community, consider doing one or more of the following:

- Take one or more of your relatives to an adoption conference.

- As a thank-you, take your social worker, facilitator, or adoption attorney to lunch. Let them know the positive things they did to prepare you or support you.

- Offer your home to a family who is traveling to your area to finalize an adoption.

- Offer a weekend respite to a stressed adoptive family.

- Write a letter to the editor of your newspaper on an adoption issue.

- Contact local radio stations and dedicate a song to those seeking and waiting for adoption.

- Throw an adoption party to celebrate AAM.

Unofficially...
The North American Council on Adoptable Children, a national adoption support group, developed Adoption Awareness Month. November has been Adoption Awareness Month for over 20 years.

If your support group is looking for ways to celebrate AAM, here are some suggestions from existing support groups around the country:

- Plant a tree at a local park or zoo with a plaque honoring adoptive families in general.

- Donate to an adoption activist organization.

- Contact your local library, local school library, or bookstore to help them create a display of books about adoption.

- Have bumper stickers made that say "Adoption is an Option."

Big events, which may need funding and up to a year of planning, can be done with the help of other local groups and state agencies. Local businesses such as grocery stores and banks might sponsor some of the events. Ideas for larger events include:

- An adoption information fair

- A workshop with guest speakers who are considered experts (including adoptive parents) on a subject

- A breakfast for state legislators to explain adoption issues to them

According to experienced activists, coalitions of related organizations attract more attention from the media and encourage more donations from agencies and organizations single groups acting alone.

Advocating for reform

Many serious issues will need to be addressed over the next several years including open records, uniform adoption laws, and state legislation that will provide funding for post-adoption support services. It will be necessary for adoptive families to become

Moneysaver
Ask to hold meetings and information nights in public buildings such as libraries. Ask a religious organization or bank to sponsor your organization and donate space for meetings.

involved in the meetings to craft legislative bills and budget decisions that will directly affect them.

Researchers have found that in the past legislators were not well-informed about the issues concerning families, including adoptive families, in their districts. They have also reported that legislators view parent advocates as amateurs and found them ineffective advocates due to the following:

Timesaver
Parents can obtain important behind-the-scenes reports on adoption-related issues from Adoptive Families of America (AFA) or the North American Council on Adoptable Children (NACAC).

- The failure to make face-to-face contact and to build long-term relationships with members of the House and Senate

- The failure to provide timely, accurate information on specific child-related issues

- The lack of focus on *specific* legislative issues

- The inability to engage in the practical legislative arts of negotiation and compromise

- The absence of local grassroots organizations

Despite these failures, legislators are more open and accessible to citizen groups than they have been in the past. Because of this, adoptive parents can work toward beneficial change by doing the following:

- Determine who the key legislators are.

- Schedule a meeting with the legislator and follow up with phone calls, faxes, and emails.

- Provide timely and accurate information. Be clear and concise.

- Avoid being perceived as too emotional.

- Be prepared to follow up again and again.

- Look for sources of technical assistance. Individuals and other organizations with lobbying experience can be helpful.

The Massachusetts Coalition for Adoption, a successful coalition of adoptive parents and adoption professionals, started as a regional group in the southeastern part of the state and expanded in 1996 for the purpose of educating the Massachusetts legislature about the need for post-adoption services. Their first action was to organize a legislative breakfast, which was co-hosted by Massachusetts Families for Kids. The two organizations subsequently joined to advocate for post-adoption legislation.

Parents made phone calls and sent letters to legislators, visited the statehouse, and testified at budget hearings. The coalition was asked to develop a program and budget so that legislators would know where the money was going. In June of 1997, the Massachusetts legislators voted to appropriate $1.25 million to fund post-adoption support and preservation. The funds are available for services to all adoptive families whether they adopted through the state or privately.

While there are a few states that do fund post-adoption services to a limited degree, most states don't have a program as comprehensive as Massachusetts. Adoptive parents were present when the decisions were made in Massachusetts.

Just the facts

- Adoptive parents may need to teach friends, relatives, and professionals how to support their families.

- Parent and child support groups can be very beneficial to the adoptive family.

- There are not enough post-adoption services available in most areas.

- Not all therapists know how to help adoptive families.

- Parents are the best advocates for adoption reform and must learn to work politically for changes.

All in the Family

PART VII

GET THE SCOOP ON...
Establishing contact in an open
adoption ▪ Making a contract with the birth
family ▪ The birth family/adoptive family
relationship ▪ Remaining in contact with
abusive birthparents ▪ Talking to
your child about adoption

Fitting the Puzzle Together

Chapter 15

B y now you've realized that building the family by adoption is different from building the family by birth. The adoptive family must resolve many unique challenges in order to be a healthy, functional family.

One of these challenges is how to fit together all the members of your child's birth family and adoptive family, physically, emotionally, or both. In some cases, you will actually be adding members of your child's birth family to your extended family, depending on how much openness you have decided to have in your adoption. On the other hand, the contact your child has with birth family members may be limited or non-existent, but your child will still have an emotional tie with a past and another family. You will need to be able to talk sensitively and effectively with your child about adoption in general and his or her birth family in particular.

Establishing contact with the birth family

No one should consider an open adoption with ongoing contact between the birth family and the adoptive family unless both sides are prepared to work through the emotions, feelings, possibilities, and pitfalls of the arrangement. Both parties must understand that the benefits of open adoption, while they do exist for both the birthparents and the adoptive parents, primarily exist for the adoptee. This kind of total commitment to the welfare of the child can be accomplished only after much counseling and introspection for all involved.

In an open adoption arrangement in which birth and adoptive families have a great deal of contact, both birthparents and adoptive parents commit to an arrangement that will, in effect, add the other to their own family.

As with all relationships, this new relationship requires constant work and reevaluation if it is to succeed. Each participant in the agreement must be aware of his or her role and be willing to work on the established relationship throughout the years.

Establishing the birthparent/adoptive parent relationship

Two completely different sets of individuals will come together for the sake of a child. The birthparents will have a completely different set of needs, emotions, and expectations than the adoptive parents. Yet, birthparents and adoptive parents will need to connect and agree on a plan that will allow them to interact with each other over the years. In order to do this, they must work through the needs, emotions, and fears that each will bring to the table.

The birthparent is ready to commit to an open adoption plan when he or she understands the following:

- The adoption plan is in the best interests of the child.

- Feelings of grief and loss are normal after the placement has been made.

- An open adoption plan is not a way to continue parenting a child.

- He or she will continue to play a role in the child's life.

- Once the commitment is made, breaking agreements may be destructive to the child.

Prospective adoptive parents have many concerns about open adoption. Their main worry is that if the child's birthparents are in their lives, they will lose the love of their child. Adoptive parents who have experience in open adoptions maintain that the opposite is true. They stress that not only was the love and trust between them and their children not threatened, it was actually enhanced by their child's contact with the birth family.

Adoptive parents who were able to enter an open adoption successfully were able to do the following:

- Look upon the birthparents as extended family and feel that the more love available to the child, the better

- Understand that their child had a connection prior to the connection with them that will be with them whether the adoption is open or closed

- Realize that their child will not become confused about who the *parent* is in the relationship

Watch Out!
Don't consider an open adoption unless you've read all the information you can find and talked with as many experienced parents as possible. Be absolutely certain that you can follow through with your agreement. When either adoptive or birthparents don't follow the agreement, the adoptee suffers.

Bright Idea
Help your child learn to be comfortable with the concept of adoption. Provide your child with books about adoption, go to movies that have adoption themes, and attend adoption related events where your child can meet other adopted children.

- Understand that they will not lose their privacy when the birthparent visits

- Understand that parenting an adopted child is different—not better, not worse, but different—than parenting a birth child

- Realize that birthparents most likely are not going to "forget about it and disappear eventually"

The truth about imbalances

It's very important to begin any contract as equal participants, especially when determining the terms of the relationship with the child's birth family. Many caution against viewing the birthmother as less deserving to parent her child because she is not as economically well off, as well educated, or even as morally just as the adoptive mother or father. They stress the importance of keeping a respectful balance between the two parties throughout the relationship.

Other balance issues that can affect the relationship include:

- The grief of the birthparent due to the loss of a child contrasted with the joy of the adoptive parent in gaining a child.

- The need to determine to whom the child belongs.

- The need for all participants to find a comfortable level of familiarity in their relationship with each other.

- The fear that the success of the other will threaten the adoption. For example, if the adoptive parents succeed, the birthparent may feel unnecessary. If the birthparent succeeds in raising another child, the adoptive parent may feel that the adoption was unnecessary.

- Each has power over the other; the birthparent may have legal recourse, while the adoptive parent can refuse to let the birthparent see the child.

Making it work

Open adoption relationships take many forms, depending on the comfort level for all involved. Some adoptive families consider birthparents as members of their families, while others allow contact once or twice a year. It's up to you to determine what feels comfortable for you and set the ground rules early in the relationship.

Before you make an agreement with the birthparents, be sure that you and the birthparents are able to work together well because this arrangement could last for a lifetime, as long as it is in the best interests of the child. You may want to interview several different birthparents before making your decision. You need to find birthparents who will agree to your needs and desires for both a pre-adoption and post-adoption plan. As Joyce Stevens, a mother who adopted two children in separate open adoptions, explains, "The first time my husband and I were so eager to arrange to adopt a child, we decided to work with the first birthmother we met. All went well before the adoption and even for a few months after the adoption. Soon we realized that we were not a good match; our contacts have been unpleasant. The second time around, we had learned from our experience. We interviewed several different birthmothers and a few birthfathers before we made our final decision. It added a few months to the process, but it was worth it."

66
Do you know how many grown adoptees would have different lives, richer lives, had they received a special gift, a photo, even a single letter from a birthmother telling them the simple, honest truth...that their mother didn't give them away because they were somehow bad?
—Marcy Wineman Axness
99

Bright Idea
Consider the possibility of formally getting together with the birthparents for another planning session a few months after the birth of the baby. Involve a third party who can help you see how the relationship will develop over time. (Lois Gilman, *The Adoption Resource Book*)

The contract

Discuss post-adoption issues with both birthparents if both wish to remain in contact or with just the birthmother if the birthfather doesn't want to remain in contact. Put into writing the agreements you make concerning the issues of contact, frequency of communication and visitation, and other issues that will come up post-adoption. The following are some of the post-adoption issues that experts and experienced adopters recommend including in the contract:

- The amount of information that will be exchanged between the birth family and the adoptive family.

- What the adoptee will be told and when.

- How birthdays and other holidays will be celebrated. Will the birth family be part of the celebrations? Will the birth family give gifts?

- The type of contact that is going to occur. Will it be limited to letters, telephone calls, and/or visits?

- Will contact occur through a third party such as the agency or attorney, or will it be directly between the birth family and adoptive parents?

- Who in the birth family will be making contact?

- If the contacts are to be visits, how often will they occur and where?

- Who will pay the birthparents' traveling expenses, if any?

- Who will be the guardians of the child should something happen to the adoptive parents? Will the guardians be willing to continue the agreement between the birth and adoptive families?

- How will future issues and disagreements be handled? Who will mediate disagreements?

- Who will pay for any needed counseling or mediation in the future?

- What terms should the child use to refer to the birthparents?

- Will a birthparent be allowed to spend time alone with the child, especially if there is a question of the birthparent harming the child in some way?

Talk about as many details in advance as possible. Each agreement will be different, just as the needs and desires of each set of parents will be different. What remains constant is the willingness for both sets of parents to maintain an open dialogue for the benefit of the adoptee.

The reality

Most human relationships are not based on contracts, but on emotion and compromise, and the same is true of the relationship between two sets of parents in an open adoption. It is especially difficult when the birthparents are not together, but both want to remain in contact with the child. To help establish a compromise, experts suggest the following:

- Use common courtesy.

- Establish clear boundaries.

- Establish trust.

- Be forgiving.

The goal of the open adoption arrangement is to develop a relationship that works and eventually deepens into a true friendship that moves beyond the love of the same child. This is possible if both sides

Unofficially...
Children are having few problems with open adoption, according to Sharon Kaplan Roszia and Kathleen Silber, two open adoption experts. The children seem to have fewer struggles with adoption issues and see open adoption as "no big deal."

not only follow the rules, but also understand that the alliance needs to be fluid and will change over time.

When contact becomes unbalanced

Open adoption is not problem-free. Maintaining the original contact agreement is one of the most challenging problems, along with dealing with children the birthparents may have in the future, and explaining the birth family to friends and acquaintances. The latter is particularly difficult for an adolescent struggling with identity issues.

Problems with contact

The first year brings major adjustments to all participants. Each person needs to be particularly sensitive to the issues the other is facing. Some of the difficulties that may occur include the following:

- The birthparent may initiate contact more often than agreed to in the contract. This may be a way of working through grief and loss.

- The birthparent may not wish to see the child as often as agreed upon. This may be because it is too painful to see the child, or because the birthparent encounters circumstances that make it impossible to follow the contract.

- The adoptive parents may find themselves the only source of support for the birthparent, which will cause unnecessary stress for them during the adjustment period.

Over time, the birthparent may move on with life and find it more difficult to stay committed to the child. A birthparent might stop seeing your child for several reasons, including:

- The birthparent may see that you are doing a good job in raising the child; the child is happy and well-adjusted. The birthparent may feel that it's OK to establish a life and family of his or her own.

- The birthparent may move to another area for a variety of reasons and not have the time or money to see the child.

- The birthparent may have a relapse back into a drug or alcohol problem.

The birthparents and the adoptive parents should understand the impact on the child should contact lessen or, more importantly, stop altogether. A child who is accustomed to some contact with a birthparent will see the loss of contact, even if only once a year, as another rejection. To encourage the birthparent to stay in contact, you can do the following:

- Reinforce to the birthparent how important the relationship is to the child despite what people outside of the agreement may be telling them.

- If visits are impossible at the time, encourage the birthparent to stay in touch with cards, letters, and an occasional phone call for the sake of the child.

- Stay in contact with extended birth family members as much as possible. Perhaps an aunt, uncle, or grandparent is in a more stable place in life and can maintain a contact schedule.

If you are unable to stay in contact with any of the birth family, always reinforce your child's self-esteem and acknowledge your child's hurt.

There may be a time when your child is not interested in having contact with a birthparent, especially if the contact is infrequent. It may be difficult for your child to write or call someone seen only once or twice a year. Remember that the

Watch Out!
Always keep the emotional and physical welfare of your child in mind. You may have to stop contact with a birth family member when you have determined that contact could be dangerous to your child. Review the terms of the agreement at that time.

agreement to stay in contact was made by the adults, not the child. It is up to the adults to maintain the agreement and remain in contact. This will leave the door open for the adoptee to have a change of heart later in life and have contact with the birthparent.

Other children in the birth family

"One of the most difficult things I had to do was to try to explain to my seven-year-old adopted daughter why her birthmother was going to have a baby and raise the child herself," says Jill Henderson, an adoption social worker and mother of two. "She could not understand why she could keep this baby, but could not have kept her. She was simply much too young to understand the differences in her birthmother's situation that made raising this child possible. She then worried about the relationship of the child to her, but not to her sister. It was a very confusing time for her. It has been two years, and I am not sure she has really resolved the problem in her mind."

A child has little ability to understand why a birthparent made an adoption plan for one child, and subsequently decides to raise another child. Young children, especially, feel that there must have been something wrong with them, that perhaps this new child is better in some way. In this situation, the adoptive parents must remind the child of his or her importance to both themselves and the birthparents.

The birthparents, who may later have children either together or separately, may also have a difficult time explaining to younger children why they chose not to raise an older brother or sister.

More than one set of birthparents

After you have successfully negotiated an open adoption with one birth family, you may feel encouraged to try again. Keep in mind that all relationships are different, and it would be impossible to have exactly the same relationship with both, or all, birth families. The mother of three children adopted in open adoptions with varying amounts of openness describes how she handles the resulting jealousies, saying, "We have learned to deal with the jealousy by giving each child as much information as possible about the birth family. We allow each child to express the sadness and anger that results from not having the same relationship with a birthparent as another sibling has."

Questions to be answered

No matter how much you wish to insulate your child from a judgmental or unfair society, your child may be exposed to those who will make disparaging remarks about the relationship that your child has with the birth family. In order to help your child answer the inevitable questions from those outside the family, determine ahead of time how to answer the following questions:

- What will they call the members of the birth family, including children of the birthparents?

- Do they include in the number of siblings they have the children of the birthparents?

- How do they handle the birth family in their "family tree"?

- Do they tell their friends and others that they have siblings who don't live with them?

For more information on fielding questions with good answers, see Chapter 13.

Open adoption with "special needs" kids

Many of the older children adopted from the foster care system remember the abuse and neglect of

Unofficially...
Open adoption is a relatively new experience for the triad. It will take many years of research to determine if it "works." Experts already agree that it does not solve all the problems related to the adoption experience.

Bright Idea
Some agencies try to prepare adoptive families for open adoption by discussing the benefits to the child and having birthparents talk to adoptive parent groups. This helps adoptive parents see the birthparents as real people.

their birthparents; nevertheless, they have retained a strong connection to them. The truth is that children who are abused and neglected are able to love those who abused and neglected them. Therefore, many adoption social workers are advocating for supervised contact with some or all members of the birth family after the child has been placed for adoption.

Advocates also point out that seeing the dysfunctional behavior of a parent may help the child understand why the parent was not able to parent. If genetic disorders such as mental illness played a role in the parent's inability to parent, the child may have the opportunity to see how this can be controlled, if the birthparent seeks appropriate treatment. On the other hand, a birthparent who does not take prescribed medication is a poor and scary example for a child with a hereditary condition.

Some agencies have policies concerning open adoption with older children, and others do not. You have to decide if it's something you want to do, depending on the situation and the benefit to your child. Obviously, you should not consider contact if potential danger exists for either you or your child.

To alleviate any fears and lessen the danger when meeting the birthparents of special needs children, create the following boundaries:

- Meet the birthparent in a public place.
- Give the birthparent your work phone number, not your home number.
- If the visit is to be in your home, consider having a friend, neighbor, or relative join the meeting.

Although the needs of the child are of foremost concern, contact with a birthparent may have benefits for you as well. You may get new insights into your child's moods and behaviors, and you may develop a level of understanding and compassion for the birthparent of your child. You can also reassure your child of this person's love for him or her.

How to talk with your child about adoption

"My child is about to go into kindergarten; I have not told him that he is adopted. When should I tell him? What should I say? How will I answer his questions? How do I handle the negative aspects of his history?" These are the most frequently asked questions at adoption workshops and conferences. At a recent adoption conference, over 82 percent of the questions had to do with how to discuss adoption with the adoptee. It seems to be one of the most difficult problems for adoptive parents.

Whether your child entered your family as an infant or as an older child who has some recollection of the past, it will be up to you to answer questions and fill in details that are important to your child. How well you do this will have a lasting impact on your child's sense of identity and your relationship as a family.

When to tell your child

Most experienced adoptive parents and experts agree that it is best to tell a child at an early age that he or she is adopted. They don't believe that giving information to the child in the preschool years causes any lasting emotional damage, as some people maintain. Also, they believe that giving them the information from the beginning builds the relationship between parents and child with a firm base of trust and openness. From a practical standpoint, it assures adoptive parents that the information is

Timesaver
Arranging a meeting among adoptive parents, children, and birthparents in a therapeutic setting can yield answers for everyone and save years of therapy and searching for the adoptee.

given to their child with love and understanding and not mistakenly by a friend or relative. The benefits of creating an awareness of adoption when a child is young include the following:

- The parents know that they are the ones who have given the information to their child. They are the ones who initiated awareness in an atmosphere of love and understanding.

- The relationship is not based on fear of a secret being revealed, but on openness and truth.

Another theory held by some suggests that telling a child too early contributes to problems for the adopted child. Proponents believe that young children are not able to understand the information that is given to them and will have serious emotional difficulties as a result. These people give the following reasons for withholding the information from a young child:

- Telling a young child undermines the bonding process with the adoptive parents.

- Young children are busy with other issues of growing.

- Young children feel that they somehow caused the birthparents to "give them up" because of something they did.

- Young children cannot understand being "unwanted" by birthparents and "wanted" by adoptive parents.

The choice of when to tell your child that he was adopted ultimately rests with you. You are the only one who can determine when the time is right for you, your child, and your family.

What to tell your child

Tell your child the truth. All experts agree that no matter when you decide to introduce the concept of adoption into your child's life, you must be honest and give as many details as necessary, depending on the child's age and interest. More details can be added in later dialogues. If you are not honest from the beginning, your child will lose trust when the truth is revealed. The guidelines for telling your child's adoption story include the following:

- Tell the truth.

- Start at the beginning with your child's birth. Give the time, place, first names of birthparents, and related details.

- Keep it simple and give details that are age-appropriate. Don't tell your child too much at one sitting. There will be many opportunities to add to the story later.

- Always refer to the birthparents with respect, and help your child to understand why they chose to place their child for adoption. Avoid using terms like "give away," as children don't understand how someone can love them enough to give them away.

- Be compassionate when speaking of the birthparents to prevent your child from feeling that he or she comes from "bad" people.

- Emphasize that the birthparents placed your child for adoption because they were unable to parent fully, not because there was something wrong with the child.

- Emphasize that adoption is forever.

But even if you have never met Baby's birthparents and never expect to, you have a relationship with them. You will think about them; you will wonder or worry about them.
—Pat Johnston

What not to tell your child

In the past, adopted children were told that they were *chosen* and *special* by well-meaning adoptive parents. But many adoptees have expressed the belief that these two words have contributed to their feelings of insecurity, low self-esteem, and the need to be accepted, because the adoptees feel that they have not measured up to being *chosen* or *special.*

When adoptees are told that they are special, some feel they must be perfect in order to keep the love of family and friends. They may feel that they must be perfect for the adoptive parents, or the adopted parents will abandon them.

Watch Out!
Young children often believe they are either adopted or born. Make sure you make it clear to them that they are born first, then adopted. Let them know that all children are born in the same way.

How to make it easier

Adoptive parents and professionals have learned through experience how to help parents with the job of talking about adoption. Some helpful tips include the following:

- Buy videos of movies that have adoption themes. Watch the movie at home, so you can stop the movie at strategic places and discuss what's going on.

- If your child asks a question concerning adoption at an inconvenient time, it's OK to postpone the answer until later. Simply tell your child that it was a good question, and you will answer it at another time.

- Make sure you have filled in all the details of your child's story by the time your child is a teen.

- Consider having a therapist or counselor work with you as you tell your child some particularly negative details.

- Read books about adoption to your children to let them know that other children are adopted also.

- Always provide an environment in which children feel free to ask questions.

- Allow children to express all the emotions they feel when they hear the story of their adoption. These emotions may be different at each stage of their development.

- As much as possible, let adoptees decide who knows their adoption stories.

- Don't force your child to talk about adoption. Take cues from your child and try again at another time.

- Never discuss adoption when you are angry with your child.

Children of all ages can learn a great deal about adoption by reading the many books available on the subject. Many of the books discuss adoption in general, and others deal with the specific issues in transracial, intercountry, and special needs adoptions. I've listed several of these books in Appendix C.

Creating a life book

One of the most effective ways to initiate a discussion of your child's history is to create a life book. Formerly thought to be effective only for children with complex histories, now the life book is being used by parents who adopted their children as infants.

A life book is a chronological history of your child's life containing all available information. The book should be created by the adoptee with your help. Encourage your child to do all the writing

Bright Idea
A life book can also be a narrated video with occasional live performances such as concerts, ball games, and graduations. A video or videos can also supplement a written life book.

and/or illustrations while you check for accuracy. Begin by recording the information you have about your child prior to the placement for adoption, and continue with post-adoption information such as the first step, first word, and other milestones.

The life book should contain the following:

- Child's birth information: date, time, location, weight, and height

- An accurate history of the child's birth family

- Foster homes and relatives' homes where the child has lived, if any

- Photos of the hospital where the child was born and the nurses in the nursery

- The plane on which the parents traveled to meet the baby

- The judge at the adoption hearing

- School-related information: list of schools attended, dates, teachers' names, report cards, comments from teachers, and sample work

- Medical information about the child

- Letters and mementos from parents, relatives, or significant others

- Anecdotes about the child: developmental milestones; favorite activities, hobbies, or sports; favorite friends, etc.

- Drawings by the child

- Photographs and other mementos

Working on the book together with your child gives you an excellent opportunity to fill in information, answer questions, and explain difficult details for your child. You should work on the book for short periods of time, keeping in mind both the short attention span of young children as well as the emotional strain that it might put on both of you.

Just the facts

- Open adoption contracts are made to benefit the adoptee, not the birthparents or the adoptive parents.

- Open adoption does not solve all the problems with adoption.

- While experts disagree about the best age for beginning to talk to your child about adoption, all agree that adolescence is too late.

- The adoptee who is raised in a home where adoption is discussed openly and with ease has a better chance of accepting himself as a valuable human being.

GET THE SCOOP ON...
Why adult adoptees search for birthparents
■ Why adoptive parents need to understand
■ Dealing with your feelings when your child
searches ■ Why you should offer your help ■ The
benefits of disappointing reunions

The Facts About Searching

Chapter 16

The verb *to search* means to look for something that is lost. Adoption is about loss for adoptees. Many adoptees have lost their histories because their adoptions are shrouded in secrecy. It should not be surprising, then, that some adoptees, though certainly not all, cannot rest until they have uncovered the part of their history that has been unknown to them.

One of the best ways to understand your adopted child is to hear from adult adoptees about why they feel a need to search for their birth families (or why they have no desire to do so) and how contact with their birth family has affected their lives.

Why they have to search

As recently as 25 years ago, society placed strict rules on the adoption process, with the good intention of protecting the members of the triad. Adoption officials locked up adoption records and threw away the key. Today in the United States, the pendulum is swinging toward open adoption. Yet, citing the need to keep a promise of confidentiality to birth and adoptive parents, many states continue to adhere to the policy of keeping closed adoption records sealed. As a result, some adult adoptees spend years and a great deal of money trying to track down their birthparents.

Despite enlightened adoption policies and practices in this country, a number of countries overseas do not allow even the first name of the birthmother to be identified to prospective adoptive parents. In other countries, societal and cultural rules force birthmothers to "abandon" their babies, as does U.S. Immigration law, which requires that a child brought into this country meet the definition of "orphan". As a result, many adoptees from other countries cannot search for information about their birth families.

Why adoptees want to search

66
I began this way: No matter how much I loved my family, I never knew who I really was or where I came from. For all I knew, being from Illinois, I could have been related to John Wayne Gacy."
—Andrew Blum in "Digging Deep" in the November/December issue of *Adoptive Families* magazine
99

Why do adoptees search? There are as many answers to that question as there are adoptees searching. The reasons run the gamut from simple curiosity to a burning desire or a spiritual obsession. While some only want to know non-identifying information or medical history, others want to meet members of their birth family because they feel they will never really know themselves until they know their roots.

To fill in the blanks

Authors like Jayne E. Schooler, *Searching for a Past: The Adopted Adult's Unique Process of Finding Identity* (see Appendix C), have studied the reasons that adult adoptees search for their past. Some of the reasons that people search include the following:

- A simple curiosity about physical appearances drives some adoptees to seek out information about birth families. They need to answer questions such as "Who do I resemble?" or "Who else in my birth family has artistic talents?"

- Some people are naturally curious and need to solve the mystery of their past. They view the search as an adventure with knowledge of the past as the reward.

- Some people search because they are seeking a therapeutic solution to some of their problems. Those who believe that many of their personal problems stem from being adopted hope that finding their birth family will bring resolution to their problems.

- Many people find not having a complete medical history very disturbing. They worry that they may have medical issues that need to be uncovered for the sake of their own health and the health of their children.

- Most adoptees who search need to ask birthparents why they decided to arrange an adoption for them. They feel that they cannot truly forgive their birthparents until they have that answer. It gives them a sense of closure to a lifelong need to know and to forgive their birthparents for not raising them.

Questions that need answers

"Both my girls were adopted as older children. Therefore, they always knew that they were adopted. As they entered adolescence, they often expressed to me the need to know why their birthmother chose to place them for adoption. They expressed little curiosity over anything but the answer to that

Watch Out!
Often, adoptive parents inadvertently contribute to the anxiety that adult adoptees feel because they have not answered their child's questions truthfully and completely. Experts advise complete honesty when your child asks a question. See Chapter 15 for more about questions and answers.

question. It wasn't until later in their teens that they became curious about other aspects of their past," said one adoptive mother, describing a typical situation with children who are curious about their past.

It doesn't seem to matter whether children are adopted as infants or as older children, for many the need to know *why* is the first question that needs answers. As they develop and begin to think in abstract terms, the answers to the following questions become important:

- Where and what time was I born?
- Was I a normal size; were there any problems with the birth?
- Who was present at the birth?
- Did my birthmother hold me? Did my birthfather hold me?
- Did my birthparents choose my adoptive family? Did they meet my adoptive family?
- Did my birthparents give me a name?
- What are the details about my birthparents? How old were they? Were they married?
- Who were my birthparents? Did they graduate from high school? College? What were their interests?
- What is my racial/ethnic background?
- Did my birthparents marry each other? Someone else? Do I have siblings?
- What do my birthparents look like? Other family members? Do I look like anyone in the birth family?
- Are my birthparents still alive? Do they think of me?

- Are there any medical conditions I should know about?

- What name should I use to refer to my birth-parents?

Experts feel that if these questions are not answered early, some adult adoptees will spend the rest of their lives yearning for the answers. For some, just the answer to questions such as these is the end of the quest, but others need actual contact with the birth family.

When they usually search

Some adoptees know in their teens that they will search for their birthparents as soon as they reach 18. Others are older before they even contemplate seeking answers. Sometimes it takes a particular event or series of events to motivate a person to search, such as the following:

- The death of an adopted parent or parents. The adoptee feels an emptiness that he or she is experiencing can be filled with knowledge of the birthparents. The adoptee may also feel that he or she can search without being concerned about how it will affect the adoptive parent or parents.

- The birth of a child.

- The adoption of a child.

- A marriage or divorce.

Many of the significant life events that we take for granted can leave the adult adoptee feeling incomplete and unsettled. This can prompt him or her to search for the lost connection in the hope that it will fill the void.

Unofficially...
Often, the adult adoptee simply feels a sense of dissatisfaction that he hopes will be alleviated when he finds his birthparents. Also, as adult adoptees age, their search develops a sense of urgency as they fear that their birthparents may die before they can find them.

Why some do not want to search

While it seems that more adult adoptees are searching today, perhaps because of the new attitudes toward open adoption and open adoption records, the truth is that the vast majority of adoptees do not wish to search. Their reasons for not searching seem to fall into four major categories:

- A general contentment with who they are
- A loyalty to the adoptive family
- A feeling that it is wrong to search for a variety of personal reasons
- A fear of being rejected again

For many, even the idea of digging into the past and perhaps bringing up painful memories and possible rejection is too difficult to contemplate. Some are afraid that they will find that one or more of the birth family members has died, and they will have to grieve because they will never be able to meet the person. Others are very happy with the life they have now and are content to live with the memories they do have of their past.

The truth about your feelings

Imagine this scene: It is years after you adopted your child. You have read and learned everything you possibly could about adoption. You are enlightened; you know that some adopted children want to search for birth families. Deep in your heart you feel that your child is happy, well-adjusted, and will not want to search. Suddenly, your child informs you that he wants to search. You feel you are prepared. Wrong!

According to most adoptive parents, no matter how much you tell yourself that you knew this might happen, you are never fully prepared. "It caught us off-guard," one adoptive father reported. "I just didn't see it coming. [Our son] had never mentioned it before, even when we talked about his history and told him what we knew. Then several months before his wedding, he told us he wanted to find members of his birth family in the hopes they could attend the wedding. We were shocked."

Many adoptive parents describe a flood of emotions when their children tell them that they wish to search. No matter how young or old the child is, it always seems like the wrong time. Experts advise parents to be prepared for the emotional rollercoaster they can experience before and during their child's search.

Hurt

One of the emotions described by experienced adopters is hurt. The hurt that adoptive parents feel may come from a variety of issues. For some, it may bring up painful memories of infertility that the parent thought had been resolved long before adopting the child.

Other parents are hurt because they feel they were betrayed by a system that promised them they would be the only parents of their child. They are hurt because they feel their child did not find them to be enough. In *The Whole Life Adoption Book* (see Appendix C), Jayne Schooler tells the story of Linda, who was devastated when her son told her that he was interested in conducting a search. Her hurt was rooted in the words of a pre-adoption counselor who had told her that if she were "the right kind of a mother" her child would never want to search. She felt that her son's desire to search indicated her failure as a parent.

Bright Idea
Take small steps back into the past. Take a roots trip. Whether it is overseas or a nearby town, children benefit from seeing their birthplace. It will help both of you integrate the past into the present.

Fear

Adoptive parents admit to being fearful on many levels. Some of the fears they have are for their relationship with their child, but many are fears of what the results of the search will do to their child. Some of the common fears are:

- That they will "lose" their children to the birthparents. Words from the teenage years like "You are not my real parents" take on a new meaning for parents during the search process.

- That their children will be hurt by something they find. Perhaps this hurt will permanently change their children's lives in a negative way. It is very normal for a parent to want to protect a child from pain of any kind.

In reality, most fears are unfounded. Studies have shown that after reconnecting with the birth family, most adoptees report an improvement in self-esteem and self-confidence. They also report no significant negative changes in their relationship with their adoptive parents. They still have the same feelings and emotions for them. It sometimes even improves the relationship, as the adoptees have a renewed love and ability to express their appreciation of how well their parents raised them.

Jealousy

Finally, many parents are afraid that they'll have to share their children with those from the past. Adoptive parents participating in a workshop entitled "Helping Your Child Search" expressed the following concerns in regard to sharing their children with the birth family:

- Where their child would choose to spend holidays
- Whether their child would visit or call less often

Unofficially
The International Soundex Reunion Registry (www. adoptiontriad. org) is the world's largest mutual consent reunion registry and is free. Get your free registration form by sending a self-addressed stamped envelope to: I.S.R.R., P.O. Box 2312, Carson City, Nevada 89702-2312 or call 702-882-7755.

- How they would fit into the equation with the birthparents

- What the grandchildren would call the birthparents and how they would react to another set (or two) of grandparents

- How they would resolve any residual anger they might feel toward a birthparent who might have neglected or abused a child

- How the birthparents might undermine parenting decisions that the adoptive parents have made or encourage the child to rebel against such decisions.

Jealous fears usually work out to be just as unfounded as the other fears expressed by adoptive parents. Most adoptive parents report that while their children have reconnected with the "other" family, it doesn't take time away from the adoptive family. Most adoptees quickly learn how to balance both relationships.

So, should you help?

Absolutely. Your child will decide whether or not to search and when to search. The degree to which you help your child depends on how much you want to help, balanced with how much help your child wants.

The least you should do is be there for your child no matter what happens. You can be an unbiased support to whom your child can turn if the results of the search are disappointing. You need to let your child know that no matter what happens they will not lose you.

Parents should let their children know that they will support them in their search and tell them exactly what they will do to help them.

> "
> I wanted to honor my adoptive mother during the reunion period of my search. On the day I was to meet my birthmother, I sent flowers to my adoptive mother assuring her of my deep love for her and deep commitment to my adoptive family.
> —Andrea West, age 29
> "

How to search

Most people assume that they can find their genetic and medical information whenever they choose to do so. What they cannot find out from parents or relatives, they can find by researching their own records. This is not the case for many people who were adopted. No federal laws govern adoption records, so each state is left to determine how much information can be given to whom.

Some adoptees are very angry that they are not allowed to find out information regarding their past; others are amazed at how difficult it is to retrieve information.

Not everyone agrees that the records should be open. Many birthmothers have a good case against open records. Some of the reasons against open records are listed in the section "Why some don't want to be found" later in this chapter.

Despite the difficulties, adoptees can usually obtain updated medical and other non-identifying information such as medical records or other information that does not identify the birthparents. With more effort and determination, adoptees are usually able to find their birthparents. The search is made more difficult because the laws and policies vary in each state.

Obtaining non-identifying information

Generally speaking, non-identifying information is easy to obtain in most states. As of this writing, adoptees can obtain non-identifying information in all states except the District of Columbia, Louisiana, and New Jersey. New Jersey currently has several pending bills concerning release of records. The amount of information that is available depends on

Timesaver
The search itself can be a long, difficult, and emotional process for your child. Consider helping your child with the actual search. Make phone calls or write letters. Your help will not only shorten the process, it will bring the two of you closer together.

what was recorded at the time of the birth and the adoption and may include the following:

- Medical history
- Health status
- Cause of and age at death (of the birthparents' parents)
- Height, weight, eye and hair color
- Ethnic origins
- Level of education
- Professional achievement
- Religion
- Parents' ages at the time of birth
- Ages and sexes of other children
- Hobbies
- General geographic location
- Reasons for action taken

Anything that could be considered data that would lead to identification of the adopted adult, the birthmother, or birthfather is called identifying information.

There are three legal ways to obtain identifying information: the original birth certificate, registries, and court orders.

Original birth certificate
Adopted adults 18 or older have automatic access to their original birth certificate in Alaska, Kansas, and, in some cases, Ohio, Tennessee, and Montana, depending on the year the adoption was finalized. In the other states, an adoptee must obtain a court order for the release of the birth certificate.

Moneysaver
Save time, energy, and money. In New York, the number on the adoption birth certificate is the same as the number on the original birth certificate. Those numbers can be matched with the birthmother's name in a book kept by the state registrar listing births for that year.

Signing up with a registry

Reunion registries, or mutual consent registries, can be maintained by the state, private individuals, or commercial firms. Registry procedures vary greatly from state to state. Some states won't release information if one of the parties is deceased. Some states require the adoptive parents to give permission to the adopted adult to receive the information.

There are two kinds of registries:

- *Passive* (mutual consent or volunteer) requires both parties to register their consent for release of information. These registries have a match rate of approximately 10 percent.

- *Active* does not require that both parties register consent. As soon as one party requests information, an agency or court representative contacts the other party to determine their wishes for release of information. These registries have a match rate of 50 to 90 percent.

Court orders

Most states in which the adoption records are sealed allow an adoptee to petition the court to open the records. The adoptee must show "good cause," which is defined differently from court to court and state to state. Some examples of good cause include:

- A showing of compelling reasons

- The release of information is in the best interests of the adoptee or the public

- Health or medical issues

- Proving that releasing information would be of greater benefit than not releasing it

Many states have recently passed laws regarding release of records; others have bills pending. The

Bright Idea
Seventeen states have a confidential intermediary system. These states allow adoptees or birthparents to hire a state employee or individual sanctioned by the court to search for the other party. If release of information is agreed upon by both parties, the court authorizes the release.

following states are actively reassessing their statutes regarding the rights of adopted adults and birth-parents: Delaware, Illinois, New Jersey, New York, Pennsylvania, Texas, Washington, and Oregon. To check on state statutes and laws regarding adoption records, contact the state adoption specialist (see Appendix B).

Returning to the original adoption agency

Some agencies will release information to an adoptee if the birthparent has given permission to do so. Experienced searchers suggest that you contact the agency by phone to make an appointment for an interview with a social worker. Be sure to tell the social worker your reasons for wanting the interview. If the social worker will not agree to an interview for any reason, write a letter to the agency requesting the information. Include a waiver of confidentiality with the request.

Using a private investigator

Some adoptees hire an individual, search consultant, or search organization to do the searching. Some of these individuals or organizations do the investigating on a volunteer basis, while others charge a fee. Check the fee schedule before you hire anyone. Ask for references and check out the organization with the Better Business Bureau.

Investigating on your own

Once you and your child have learned about the laws in the state or states in which you'll be searching, you can actively begin your search. Several good books provide step-by-step instructions on how to do the actual search, including how to use the Internet in your search, and I list those in Appendix C.

Unofficially...
State laws vary considerably. For example, Iowa courts will release records if "good cause" is proven, but may deny the request for information if releasing it could harm a minor sibling. Kentucky courts will release records if birthparents are missing or deceased. Be sure to check the state's laws.

Timesaver
Keep all the
information that
you gather in
one notebook or
folder. Document
every
conversation,
including
original contact
and replies
received. The
success of the
search is often
the result of
putting one
small clue
together with
another small
clue.

If you do your own investigating, you'll need to budget for expenses. According to Jayne Schooler in *Searching for a Past* (see Appendix C), you can count on the following costs:

- Official certificates of record cost from $2 to $15.
- Filing in a probate court or registering in a state registry costs around $100.
- In a state with a mandated intermediary system, fees can be between $200 and $2,000.
- Some private adoption agencies charge (from $10 to $100) for opening and reviewing their files.
- Some adoptees spend over $100 in mailing fees.
- Telephone bills vary, but may be in excess of $100.
- Membership dues in an adoption, genealogical, or historical group range from $25 to $75.

Keep in mind the amount of money you are willing and able to spend on the search. The search can be frustrating and emotional enough without adding money problems to the mix. If you find yourself going over budget, you can always stop the search for the time being and resume later when you have the funds.

Connecting with the birthparents

After accumulating all the information and documentation needed to locate a birthparent, the adoptee is ready to initiate contact—either by phone or mail. The adoptee is about to reconnect with the past, or maybe not.

Why some don't want to be found

There are no easy answers to why a birthparent would hang up the phone or not reply to the letter that your child sent. The fact is that not all birth-parents are in favor of opening closed records and allowing adoptees to seek contact. In November of 1998, the citizens of Oregon voted to approve Measure 58, which granted adoptees over the age of 21 the right to their original birth certificates. Only two other states, Alaska and Kansas, have open access to adoption records. But before the law could go into effect in Oregon in December, a group of mothers filed suit against the state, claiming the law violated their right to privacy.

The debate rages in other states as well. Some women made adoption plans because they were forced to do so by parents or societal attitudes. Other women were pregnant as a result of rape. Many of these women still carry the fear of retribution by the offender if they are found. In his article, "Tracking Down Mom" in the February 22, 1999, issue of *Time* magazine, John Cloud describes the plight of one woman who became pregnant as a result of being beaten and raped in college. She had the baby, but placed her for adoption. Twenty years later, the child found her, and they exchanged letters. The child seemed to take the news of her father being a rapist in stride and wanted to know how she could contact him in prison. Today, the birthmother lives in terror of being found by the man she helped send to prison.

Whatever the reason, these women made a plan that purportedly guaranteed they would be able to go on with their lives without the fear of the past reintroducing itself. The possible end to that guarantee is very threatening to these women.

Experts stress that as difficult as rejection is for the adoptee, it should not be taken as a personal rejection. The birthparent does not know the adoptee, but is working on a personal agenda that does not allow for reunification with a painful past.

Some of the other reasons that your child might not receive a reply include:

- It's not a good time in the birthparent's life to reconnect. The birthparent may be busy raising a family, for example.

- The birthparent may want to honor the agreement made with the adoptive parents years ago.

- The birthparent may be seriously ill or even deceased.

Your child may wish to try to establish contact again at a later date.

Reality check?

Of course, there may be an answer to the phone call or a reply to the letter. Many birthparents are eager to reconnect with the child they thought was lost to them forever. If the birthparent agrees to a reunion, one of the following could be the result:

- There is a one-time meeting that solves enough of the mystery for both parties.

- A relationship is established with the birthparent, but the adoptive parents remain the primary parents. Usually the adult adoptee refers to the birthparents by their first names while continuing to call their adoptive parents mother and father.

- The birthparents become the primary parents.

- A relationship with the birthparents starts out strong but fizzles out.

Often, adoptees are disappointed in what they find. Nothing could live up to the fantasies that

Moneysaver
During the search and after contact, phone bills may grow large. Use email, find the cheapest times to make calls, and seek the best rates to keep your phone bill down. Be careful, the cheapest rates are usually after business hours, which may be too late in another time zone.

filled their minds for years, or they find their birth-parents to be needy, drug involved, greedy, cruel, or just disinterested. On the other hand, most report that the search was worth all the effort, as their worst fears were not realized, and they were able to find answers to questions that had plagued them their entire life.

Adoptees who have searched and found birth-parents warn others to be prepared for anything and everything. The best place to prepare for any-thing and everything is in a support group of other adult adoptees who are also in the process of search-ing. The support group will be there for your child both during and after the reunion.

Happily ever after?

Unfortunately, orchestrating a reunion and making a few practical changes in scheduling and lifestyle in order to incorporate another family into the adoptee's life is not the end of the story. The adoptee will still be on a roller-coaster of conflicting emotions. Some adoptees who have searched have gone through a series of stages immediately after their reunion, including anger, sadness, and depres-sion, but they report working through their emo-tions and going on with their lives.

For many, the search is a journey that brings the adoptee full circle back to the adoptive family with an even greater appreciation of the security that family provided.

Watch Out! Siblings in the birth family are not always eager to have the adoptee "back" in the family. Perhaps they were never told about the adoptee, or they see the adoptee receiving attention and love they're not ready to share. It may take time to win them over.

Just the facts

- Even though it takes time to find the answers, the search is worth the effort and results in increased self-esteem and self-worth for most adoptees who do search.

- As with most state adoption laws, those concerning open records and release of information are changing rapidly and vary from state to state.

- There is an ongoing heated debate between opponents of open records and adoptees who feel the records are their birthright.

- Only in rare instances do adoptees give up the relationship with adoptive parents as a result of a search. Often the relationship is enhanced as a result.

Glossary

adoptee   A person who has been adopted.

adoption   The legal process in which parental rights are transferred from birthparents to adoptive parents.

adoption agency   An organization that places children for adoption. It can be a county agency or private agency licensed by the state.

adoption attorney   An attorney who arranges adoptive placements. Some attorneys specialize in adoption issues.

adoption cancellation insurance   Insurance that covers some of the financial losses incurred by prospective adoptive parents should a birthparent choose not to continue with the adoption plan.

adoption exchange   An organization designed to provide connections between prospective adoptive parents and adoption agencies that place children. Many states have state-operated exchanges and publish photolistings of waiting children. There are also regional, national, and international exchanges that are non-profit organizations.

adoption facilitators　Individuals who help prospective adopters with the various aspects of the adoption process. Some adoption facilitators are licensed social workers, some are attorneys; others are not licensed by the state. Adoption facilitators are illegal in many states.

adoption professional　An employee of a licensed adoption agency or a trained, educated, and experienced authority who has been authorized to provide adoption services.

adoption ritual　A ceremony that acknowledges that a child has been adopted into the family. Adoption rituals may be religious or non-religious.

adoption triad/triangle　The three parties involved in an adoption—adoptive parents, birthparents, and adoptee.

adoptive parent　A person who legally assumes the parental rights and responsibilities for an adopted child. Some adoptive parents are related to the child; others are not.

agency adoption　An adoption that is arranged by professionals at a licensed adoption agency. In some areas it may also be referred to as an agency placement.

biological child　The child of parents by birth.

biracial　A term used to describe a person who has biological parents of different races, usually black and white.

birth certificate (amended)　The legal document issued after the adoption is finalized. It replaces the original birth certificate as indicated by the court in the adoption decree with the adoptive parents' names replacing the birthparents' names.

birth certificate (original) The legal document issued at the time of birth with the child's biological history including the identity of one or both biological parents.

birth family The extended biological family of an adoptee.

birthfather The biological father of an adoptee.

birthgrandparents The biological grandparents of an adoptee.

birthmother The biological mother of an adoptee.

black market adoption The illegal buying and selling of children.

chosen child A term used in the past to refer to an adopted child. Today, many experts and adoptees caution against using the term because it puts too much pressure on adoptees to be special.

closed adoption An adoption in which the confidentiality of both adoptive parents and birthparents is protected under the law. All records are sealed by the courts. Also called a confidential adoption.

confidential adoption See **closed adoption**.

confidential intermediary system The system in a state that allows the adoptee to search for a birthparent. The birthparent is identified and contacted. If the birthparent agrees, identifying information is given to the adoptee.

consent form The legal document signed by both the birthparents allowing the child to be placed for adoption. If a birthparent is unavailable, the courts can validate the consents without the birthparent's signature. A consent is also referred to as a surrender or relinquishment.

cooperative adoption   An adoption in which an adoptee has access to both his adoptive parents and his birthparents who participate in decisions affecting his life.

custody   The legal guardianship of a child, which includes the right to have physical possession of the child along with the right and duty to protect, train, and discipline the child. It also includes the responsibility to provide the child with food, shelter, and medical care along with the authority to consent to surgery or other medical care in the event of an emergency.

developmental disability   Any handicapping condition related to delays in maturation of or difficulties with skills or intellect.

direct placement adoption   An adoption in which the birthmother chooses the adoptive mother and/or father.

disruption   Most commonly used to refer to an adoption that fails before finalization. Also, used to refer to any adoption that fails. (See **dissolution**.)

dissolution   Refers to an adoption that fails after finalization.

dossier   The legal documents that must be completed in order to adopt a child from another country.

entitlement   The feeling of an adopter that he or she has a right to parent a child.

Final Adoption Decree   The legal document issued by the court that completes the adoption.

finalization   The court action that grants permanent legal custody of a child to the adoptive parents.

foster adoption placement The foster placement of a child with adoption being the final goal once all legal requirements have been met. There is no guarantee that the child will be available for adoption. Also called legal risk adoption.

foster care The substitute parental care for a short or extended period of time for a child whose biological parents are unable to provide care.

foster child A child in foster care.

foster parent A person who cares for a foster child.

home study The process by which prospective adoptive parents are approved to adopt a child. The process varies from agency to agency, but usually includes interviews, home visits, reference checks, and reviews of financial and medical information. The terms used to describe the process also vary from agency to agency.

Immigration and Naturalization Service (INS) A federal agency that oversees international adoptions.

independent adoption An adoption arranged through an intermediary, such as a lawyer or physician, rather than through a licensed adoption agency. The intermediary may find the birthmother, who plans to place her child for adoption, or may help the birthmother locate a family interested in adopting her child. The term also refers to adoptions completed without the help of an intermediary. Note: Independent adoptions are not legal in all states; check with your state department of social services or your state adoption specialist.

international adoption The adoption of a child from outside the United States. Also called intercountry adoption.

interstate compact   The legal compact among states that allows for the placement of children for adoption across state lines.

legal risk adoption   See **foster adoption placement**.

nonrelative adoption   The adoption of a child who is not a biological relative.

open adoption   An adoption in which the birth-parents and adoptive parents exchange identifying information, may meet, and may continue communication indefinitely. The amount of openness in the adoption is agreed upon by both parties.

open records   Refers to a system in which an adult adoptee can obtain the original birth certificate without a court order.

orphan visa   The permission granted to a child living in another country by the U.S. State Department. This permission allows the child to enter the United States for the purpose of living with adoptive parents.

post-adoption support   Ongoing support for adoptive families experiencing challenges with adopted children. Support may be provided by public and private agencies.

post-placement   This is the time after the child has been placed in your home and before finalization of the adoption. In some cases, a post-placement home study is required by the court.

post-placement services   Pre-finalization services offered by an agency or intermediary, which provide support for the adoptive family to make the placement successful.

private adoption   See **independent adoption.**

private adoption agency   A non-profit or for-profit agency that depends on fees and donations for support rather than on tax dollars and is licensed by the state.

public adoption agency A state or county agency (known as social service, human service, children and family service, and so on) responsible for placing waiting children from foster care or institutional settings with adoptive families.

putative father The alleged father of the child.

putative father registry A registry provided in many states for men who believe they may have fathered a child. Registered birthfathers may protest a birthmother's adoption plans.

readoption The second adoption of a child by international adopters of the child. The first time was in the country of the child's birth. The readoption is completed by a U.S. court.

reunion The in-person meeting between an adoptee and a birth relative.

revoke consent The change of mind by a birthparent to place a child for adoption. Some states have a designated time period in which a birthparent can revoke consent; other states do not.

search The process by which a birth family member and/or an adoptee look for each other.

search (support) group A group that aids an adoptee and/or birth family member with the search process.

second-parent adoption The adoption of a partner's child by a gay or lesbian individual. This is not legal in all states.

semi-open adoption An adoption in which the sharing of information between birthparents and adoptive parents is limited. Often, all communication takes place through a third party.

special needs child   A child waiting to be adopted who is characterized by one or more of the following: a member of a sibling group to be placed together; minority ethnic background; mental, physical, or emotional challenge; over three (or five in some states) years of age; history of physical, mental, sexual, and/or emotional abuse; and not yet legally free for adoption.

subsidy   A state program committing financial support or specific services for qualifying children after a legal adoption.

transracial adoption   An adoption in which parents of one race or ethnic group adopt a child of another race or ethnic group.

waiting child   In some states a special needs child is called a waiting child. See **special needs child**.

wrongful adoption   An adoption in which the adoptive parents would not have adopted the child if information that was purposely withheld or misrepresented had been available.

Resource Guide

T he following is a state-by-state list of selected organizations that deal with adoption issues. To find public and private agencies in your area, contact your state licensing specialist or your state adoption specialist.

Alabama
State Adoption Specialist:
Office of Adoption, Family Services Division
Alabama Department of Human Resources
Carole Burton
50 N. Ripley Street
Montgomery, AL 36130-4000
(334) 242-9500
Fax: (334) 242-0939

State Licensing Specialist:
Office of Residential Licensing,
Family Services Division
Alabama Department of Human Resources
Carola Kelly
50 N. Ripley Street
Montgomery, AL 36130-4000
(334) 242-9500

State Adoption Exchange/
State Photolisting Service:
Alabama Adoption Resource Exchange
Alabama Department of Human Resources,
Office of Adoption
50 N. Ripley Street
Montgomery, AL 36310-4000
(334) 242-9500

Attorney Referral Service:
Alabama State Bar
P.O. Box 671, 415 Dexter Avenue
Montgomery, AL 36101
(334) 269-1515
Fax: (334) 261-6310
World Wide Web: http://www.alabar.org

Alaska
State Adoption Specialist:
Alaska Department of Health and Social Services
Suzanne Maxson
P.O. Box 110630
Juneau, AK 99811-0630
(907) 465-3397
Fax: (907) 465-3397
E-mail: smaxson@health.state.ak.us

State Licensing Specialist:
Alaska Department of Health and Social Services
Division of Family and Youth Services
Phillip J. Snyder
P.O. Box 110630
Juneau, AK 99811-0630
(907) 465-2817
E-mail: PSnyder@health.state.ak.us

State Adoption Exchange/
State Photolisting Service:
Northwest Adoption Exchange
600 Stewart Street, Suite 1313
Seattle, WA 98101
(206) 292-0082

Attorney Referral Service:
Alaska Bar Association
P.O. Box 100279
Anchorage, AK 99510
(907) 272-7469
Fax: (907) 272-2932
World Wide Web: http://www.alaskabar.org
E-mail: alaskabar@alaskabar.org

Arizona

Arizona State Adoption Specialist:
Arizona Department of Economic Security Linker
P.O. Box 6123
Phoenix, AZ 85005
(602) 542-2359
Fax: (602) 542-3330

State Licensing Specialist:
Arizona Department of Economic Security
Wayne Wallace
P.O. Box 6123
Phoenix, AZ 85005
(602) 542-2289

State Adoption Exchange/
State Photolisting Service:
Arizona Adoption Exchange Book
c/o Arizona Families for Children
P.O. Box 17951
Tucson, AZ 85731
(520) 327-3324

Attorney Referral Service:
State Bar of Arizona
111 W. Monroe, Suite 1800
Phoenix, AZ 85003-1742
(602) 252-4804
Fax: (602) 271-4930
World Wide Web: http://www.azbar.org
E-mail: azbar@azbar.org

Arkansas
State Adoption Specialist:
Arkansas Department of Human Services
June Flye
P.O. Box 1437, Slot 808
Little Rock, AR 72203-1437
(501) 682-9273
World Wide Web: http://www.state.ar.us/dhs/
adoption/adoption.html

State Licensing Specialist:
Arkansas Department of Human Services
Division of Child and Family Services
Child Welfare Agency Licensing Unit
523 S. Louisiana, Slot 626
Little Rock, AR 72203
(501) 682-9978

State Adoption Exchange/
State Photolisting Service:
Department of Human Services
P.O. Box 1437, Slot 808
Little Rock, AR 72203-1437
(501) 682-8462

Attorney Referral Service:
Arkansas Bar Association
400 W. Markham
Little Rock, AR 72201
(501) 375-4606
Toll-free: (800) 609-5668
World Wide Web: http://www.arkbar.com
E-mail: arkbar@ipa.net

California
State Adoption Specialist:
California Department of Social Services
Adoptions Branch
Wesley Beers
744 P Street, MS 19-69
Sacramento, CA 95814
(916) 445-3146
Fax: (916) 445-9125
Toll-free: (800) 543-7487
TTY: (916) 445-5837
World Wide Web:
http://www.dss.cahwnet.gov/getser/cfsadopt.html
E-mail: WBeers@dss.ca.gov

State Licensing Specialist:
California Department of Social Services
Martha Lopez
744 P Street, MS 17-17
Sacramento, CA 95814
(916) 657-2346

State Adoption Exchange/
State Photolisting Service:
California Waiting Children—Photolisting Service
California Department of Social Services
744 P Street, MS 19-68
Sacramento, CA 95814
(916) 323-0590
Toll-free: (800) 543-7487
World Wide Web: http://www.childsworld.org/

Attorney Referral Service:
State Bar of California
555 Franklin Street
San Francisco, CA 94102
(415) 561-8200
World Wide Web: http://www.calbar.org

Colorado
State Adoption Specialist:
Colorado Department of Human Services
Child Welfare Services
Barbara Killmore
1575 Sherman Street, Ground Floor
Denver, CO 80203-1714
(303) 866-3209
Fax: (303) 866-2214
E-mail: barbara.killmore@state.co.us

State Licensing Specialist:
Colorado Department of Human Services
Division of Child Care Services
Oxana Golden
1575 Sherman Street, 1st Floor
Denver, CO 80203-1714
(303) 866-5961
Toll-free: (800) 799-5876

State Adoption Exchange/
State Photolisting Service:
Colorado Adoption Resource Registry (CARR)
Colorado Department of Human Services Child
Welfare Services
1575 Sherman Street, Ground Floor
Denver, CO 80203-1714
(303) 866-3209

The Adoption Exchange
14232 East Evans Avenue
Aurora, CO 80014
(303) 755-4756
Toll-free: (800) 451-5246
World Wide Web: http://www.adoptex.org
E-mail: kids@adoptex.org

The Adoption Exchange
Colorado Adoption Resource Registry (CARR)
Colorado Department of Human Services Child
Welfare Services
1575 Sherman Street, 2nd Floor
Denver, CO 80203-1714
(303) 866-3209
Toll-free: (800) 451-5246

Attorney Referral Service:
Colorado Bar Association
1900 Grant Street, Ninth Floor
Denver, CO 80203
(303) 860-1115
Fax: (303) 894-0821
World Wide Web: http://www.cobar.org

Connecticut
State Adoption Specialist:
Connecticut Department of Children and Families
Office of Foster & Adoption Services
Liz Tyson
505 Hudson Street
Hartford, CT 06106
(860) 550-6463
Fax: (860) 566-3453
World Wide Web: http://www.state.ct.us/dcf/
foster.htm

State Licensing Specialist:
Connecticut Department of Children and Families
Dr. Michael J. Schultz
505 Hudson Street
Hartford, CT 06106
(860) 550-6385

State Adoption Exchange/
State Photolisting Service:
Office of Foster and Adoption Services
550 Hudson Street
Hartford, CT 06106
(860) 550-6585
World Wide Web: http://www.state.ct.us/dcf

Attorney Referral Service:
Connecticut Bar Association
101 Corporate Place
Rocky Hill, CT 06067
(860) 721-0025
World Wide Web: http://www.ctbar.org
E-mail: ctbar@ctbar.org

Delaware
State Adoption Specialist:
Delaware Department of Services for Children,
Youth and Their Families
Mariann Kenville-Moore
1825 Faulkland Road
Wilmington, DE 19805
(302) 633-2655
Fax: (302) 633-2654

State Licensing Specialist:
Delaware Department of Services for Children,
Youth and Their Families
Christine Hill
1825 Faulkland Road
Wilmington, DE 19805
(302) 739-6596

State Adoption Exchange/
State Photolisting Service:
Deladopt
Delaware Department of Services for Children,
Youth and Their Families
1825 Faulkland Road
Wilmington, DE 19805
(302) 633-2655

Attorney Referral Service:
Delaware State Bar Association
1201 Orange Street, Suite 1100
Wilmington, DE 19801
(302) 658-5279
Fax: (302) 658-5212
World Wide Web: http://www.dsba.org

District of Columbia
State Adoption Specialist:
District of Columbia Child and Family Services
Agency
J. Toni Oliver
609 H Street, N.E.
Washington, DC 20002
(202) 724-8602
Fax: (202) 546-1253

State Licensing Specialist:
Department of Health—Licensing and Regulatory
Administration
Human Social Services Facility Division
825 North Capital Street NE
Washington, DC 20002
(202) 442-5929
Fax: (202) 442-9430

Attorney Referral Service:
District of Columbia Bar Association
1250 H Street, N.W., 6th Floor
Washington, DC 20005
(202) 737-4700
Fax: (202) 626-3471
World Wide Web: http://www.dcbar.org
E-mail: feedback@dcbar.org

Florida
State Adoption Specialist:
Florida Department of Children and Families
Gloria Walker
2811-E Industrial Plaza Drive
Tallahassee, FL 32308
(850) 487-2383
Fax: (850) 488-0751
World Wide Web:
http://sun6.dms.state.fl.us/cf_web/adopt

State Licensing Specialist:
Florida Department of Children and Families
2811-E Industrial Plaza Drive
Tallahassee, FL 32308
(850) 487-2383
Fax: (850) 488-0751

State Adoption Exchange/
State Photolisting Service:
Adoption Information Center Daniel Memorial, Inc.
134 E. Church Street
Jacksonville, FL 32202-3130
(904) 353-0679
Toll-free: (800) 962-3678

Florida's Waiting Children
Florida Department of Children and Families
2811-E Industrial Plaza Drive
Tallahassee, FL 32308
(850) 487-2383
Fax: (850) 488-0751
World Wide Web:
http://sun6.dms.state.fl.us/cf_web/adopt/

Attorney Referral Service:
The Florida Bar
650 Apalachee Parkway
Tallahassee, FL 32399
(850) 561-5600
World Wide Web: http://www.flabar.org
E-mail: flabarwm@flabar.org

Georgia
State Adoption Specialist:
Georgia Department of Human Resources
State Office of Adoptions
Forrest Burson
Suite 3-300, 2 Peachtree Street, NW
Atlanta, GA 30303-3142
(404) 651-6067
Fax: (404) 657-9498
World Wide Web:
http://www.adoptions.dhr.state.ga.us/
E-mail: fbb@dhr.state.ga.us

State Licensing Specialist:
Georgia Department of Human Resources
Office of Regulatory Services
Jo Cato
Suite 32-452, 2 Peachtree Street, NW
Atlanta, GA 30303-3142
(404) 657-5562
Fax: (404) 657-5708
World Wide Web:
http://www.adoptions.dhr.state.ga.us

State Adoption Exchange/
State Photolisting Service:
Georgia State Adoption Exchange
Office of Adoptions
Suite 11-210, 2 Peachtree Street, NW
Atlanta, GA 30303-3142
(404) 657-3550

My Turn Now, Inc.
Suite 13-101, 2 Peachtree Street, NW
Atlanta, GA 30303-3142
(404) 657-3479

Attorney Referral Service:
State Bar of Georgia
800 The Hurt Building, 50 Hurt Plaza
Atlanta, GA 30303
(404) 527-8700
World Wide Web: http://www.gabar.org

Hawaii
State Adoption Specialist:
Hawaii Department of Human Services
Lynn Mirikidani
810 Richards Street, Suite 400
Honolulu, HI 96813
(808) 586-5698
Fax: (808) 586-5700

State Licensing Specialist:
Hawaii Department of Human Services
Lynn Mirikidani
810 Richards Street, Suite 400
Honolulu, HI 96813
(808) 586-5698
Fax: (808) 586-5700

State Adoption Exchange/
State Photolisting Service:
Central Adoption Exchange of Hawaii
810 Richards Street, Suite 400
Honolulu, HI 96813
(808) 586-5698
Fax: (808) 586-5700

Attorney Referral Service:
Hawaii State Bar Association
1136 Union Mall, 9th Floor, Penthouse 1
Honolulu, HI 96813
(808) 537-1868
Fax: (808) 521-7936
World Wide Web: http://www.hsba.org

Idaho
State Adoption Specialist:
Idaho Department of Health and Welfare
Meri Brennan
5th Floor
Boise, ID 83720-0036
(208) 334-5700
Fax: (208) 334-6664

State Licensing Specialist:
Idaho Department of Health and Welfare
Ed Van Dusen
5th Floor
Boise, ID 83720-0036
(208) 334-5700
Fax: (208) 334-6664

State Adoption Exchange/
State Photolisting Service:
Idaho Department of Health and Welfare
P.O. Box 83720
Boise, ID 83720-0036
(208) 334-5700

Attorney Referral Service:
Idaho State Bar
P.O. Box 895
Boise, ID 83701
(208) 334-4515
Fax: (208) 334-4500
World Wide Web: http://www2.state.id.us/isb

Illinois
State Adoption Specialist:
Illinois Department of Children and Family
Services
Jane Elmore
406 E. Monroe Street, Station 225
Springfield, IL 62701-1498
(217) 524-2422
Fax: (217) 524-3966

State Licensing Specialist:
Illinois Department of Children and Family
Services
Ginny Conlee
406 E. Monroe Street
Springfield, IL 62701
(217) 785-2688
World Wide Web: http://www.state.il.us/dcfs

State Adoption Exchange/
State Photolisting Service:
Adoption Information Center of Illinois (AICI)
188 W. Randolph, Suite 600
Chicago, IL 60606
(312) 346-1516
Fax: (312) 346-0004
Toll-free: (800) 572-2390
World Wide Web: http://www.adoptinfo-il.org
E-mail: aici@adoptinfo-il.org

Attorney Referral Service:
Illinois State Bar Association
Illinois Bar Center
Springfield, IL 62701
(217) 525-1760
Fax: (217) 525-0712
Toll-free: (800) 252-8908
World Wide Web: http://www.illinoisbar.org

Indiana
State Adoption Specialist:
Indiana Division of Family & Children
Family Protection/Preservation
Kaye Clark
402 W. Washington Street, Third Floor, W-364
Indianapolis, IN 46204-2739
(317) 233-1743
Fax: (317) 232-4436
Toll-free: (888) 204-7466

State Licensing Specialist:
Residential Licensing Unit
Indiana Division of Family and Children
402 W. Washington Street
Indianapolis, IN 46204-2739
(317) 232-3476

State Adoption Exchange/
State Photolisting Service:
Indiana Adoption Resource Exchange
Indiana Division of Family and Children
402 W. Washington Street, Third Floor, W-364
Indianapolis, IN 46204-2739
(317) 232-5613

Attorney Referral Service:
Indiana State Bar Association
230 E. Ohio Street
Indianapolis, IN 46204
(317) 639-5465
Fax: (317) 266-2588
Toll-free: (800) 266-2581
World Wide Web: http://www.ai.org/isba
E-mail: isbaadmin@inbar.org

Iowa
State Adoption Specialist:
Iowa Department of Human Services
Charlcie Y. Carey
Hoover State Office Building, 5th Floor
Des Moines, IA 50319-0114
(515) 281-5358
Fax: (515) 281-7791
E-mail: ccarey@dhs.state.ia.us

State Licensing Specialist:
Iowa Department of Inspections & Appeals
Art Anderson
Lucas State Office Building
Des Moines, IA 50319
(515) 281-3186

State Adoption Exchange/
State Photolisting Service:
Iowa Adoption Resource Exchange
Bureau of Adults, Children, and Family Services
Hoover State Office Building, 5th Floor
Des Moines, IA 50319
(515) 281-5358

Attorney Referral Service:
Iowa State Bar Association
521 E. Locust, 3rd Floor
Des Moines, IA 50309
(515) 243-3179
Fax: (515) 243-2511
World Wide Web: http://www.iowabar.org

Kansas
State Adoption Specialist:
Kansas Department of Social and Rehabilitation
Services
Shannon Manzanares
300 S.W. Oakley, West Hall, Room 226
Topeka, KS 66606
(785) 368-8190
Fax: (785) 296-4649

Kansas Department of Social and
Rehabilitation Services
Lois Mitchell
300 S.W. Oakley, West Hall, Room 226
Topeka, KS 66606
(785) 296-0918

Lutheran Social Services of Kansas
Sharri Black
2942 S.W. Wanamaker Drive
Topeka, KS 66614
(785) 272-7883
Fax: (785) 228-9405
Toll-free: (800) 210-5387
E-mail: bkarstensen@lss.org

State Licensing Specialist:
Department of Health & Environment Childcare
Licensing/Registration
Russell Northrup
Mills Building, Suite 400C
Topeka, KS 66612
(785) 296-1270

State Adoption Exchange/
State Photolisting Service:
Lutheran Social Services
Kansas Families for Kids (KFFK)
603 S. Topeka Blvd., Suite 206
Topeka, KS 66603
(785) 354-4663
Fax: (785) 354-4684
Toll-free: (800) 210-5387
World Wide Web: http://www.kffk.org
E-mail: patricial@kffk.org

Attorney Referral Service:
Kansas Bar Association
P.O. Box 1037, 1200 Harrison Street
Topeka, KS 66612
(785) 234-5696
Fax: (785) 234-3813
World Wide Web: http://www.ksbar.org

Kentucky
State Adoption Specialist:
Cabinet for Families and Children
Ryce E. Hatchett
275 E. Main Street
Frankfort, KY 40621
(502) 564-2147
Fax: (502) 564-9554

State Licensing Specialist:
Cabinet for Health Services
Rebecca Cecil
275 E. Main Street
Frankfort, KY 40621
(502) 564-2800

State Adoption Exchange/
State Photolisting Service:
Kentucky Adoption Resource Exchange
Department of Social Services
275 E. Main Street, 6th Floor, West
Frankfort, KY 40621
(502) 564-2147

Special Needs Adoption Program
Cabinet For Family and Children,
Department for Community Based Services
908 W. Broadway, 8W
Louisville, KY 40203
(502) 595-4303

Special Needs Adoption Project (SNAP)
Department for Social Services
710 W. High Street
Lexington, KY 40508
(606) 252-1728

Attorney Referral Service:
Kentucky Bar Association
514 W. Main Street
Frankfort, KY 40601
(502) 564-3795
Fax: (502) 564-3225
World Wide Web: http://www.kybar.org

Louisiana

State Adoption Specialist:
Louisiana Department of Social Services
Office of Community Services
Ada K. White
P.O. Box 3318
Baton Rouge, LA 70821
(504) 342-4059
E-mail: fcada@ocs.dss.state.la.us

State Licensing Specialist:
Louisiana Department of Social Services
Office of the Secretary, Licensing
Thalia Millican
P.O. Box 3767
Baton Rouge, LA 70821
(504) 922-0015

State Adoption Exchange/
State Photolisting Service:
Louisiana Adoption Resource Exchange (LARE)
Louisiana Department of Social Services
P.O. Box 3318
Baton Rouge, LA 70821
(504) 342-4040
Toll-free: (800) 259-3428

Attorney Referral Service:
Louisiana State Bar Association
601 St. Charles Avenue
New Orleans, LA 70130
(504) 566-1600
World Wide Web: http://www.lsba.org
E-mail: infolsba@lsba.org

Maine

State Adoption Specialist:
Maine Department of Human Services
John Levesque
221 State Street, State House
Augusta, ME 04333
(207) 287-5060
E-mail: john.levesque@state.me.us

State Licensing Specialist:
Department of Human Services
Tom Bancroft
221 State Street, State House
Augusta, ME 04333
(207) 287-5060
E-mail: tom.bancroft@state.me.us

State Adoption Exchange/
State Photolisting Service:
Northern New England Adoption Exchange
Department of Human Services
221 State Street, State House
Augusta, ME 04333
(207) 287-5060

Attorney Referral Service:
Maine State Bar Association
P.O. Box 788, 124 State Street
Augusta, ME 04332-0788
(207) 622-7523
Fax: (207) 623-0083
World Wide Web: http://www.mainebar.org
E-mail: info@mainebar.org

Maryland

State Adoption Specialist:
Maryland Department of Human Resources
Social Services Administration
Stephanie Johnson-Pettaway
311 W. Saratoga Street
Baltimore, MD 21201
(410) 767-7506

State Licensing Specialist:
Maryland Department of Human Resources
Social Services Administration
Grace Turner
311 W. Saratoga Street
Baltimore, MD 21201
(410) 767-7903

State Adoption Exchange/
State Photolisting Service:
Maryland Adoption Resource Exchange (MARE)
Social Services Administration
311 W. Saratoga Street
Baltimore, MD 21201
(410) 767-7359

Attorney Referral Service:
Maryland State Bar Association
Maryland Bar Center, 520 W. Fayette Street
Baltimore, MD 21201
(410) 685-7878
Fax: (410) 837-0518
Toll-free: (800) 492-1964
World Wide Web: http://www.msba.org
E-mail: msba@msba.org

Massachusetts
State Adoption Specialist:
Massachusetts Department of Social Services
Mary Gambon
24 Farnsworth Street
Boston, MA 02210
(617) 727-0900, Ext: 589
Fax: (617) 261-7435
TTY: (617) 261-7440

State Licensing Specialist:
Massachusetts Department of Social Services
Donna Morrison
24 Farnsworth Street
Boston, MA 02210
(617) 727-0900

State Adoption Exchange/
State Photolisting Service:
Massachusetts Adoption Resource Exchange, Inc.
(MARE)
45 Franklin Street, 5th Floor
Boston, MA 02110-1301
(617) 542-3678
Fax: (617) 542-1006
Toll-free: (800) 882-1176
World Wide Web: http://www.mareinc.org

Attorney Referral Service:
Massachusetts Bar Association
20 West Street
Boston, MA 02111
(617) 338-0500
World Wide Web: http://www.massbar.org

Michigan
State Adoption Specialist:
Family Independence Agency
Jean Hoffman
P.O. Box 30037
Lansing, MI 48909
(517) 373-4021
Fax: (517) 335-4019

State Licensing Specialist:
Family Independence Agency
Bob Cable
P.O. Box 30650
Lansing, MI 48909
(517) 373-8383
Fax: (517) 335-6121

State Adoption Exchange/
State Photolisting Service:
Kinship/Family Adoption Registry
30215 Southfield Road
Southfield, MI 48076
(248) 443-0306
Toll-free: (800) 267-7144

Michigan Adoption Resource Exchange
P.O. Box 6128
Jackson, MI 49201
(517) 783-6273
Fax: (517) 783-5904
Toll-free: (800) 589-6273
World Wide Web: http://www.mare.org
E-mail: njennings@voyager.net

Attorney Referral Service:
State Bar of Michigan
306 Townsend Street
Lansing, MI 48933-2083
(517) 346-6300
Fax: (517) 482-6248
Toll-free: (800) 968-1442
World Wide Web: http://www.michbar.org

Minnesota
State Adoption Specialist:
Minnesota Department of Human Services
Family & Children's Services
Robert DeNardo
444 Lafayette Road, Human Services Building
St. Paul, MN 55155-3832
(612) 296-3740
Fax: (612) 297-1949
E-mail: bob.denardo@state.mn.us

State Licensing Specialist:
Minnesota Department of Human Services
Division of Licensing
444 Lafayette Road, Human Services Building
St. Paul, MN 55155
(651) 296-3971

State Adoption Exchange/
State Photolisting Service:
Minnesota Adoption Resource Network
2409 West 66th Street
Minneapolis, MN 55423
(612) 861-7115
Fax: (612) 861-7112
World Wide Web: http://www.mnadopt.org/
E-mail: MNadopt@aol.com

Attorney Referral Service:
Minnesota State Bar Association
514 Nicollet Mall, Suite 300
Minneapolis, MN 55402
(612) 333-1183
Fax: (612) 333-4927
Toll-free: (800) 882-6722
World Wide Web: http://www.mnbar.org

Mississippi
State Adoption Specialist:
Adoption Unit Mississippi
Department of Human Services (LMSW)
Wanda Gillom
750 N. State Street
Jackson, MS 39202
(601) 359-4981
Fax: (601) 359-4978

State Licensing Specialist:
Mississippi Department of Human Services
Ruby Wiggins
750 N. State Street
Jackson, MS 39202
(601) 359-4994
Fax: (601) 359-4978

State Adoption Exchange/
State Photolisting Service:
Mississippi Adoption Resource Exchange
P.O. Box 352
Jackson, MS 39205
(601) 359-4407
Toll-free: (800) 821-9157

Attorney Referral Service:
Mississippi State Bar
P.O. Box 2168, 643 North State Street
Jackson, MS 39225
(601) 948-4471
Fax: (601) 355-8635
World Wide Web: http://www.msbar.org
E-mail: msbar@msbar.org

Missouri
State Adoption Specialist:
Missouri Department of Social Services
Kathryn Wilson
615 Howerton Court
Jefferson City, MO 65103-0088
(573) 751-8981
Fax: (573) 526-3971
World Wide Web:
http://www.dss.state.mo.us/dfs/csp.htm

State Licensing Specialist:
Missouri Department of Social Services
Keith Krueger
P.O. Box 88
Jefferson City, MO 65103-0088
(573) 751-4920

State Adoption Exchange/
State Photolisting Service:
Missouri Adoption Exchange
Missouri Division of Family Services
P.O. Box 88
Jefferson City, MO 65103-0088
(573) 751-2502
Toll-free: (800) 554-2222

Attorney Referral Service:
The Missouri State Bar
P.O. Box 119
Jefferson City, MO 65102
(573) 635-4128
Fax: (573) 659-8931
World Wide Web: http://www.mobar.org
E-mail: mobar@mobar.org

Montana
State Adoption Specialist:
Montana Department of Public Health and
Human Services
Lynda Korth
P.O. Box 8005
Helena, MT 59604
(406) 444-5919
Fax: (406) 444-5956

State Licensing Specialist:
Montana Department of Public Health and
Human Services
Lynda Korth
P.O. Box 8005
Helena, MT 59604
(406) 444-5919
Fax: (406) 444-5956

State Adoption Exchange/
State Photolisting Service:
Treasure Book Photo Listing
Helena, MT
Toll-free: (888) 937-5437

Attorney Referral Service:
State Bar of Montana
P.O. Box 577
Helena, MT 59624
(406) 442-7660
Fax: (406) 442-7763
World Wide Web: http://www.montanabar.org

Nebraska
State Adoption Specialist:
Division of Protection & Safety
Nebraska Health & Human Services
Mary Dyer
P.O. Box 95044
Lincoln, NE 68509
(402) 471-9331
World Wide Web:
http://www.hhs.state.ne.us/chs/chsindex.htm
E-mail: mary.dyer@HHSS.state.ne.us

State Licensing Specialist:
Nebraska Health & Human Services
Vanessa Nownes
P.O. Box 95044
Lincoln, NE 68509
(402) 471-9138

State Adoption Exchange/
State Photolisting Service:
Nebraska Adoption Resource Exchange
Division of Protection & Safety, Nebraska Health &
Human Services
P.O. Box 95044
Lincoln, NE 68509
(402) 471-9331

Attorney Referral Service:
Nebraska State Bar Association
P.O. Box 81809, 635 S. 14th Street
Lincoln, NE 68501
(402) 475-7091
Toll-free: (800) 927-0117
World Wide Web: http://www.nebar.com

Nevada
State Adoption Specialist:
Division of Child and Family Services
Wanda Scott
6171 W. Charleston Blvd., Building 15
Las Vegas, NV 89102
(702) 486-7650
Fax: (702) 486-7626
E-mail: wscott@govmail.state.nv.us

State Licensing Specialist:
Division of Child and Family Services
Wanda Scott
6171 W. Charleston Blvd., Building 15
Las Vegas, NV 89102
(702) 486-7650
Fax: (702) 486-7626

State Adoption Exchange/
State Photolisting Service:
Nevada Adoption Exchange Division of Child
and Family Services
610 Belrose Street
Las Vegas, NV 89107
(702) 486-7800

Attorney Referral Service:
State Bar of Nevada
Las Vegas Office
600 East Charleston Blvd.
Las Vegas, NV 89101
(702) 382-2200
Fax: (702) 385-2878
Toll-free: (800) 254-2797
World Wide Web: http://www.nvbar.org

State Bar of Nevada
Reno Office
1325 Airmotive Way, Suite 140
Reno, NV 89502
(702) 329-4100
Fax: (702) 329-0522
World Wide Web: http://www.nvbar.org

New Hampshire
State Adoption Specialist:
New Hampshire Division for Children,
Youth and Families
Catherine Atkins
129 Pleasant Street
Concord, NH 03301
(603) 271-4707
Fax: (603) 271-4729

State Licensing Specialist:
New Hampshire Division for Children,
Youth and Families
Gail DeGoosh
129 Pleasant Street
Concord, NH 03301
(603) 271-4711
Fax: (603) 271-4729

State Adoption Exchange/
State Photolisting Service:
New Hampshire Division for Children,
Youth and Families
129 Pleasant Street
Concord, NH 03301
(603) 271-4707

Attorney Referral Service:
New Hampshire Bar Association
112 Pleasant Street
Concord, NH 03301-2947
(603) 224-6942
Fax: (603) 224-2910
World Wide Web: http://www.nhbar.org

New Jersey
State Adoption Specialist:
New Jersey Division of Youth and Family Services
Eileen Crummy
P.O. Box 717
Trenton, NJ 08625-0717
(609) 984-2380
Fax: (609) 984-5449
E-mail: ecrummy@dhs.state.nj.us

State Licensing Specialist:
New Jersey Division of Youth and Family Services
Ana Montes
50 E. State Street, C.N. 719
Trenton, NJ 08625
(609) 292-8255

State Adoption Exchange/
State Photolisting Service:
Division of Youth and Family Services
Adoption Exchange
Operations Support Unit
50 E. State Street, C.N. 717
Trenton, NJ 08625
(609) 984-5453

Attorney Referral Service:
New Jersey State Bar Association
1 Constitution Square
New Brunswick, NJ 08901-1500
(732) 249-5000
Fax: (732) 249-2815
World Wide Web: http://www.njsba.com

New Mexico
State Adoption Specialist:
Central Adoption Unit
New Mexico Children, Youth and
Families Department
Susan Washam
P.O. Drawer 5160
Santa Fe, NM 87502
(505) 827-8419
Fax: (505) 827-8480
World Wide Web:
http://cyf_abq.state.nm.us/adopt/ninos.html
E-mail: s_washam@cysd.aol.com

State Licensing Specialist:
Central Adoption Unit
New Mexico Children, Youth and Families
Department
Barbara Evans
P.O. Drawer 5160
Santa Fe, NM 87502
(505) 827-8478
Fax: (505) 827-8480

State Adoption Exchange/
State Photolisting Service:
New Mexico Adoption Exchange
New Mexico Children, Youth and
Families Department
P.O. Drawer 5160
Santa Fe, NM 87502
(505) 827-8422
World Wide Web:
http://cyf_abq.state.nm.us/adopt/ninos.html
E-mail: clgarcia@cyf_abq.state.nm.us

Attorney Referral Service:
State Bar of New Mexico
P.O. Box 25883
Albuquerque, NM 87125
(505) 797-6000
Fax: (505) 828-3765
World Wide Web: http://www.nmbar.org
E-mail: sbnm@nmbar.org

New York
State Adoption Specialist:
New York State Office of Children and
Family Services
Anne Furman
40 N. Pearl Street
Albany, NY 12243
(518) 474-9406
Fax: (518) 486-6326

State Licensing Specialist:
New York State Office of Children and
Family Services
Bruce Bushart
40 North Pearl Street—Mezzanine
Albany, NY 12243
(518) 474-9447

State Adoption Exchange/
State Photolisting Service:
New York State Adoption Service
40 North Pearl Street—Mezzanine
Albany, NY 12243
Toll-free: (800) 345-KIDS
World Wide Web: http://www.dfa.state.ny.us/adopt

Attorney Referral Service:
New York State Bar Association
1 Elk Street
Albany, NY 12207
(518) 463-3200
World Wide Web: http://www.nysba.org

North Carolina
State Adoption Specialist:
North Carolina Department of Health and
Human Services
Division of Social Services
Esther T. High
325 N. Salisbury Street
Raleigh, NC 27603-5905
(919) 733-4622
Fax: (919) 715-6714
E-mail: ehigh@dhr.state.nc.us

State Licensing Specialist:
North Carolina Department of Health and
Human Services
Division of Social Services
Pam Grantham-Ngeve
325 N. Salisbury Street
Raleigh, NC 27603-5905
(919) 733-9464

State Adoption Exchange/
State Photolisting Service:
North Carolina Adoption Resource Exchange
Division of Social Services
325 N. Salisbury Street
Raleigh, NC 27603-5905
(919) 733-3801

Attorney Referral Service:
North Carolina State Bar
208 Fayetteville Street
Raleigh, NC 27601
(919) 828-4620
Fax: (919) 821-9168

North Dakota
State Adoption Specialist:
North Dakota Department of Human Services
Julie Hoffman
600 E. Blvd., State Capitol Building
Bismarck, ND 58505
(701) 328-4805
Fax: (701) 328-2359
E-mail: sohoff@state.nd.us

State Licensing Specialist:
North Dakota Department of Human Services
Julie Hoffman
600 E. Blvd., State Capitol Building
Bismarck, ND 58505
(701) 328-4805
Fax: (701) 328-2359
E-mail: sohoff@state.nd.us

State Adoption Exchange/
State Photolisting Service:
Department of Human Services Children and
Family Services
600 E. Blvd., State Capitol Building
Bismarck, ND 58505
(701) 328-2316

Attorney Referral Service:
State Bar Association of North Dakota
515 1/2 E. Broadway, Suite 101
Bismarck, ND 58501
(701) 255-1404
Fax: (701) 224-1621

Ohio

State Adoption Specialist:
Office of Child and Adult Protection
Ohio Department of Human Services
Rhonda Abban
65 E. State Street, 5th Floor
Columbus, OH 43266-0423
(614) 466-9274
Fax: (614) 466-0164

State Licensing Specialist:
Office of Child and Adult Protection
Ohio Department of Human Services
Sheralyn Graise
65 E. State Street
Columbus, OH 43266-0423
(614) 466-3438

Office of Child and Adult Protection
Ohio Department of Human Services
Barbara Cannon
65 E. State Street
Columbus, OH 43266-0423
(614) 728-6983

State Adoption Exchange/
State Photolisting Service:
Ohio Adoption Photo Listing (OAPL)
Bureau of Children Services,
Adoption Services Section
65 E. State Street, 9th Floor
Columbus, OH 43266-0423
(614) 466-9274

Southwest Ohio Adoption Exchange
Department of Human Services
628 Sycamore Street
Cincinnati, OH 45202
(513) 632-6366

Attorney Referral Service:
Ohio State Bar Association
P.O. Box 16562
Columbus, OH 43204
Toll-free: (800) 282-6556
World Wide Web: http://www.ohiobar.org

Oklahoma
State Adoption Specialist:
Oklahoma Department of Human Services
Permanency Planning Section
Jane Morgan
P.O. Box 25352
Oklahoma City, OK 73125
(405) 521-2475
E-mail: Jane.Morgan@oklaosf.state.ok.us

State Licensing Specialist:
Oklahoma Department of Human Services
Prins Anderson
P.O. Box 25352
Oklahoma City, OK 73125
(405) 521-3561

Attorney Referral Service:
Oklahoma Bar Association
P.O. Box 53036
Oklahoma City, OK 73152
(405) 416-7000
Fax: (405) 416-7001
World Wide Web: http://www.okbar.org
E-mail: web@okbar.org

Oregon

State Adoption Specialist:
Oregon State Office for Services to
Children and Families
Kathy Ledesma
HRB 2nd Floor South, 500 Summer Street, N.E.
Salem, OR 97310-1017
(503) 945-5677
Fax: (503) 945-6969

State Licensing Specialist:
Oregon State Office for Services to
Children and Families
Dale Paulson
HRB 2nd Floor South, 500 Summer Street NE
Salem, OR 97310-1017
(503) 945-6687

State Adoption Exchange/
State Photolisting Service:
Boys and Girls Aid Society
018 SW Boundary Court
Portland, OR 97201
(503) 222-9661

Attorney Referral Service:
Oregon State Bar
P.O. Box 1689
Lake Oswego, OR 97035
(503) 620-0222
Fax: (503) 684-1366
Toll-free: (800) 452-8260
World Wide Web: http://www.osbar.org
E-mail: info@osbar.org

Pennsylvania
State Adoption Specialist:
Pennsylvania Department of Public Welfare
Eileen West
Health and Welfare Annex, P.O. Box 2675
Harrisburg, PA 17105-2675
(717) 787-7758
Fax: (717) 705-0364

State Licensing Specialist:
Pennsylvania Department of Public Welfare
Lee Miller
P.O. Box 2675
Harrisburg, PA 17105
(717) 787-3984
Fax: (717) 705-0364

State Adoption Exchange/
State Photolisting Service:
Pennsylvania Adoption Exchange Office of
Children, Youth and Families
P.O. Box 2675
Harrisburg, PA 17105
(717) 772-7015
Toll-free: (800) 227-0225
E-mail: JewellM@dpw.state.pa.us

Statewide Adoption Network
Pennsylvania Office of Children,
Youth and Families
P.O. Box 2675
Harrisburg, PA 17105
(717) 772-7040
Fax: (717) 772-6857
Toll-free: (800) 227-0225

Statewide Adoption Network
5021 E. Triangle Road
Mechanicsburg, PA 17055
Fax: (717) 766-8015
Toll-free: (800) 445-2444

Attorney Referral Service:
Pennsylvania Bar Association
P.O. Box 186, 100 South Street
Harrisburg, PA 17108
(717) 238-6715
Fax: (717) 238-1204
World Wide Web: http://www.pa-bar.org
E-mail: info@pabar.org

Rhode Island
State Adoption Specialist:
Rhode Island Department for Children and
Their Families
Barbara Dobbyn
530 Wood Street
Bristol, RI 02809
(401) 254-7010
Fax: (401) 254-7068

State Licensing Specialist:
Rhode Island Department for Children and
Their Families
Lee Sperduti
610 Mt. Pleasant Avenue
Providence, RI 02908-1935
(401) 457-4763
Fax: (401) 457-5331

State Adoption Exchange/
State Photolisting Service:
Adoption Rhode Island
500 Prospect Street
Pawtucket, RI 02860
(401) 724-1910
Fax: (401) 724-1910
World Wide Web: http://www.adoptionri.org/
E-mail: adoptionri@ids.net

Attorney Referral Service:
Rhode Island Bar Association
115 Cedar Street
Providence, RI 02903
(401) 421-5740
Fax: (401) 421-2703
World Wide Web: http://ribar.com

South Carolina
State Adoption Specialist:
South Carolina Department of Social Services
Division of Adoption and Birth Parent Services
Eddie Bogan
P.O. Box 1520
Columbia, SC 29202-1520
(803) 898-7561
Fax: (803) 734-6285
Toll-free: (800) 922-2504

State Licensing Specialist:
South Carolina Department of Social Services
Children, Family, and Adult Services
Jackie Holland-Davis
P.O. Box 1520
Columbia, SC 29202-1520
(803) 734-5670
Fax: (803) 734-6285

State Adoption Exchange/
State Photolisting Service:
South Carolina Seedlings
P.O. Box 1453
Greenville, SC 29602-1453
(864) 239-0303

Attorney Referral Service:
South Carolina Bar
950 Taylor Street
Columbia, SC 29202
(803) 799-6653
Fax: (803) 799-4118
World Wide Web: http://ww.scbar.org

South Dakota
State Adoption Specialist:
South Dakota Department of Social Services
DiAnn Kleinsasser
700 Governor's Drive, Richard F. Kneip Building
Pierre, SD 57501-2291
(605) 773-3227
Fax: (605) 773-6834

State Licensing Specialist:
South Dakota Department of Social Services
David Hanson
700 Governor's Drive, Richard F. Kneip Building
Pierre, SD 57501
(605) 773-3227

Attorney Referral Service:
State Bar of South Dakota
222 East Capitol Avenue
Pierre, SD 57501
(605) 224-7554
Toll-free: (800) 952-2333
World Wide Web: http://www.sdbar.org
E-mail: tbarnett@sdbar.org

Tennessee
State Adoption Specialist:
Tennessee Department of Children's Services
Jane Chittick
436 Sixth Avenue North, Cordell Hull Building,
8th Floor
Nashville, TN 37243-1290
(615) 532-5637
Fax: (615) 532-6495
E-mail: jchittick@mad.state.tn.us

State Licensing Specialist:
Tennessee Department of Human Services
Jerry Hughett
400 Deaderick Street, Citizens Plaza, 14th Floor
Nashville, TN 37248-9000
(615) 313-4744

State Adoption Exchange/
State Photolisting Service:
Resource Exchange for Adoptable Children
in Tennessee
201 23rd Avenue, North
Nashville, TN 37203-9000
(615) 321-3867

Attorney Referral Service:
Tennessee Bar Association
3622 W. End Avenue
Nashville, TN 37205
(615) 383-7421
World Wide Web: http://www.tba.org

Texas

State Adoption Specialist:
Texas Department of Protective and
Regulatory Services
Patsy Buida
P.O. Box 149030, M.C. E-557
Austin, TX 78714-9030
(512) 438-4986
Fax: (512) 438-3782
World Wide Web: http://www.tdprs.state.tx.us

Texas Department of Protective and
Regulatory Services
Susan Klickman
P.O. Box 149030, M.C. E-557
Austin, TX 78714-9030
(512) 438-3302
Fax: (512) 438-3782
World Wide Web: http://www.tdprs.state.tx.us

State Licensing Specialist:
Texas Department of Protective and
Regulatory Services
Nanci Gibbons
P.O. Box 149030, M.C. E-557
Austin, TX 78714-9030
(512) 438-3245
Fax: (512) 438-3782
World Wide Web: http://www.tdprs.state.tx.us

State Adoption Exchange/
State Photolisting Service:
Texas Adoption Resource Exchange
Texas Department of Protective and
Regulatory Services
P.O. Box 149030, M.C. E-557
Austin, TX 78714-9030
Toll-free: (800) 233-3405
World Wide Web:
http://www.tdprs.state.tx.us/adoption/tare.html
E-mail: TARE@auste654c.aust.tdprs.state.tx.us

Attorney Referral Service:
State Bar of Texas
1414 Colorado Street
Austin, TX 78701
(512) 463-1463
Fax: (512) 463-1475
Toll-free: (800) 204-2222
World Wide Web:
http://www.texasbar.com/start.html
E-mail: webmaster@texasbar.com

Utah

State Adoption Specialist:
Utah Department of Human Services
Division of Child and Family Services
Leroy Franke
Adoptions/ ICPC, 120 North, 200 West
Salt Lake City, UT 84103
(801) 538-4100
Fax: (801) 538-3993
World Wide Web: http://www.dhs.state.ut.us/
E-mail: hsadm1.lfranke@email.state.ut.us

State Licensing Specialist:
Utah Department of Human Services
Office of Licensing
Caroline K. Lepreau
120 North, 200 West, 3rd Floor
Salt Lake City, UT 84103
(801) 538-8222

State Adoption Exchange/
State Photolisting Service:
Department of Human Services
Division of Child and Family Services
P.O. Box 45500
Salt Lake City, UT 84145-0500
(801) 538-4100

Attorney Referral Service:
Utah State Bar
645 South, 200 East, Suite 310
Salt Lake City, UT 84111
(801) 531-9077
World Wide Web: http://www.utahbar.org
E-mail: info@utahbar.org

Vermont
State Adoption Specialist:
Department of Social and Rehabilitation Services
Diane Dexter
103 S. Main Street
Waterbury, VT 05671
(802) 241-2142
Toll-free: (800) 746-7000
World Wide Web:
http://www.state.vt.us/srs/adopt/adopt.htm
E-mail: diane@srs.ahs.state.vt.us

State Licensing Specialist:
Vermont Department of Social and
Rehabilitation Services
Paul Hager
103 S. Main Street
Waterbury, VT 05671
(802) 241-2159

State Adoption Exchange/
State Photolisting Service:
Northern New England Adoption Exchange
Department of Human Services
221 State Street, State House
Augusta, ME 04333
(207) 287-5060

Attorney Referral Service:
Vermont Bar Association
P.O. Box 100
Montpelier, VT 05601
(802) 223-2020
Fax: (802) 223-1573
World Wide Web: http://www.vtbar.org

Virginia
State Adoption Specialist:
Virginia Department of Social Services
Brenda Kerr
730 E. Broad Street
Richmond, VA 23219-1849
(804) 692-1290
Fax: (804) 692-1284
E-mail: bjk@dss.state.va.us

State Licensing Specialist:
Virginia Department of Social Services
Carolynne Stevens
730 E. Broad Street
Richmond, VA 23219-1849
(804) 692-1787

State Adoption Exchange/
State Photolisting Service:
Adoption Resource Exchange of Virginia (AREVA)
Virginia Department of Social Services
730 E. Broad Street
Richmond, VA 23219-1849
(804) 692-1280
Toll-free: (800) 362-3678
E-mail: lxl2@dss.state.va.us

Attorney Referral Service:
Virginia State Bar
707 East Main Street, Suite 1500
Richmond, VA 23219
(804) 775-0500
Fax: (804) 775-0501
TTY: (804) 775-0502
World Wide Web: http://www.vsb.org
E-mail: vsb@vsb.org

Washington
State Adoption Specialist:
Washington Department of Social and
Health Services
Patricia Ossorio
P.O. Box 45713
Olympia, WA 98504
(360) 902-7968
Fax: (360) 902-7904
E-mail: ospa300@dshs.wa.gov

State Licensing Specialist:
Division of Licensed Resources
Susan Corwin
P.O. Box 45700
Olympia, WA 98504
(360) 902-8009

State Adoption Exchange/
State Photolisting Service:
Northwest Adoption Exchange
600 Stewart Street, Suite 1313
Seattle, WA 98101
(206) 292-0082

Washington Adoption Resource Exchange
Washington Department of Social and
Health Services
P.O. Box 45713
Olympia, WA 98504
(360) 753-2178

Attorney Referral Service:
Washington State Bar Association
2101 Fourth Avenue, Fourth Floor
Seattle, WA 98121-2330
(206) 727-8200
Fax: (206) 727-8320
World Wide Web: http://www.wsba.org

West Virginia
State Adoption Specialist:
West Virginia Department of Health and
Human Resources
Christine Craig
DHHR Capitol Complex, Bldg. 6, Rm. B-850
Charleston, WV 25305
(304) 558-7980
Fax: (304) 558-8800
World Wide Web:
http://www.wvdhhr.org/pages/bcf/cf-social.htm
E-mail: ccraig@wvdhhr.org

State Licensing Specialist:
West Virginia Department of Health and Human
Resources—Ohio District
Peggy Cartus
P.O. Box 6165
Wheeling, WV 26003
(304) 232-4411

State Adoption Exchange/
State Photolisting Service:
West Virginia's Adoption Resource Network
Capitol Complex Building 6, Room B-850
Charleston, WV 25330
(304) 558-2891
Fax: (304) 558-8800

Attorney Referral Service:
West Virginia State Bar
2006 Kanawha Blvd., East
Charleston, WV 25311
(304) 558-2456
Fax: (304) 558-2467
World Wide Web: http://www.wvbar.org

Wisconsin

State Adoption Specialist:
Wisconsin Department of Health and
Family Services
Karen Oghalai
P.O. Box 8916
Madison, WI 53708-8916
(608) 266-0690
Fax: (608) 264-6750
World Wide Web:
http://www.dhfs.state.wi.us/Children/adoption/
index.html
E-mail: oghalkg@dhfs.state.wi.us

State Licensing Specialist:
Wisconsin Department of Health and
Family Services
Donald Dorn
P.O. Box 8916
Madison, WI 53708-8916
(608) 266-0415
E-mail: DORNDF@dhfs.state.wi.us

State Adoption Exchange/
State Photolisting Service:
Special Needs Adoption Network
1126 S. 70th Street, Suite N509A
Milwaukee, WI 53214-3151
(414) 475-1246
Fax: (414) 475-7007
Toll-free: (800) 762-8063
World Wide Web: http://www.wiadopt.com
E-mail: wiadopt@execpc.com

Wisconsin Adoption Information Exchange
1126 S. 70th Street, Suite N509A
Milwaukee, WI 53214
(414) 475-0596
Fax: (414) 475-7007
Toll-free: (800) 571-1105
World Wide Web: http://www.wiadoptioninfocen-
ter.org
E-mail: wiaic@execpc.com

Attorney Referral Service:
State Bar of Wisconsin
P.O. Box 7158
Madison, WI 53707
(608) 257-3838
World Wide Web: http://www.wisbar.org

Wyoming

State Adoption Specialist:
Wyoming Department of Family Services
Bill Rankin
2300 Capitol Avenue, Hathaway Building, 3rd
Floor
Cheyenne, WY 82002
(307) 777-3570
Fax: (307) 777-3693
E-mail: wranki@missc.state.wy.us

State Licensing Specialist:
Wyoming Department of Family Services
Linda Collins
2300 Capitol Avenue, Hathaway Building, 3rd
Floor
Cheyenne, WY 82002
(307) 777-6479

State Adoption Exchange/
State Photolisting Service:
The Adoption Exchange
Colorado Adoption Resource Registry (CARR)
Colorado Department of Human Services Child
Welfare Services
1575 Sherman Street, 2nd Floor
Denver, CO 80203-1714
(303) 866-3209
Toll-free: (800) 451-5246

Attorney Referral Service:
Wyoming State Bar
P.O. Box 109, 500 Randall Avenue
Cheyenne, WY 82003-0109
(307) 632-9061
Fax: (307) 632-3737
World Wide Web:
http://www.wyomingbar.org/index.asp

Selected national adoption organizations

Adoptive Families of America
2309 Como Avenue
St. Paul, MN 55108
(800) 372-3300 or (612) 645-9955
World Wide Web: www.adoptivefam.org
Provides adoption support, education, and advocacy. Publishes *Adoptive Families Magazine.*

American Academy of Adoption Attorneys
P.O. Box 33053
Washington, DC 20033-0053
202-832-2222
World Wide Web: www.adoptionattorneys.org
Organization of attorneys concerned with improving adoption laws and practice.

American Adoption Congress
1000 Connecticut Avenue, NW
Suite 1012
Washington, DC 20036
(202) 483-3399
World Wide Web: www.american-adoption-cong.org
Educational network dedicated to truth in
adoption.

Families for Private Adoption
P.O. Box 6375
Washington, DC 20015
(202) 722-0338
Independent adoption support group.

Family Pride Coalition
P.O. Box 34337
San Diego, CA 92163
(619) 296-0199, Fax: (619) 296-0699
E-mail: pride@familypride.org
National support group for gays and lesbians.

International Concerns for Children
911 Cypress Drive
Boulder, CO 80303
(303) 494-8333
World Wide Web: www.fortnet.org/icc/
Publishes *Report on International Adoption* and a
newsletter.

Joint Council on International Children's Services
7 Cheverly Circle
Cheverly, MD 87903
(301) 322-1906, Fax: (301) 322-3425
World Wide Web: www.jcics.org
E-mail: Mevans@jcics.org
Consortium of intercountry adoption agencies.

National Adoption Center
1500 Walnut Street, Suite 701
Philadelphia, PA 19102
(800) TO-ADOPT or (215) 735-9988
World Wide Web: www.nac.adopt.org
Works closely with adoption agencies across the
country, providing information about adopting
children with special needs and those from minority cultures.

National Adoption Information Clearinghouse
330 C Street, SW
Washington, DC 20447
(888) 251-0075 or (703) 352-3488
World Wide Web: www.calib.com.naic
Adoption information for adoptees, adoptive parents and birthparents

National Council for Adoption
1930 17th Street, NW
Washington, DC 20009
(202) 328-8072, Fax: (202) 332-0935
World Wide Web: www.ncfa-usa.org
Advocacy and information.

National Council for Single Adoptive Parents
P.O. Box 15084
Chevy Chase, MD 20825
(202) 966-6367
Publishes *The Handbook for Single Adoptive Parents.*

North American Council on Adoptable Children
(NACAC)
970 Raymond Avenue, Suite 106
St. Paul, MN 55114-1149
(612) 644-9848
Promotes special needs adoption. Provides information and assistance.

Office of Children's Issues
Bureau of Consular Affairs of the U.S. State
Department
(202) 736-7000 or (202) 647-3444
World Wide Web: www.travel.state.gov
Information about adopting internationally

RESOLVE, Inc.
1310 Broadway
Somerville, MA 02144-1731
(617) 623-0744
World Wide Web: www.resolve.org
E-mail: resolveinc@aol.com
National infertility information group.

Stars of David International, Inc.
3175 Commercial Avenue, Suite 100
Northbrook, IL 60062-1915
(800) STAR-349
World Wide Web: www.starsofdavid.org
Information and support for Jewish and interfaith
adoptive families.

Selected adoption magazines and newsletters

Adoptalk
North American Council on Adoptable Children
970 Raymond Avenue, Suite 106
St. Paul, MN 55114-1149
(612) 644-9848

Adopted Child
P.O. Box 962
Moscow, ID 83843
(888) 882-1794

Adoptive Families
2309 Como Avenue
St. Paul, MN 55108
(800) 372-3300 or (612) 645-9955
World Wide Web: www.adoptivefam.org

Attachments
Attachment Center at Evergreen
P.O. Box 2764
Evergreen, CO 80439
(303) 674-1910

The Decree
American Adoption Congress
100 Connecticut Avenue, NW, Suite 9
Washington, DC 20036
(800) 274-6736 or (202) 483-3399

FACE Facts
Families Adopting Children Everywhere
P.O. Box 28058
Northwood Station
Baltimore, MD 21239
(301) 239-4252

The Handbook for Single Adoptive Parents
National Council for Single Adoptive Parents
P.O. Box 15084
Chevy Chase, MD 20825
(202) 966-6367

National Adoption Reports
National Council for Adoption
1930 17th Street, NW
Washington, DC
(202) 328-1200
World Wide Web: www.NCFA.usa.org

PACT Press
Pact—An Adoption Alliance, Inc.
3450 Sacramento Street, Suite 239
San Francisco, CA 94118
(415) 221-6957

Report on Intercountry Adoption
International Concerns for Children
911 Cypress Drive
Boulder, CO 80303-2821
(303) 494-8333
World Wide Web: www.fortnet.org/icc

Roots and Wings
Roots and Wings Publications
P.O. Box 577
Hackettstown, NJ 07840
(908) 637-8828
World Wide Web: www.adopt-usa.com/
rootsandwings

Adoption resources on the Internet

The following are some examples of starting points
for locating adoption resources on the Net. For
more information on how to find information on
the Internet, see the National Adoption
Information Clearinghouse publication "Adoption
Web Sites: How to find reliable information."

Adopt: Assistance, Information, Support
http://www.adopting.org
Comprehensive information for all members of the
adoption triad.

Adopting.com
http://www.adopting.com
Largest listing of adoption-related Web sites, list-
serves, photolistings, and resources.

Adoptive Families of America
http://www.adoptivefam.org
Nation's largest adoptive parent support organization.

American Academy of Adoption Attorneys
http://www.adoptionattorneys.org
National directory of attorneys who practice adoption law.

Evan B. Donaldson Adoption Institute
http://www.adoptioninstitute.org
Adoption research, policy, and analysis.

Joint Council on International Children's Services
http://www.jcics.org
Affiliation of intercountry adoption agencies promoting ethical practice and child welfare services.

National Adoption Center
http://www.adopt.org
National photolisting of waiting children; information and resources.

National Adoption Information Clearinghouse
http://www.calib.com/naic
Fact sheets, resource listings, and information.

North American Council on Adoptable Children
http://members.aol.com/nacac
Parent support groups and subsidy information.

RainbowKids
http://www.rainbowkids.com
International adoption newsletter.

U.S. State Department Office of Children's Issues
http://travel.state.gov/children's_issues.
html#adoption
Official information on international adoption programs.

Recommended Reading List

Finding books about adoption

Tapestry Books—*Adoption Book Catalog*
Call for a free catalog at (800) 765-2367.
Web site: http://www.tapestrybooks.com

William Gage—*Readers' Guide to Adoption-Related Literature*
Web site: http://members.aol.com/billgage/lit-list.htm

PACT's Book Source: *A Reference Guide to Books on Adoption and Race for Adults and Children*
A large volume of reviews and ratings of hundreds of books about adoption. Available for $14.95 ($9.95 if you join the organization, which includes a magazine and other services). You will receive the revised second edition. Contact Pact to place an order.
Phone: (415) 221-6957
E-mail: info@pactadopt.org
Web site: http://www.pactadopt.org

Perspectives Press
Phone: (317) 872-3055
Web site: http://www.perspectivespress.com

Adoptive Families of America—The Bookstore
Phone: (800) 372-3300
Web site: http://www.adoptivefam.org

Books for adults

Adamec, Chris. *There ARE Babies to Adopt.* New York: Pinnacle Books, 1991.

Arms, Suzanne. *Adoption: A Handful of Hope.* Berkley: Celestial Arts, 1990.

Beauvais-Godwin, Laura, and Raymond Godwin. *The Complete Adoption Book.* Holbrook, MA: Adams Media Corporation, 1997.

Best, Mary Hopkins. *Toddler Adoption: The Weaver's Craft.* Indianapolis: Perspectives Press, 1998.

Brodzinsky, David M., Marshall D. Schechter, and Robin Marantz Henig. *Being Adopted: The Lifelong Search for Self.* New York: Doubleday, 1992.

Davis, Diane. *Reaching Out to Children with FAS/FAE: A Handbook for Teachers, Counselors and Parents Who Work with Children Affected by Fetal Alcohol Syndrome and Fetal Alcohol Effects.* West Nyack, NY: The Center for Applied Research in Education, 1994.

Delaney, Richard J., Ph.D., and Frank R. Kunstal, Ed.D. *Troubled Transplants: Unconventional Strategies for Helping Disturbed Foster and Adopted Children.* University of Southern Maine, 1993.

DeMuth, Carol. *Courageous Blessing: Adoptive Parents and the Search.* Garland, TX: Aries Center, 1993.

Fahlberg, Vera, M.D. *A Child's Journey Through Placement.* Indianapolis: Perspectives Press, 1991.

Gabel, Susan. *Filling in the Blanks: A Guided Look At Growing Up Adopted.* Indianapolis: Perspectives Press, 1988.

Harnack, Andrew. *Adoption: Opposing Viewpoints.* San Diego: Greenhaven Press, 1995.

Harris, Judith Rich. *The Nurture Assumption.* New York: The Free Press, 1998.

Hopson, Dr. Darlene Powell, and Dr. Derek S. Hopson with Thomas Clavin. *Raising the Rainbow Generation.* New York: Fireside, 1993.

Hughes, Daniel A., Ph.D. *Building the Bonds of Attachment: Awakening Love in Deeply Troubled Children.* Northvale, NJ: Jason Aronson, Inc., 1998.

Hughes, Daniel A., Ph.D. *Facilitating Developmental Attachment: The Road to Emotional Recovery and Behavioral Change in Foster and Adopted Children.* Northvale, NJ: Jason Aronson, Inc., 1997.

James, Beverly. *Handbook for Treatment of Attachment-Trauma Problems in Children.* New York: Lexington Books, 1994.

Johnston, Patricia Irwin. *Adopting After Infertility.* Indianapolis: Perspectives Press, 1992.

Johnston, Patricia Irwin. *Launching a Baby's Adoption: Practical Strategies for Parents and Professionals.* Indianapolis: Perspectives Press, 1997.

Keck, Gregory, and Regina M. Kupecky. *Adopting the Hurt Child: Hope for Families with Special Needs Kids, A Guide for Parents and Professionals.* Colorado Springs: Pinon Press, 1995.

Kirk, David H. *Shared Fate: A Theory and Method of Adoptive Relationships.* Port Angeles, WA: Ben-Simon Publications, 1984.

Komar, Miriam. *Communicating With the Adopted Child.* New York: Walker and Co., 1991.

Lindsay, Jeanne Warren. *Open Adoption: A Caring Option.* Buena Park, CA: Morning Glory Press, 1987.

Mansfield, Lynda Gianforte, and Christiopher H. Waldmann. *Don't Touch My Heart.* Colorado Springs: Pinon Press, 1994.

Melina, Lois Ruskai. *Making Sense of Adoption: A Parent's Guide.* New York: Harper & Row, 1989.

Melina, Lois Ruskai. *Raising Adopted Children.* New York: HarperCollins, 1998.

Melina, Lois Ruskai, and Sharon Kaplan Roszia. *The Open Adoption Experience.* New York: HarperCollins, 1993.

McColm, Michelle. *Adoption Reunions: A Book for Adoptees, Birth Parents, and Adoptive Families.* Toronto: Second Story Press, 1993.

Pavao, Joyce Maguire. *The Family of Adoption.* Boston: Beacon Press, 1997.

Powell-Hopson, Dr. Darlene, and Dr. Derrick Hopson. *Different and Wonderful—Raising Black Children in a Race-Conscious Society.* New York: Prentice Hall, 1990.

Register, Cheri. *Are Those Kids Yours? American Families with Children Adopted from Other Countries.* New York: Free Press, 1991.

Rosenberg, Elinor B. *Adoption Life Cycle: The Children and Their Families Through the Years*. New York: Free Press, 1992.

Schaeffer, Judith, and Christina Lindstrom. *How to Raise an Adopted Child*. New York: Plume, Penguin Books USA, 1991.

Schooler, Jayne E. *Searching for a Past: The Adopted Adult's Unique Process of Finding Identity*. Colorado Springs: Pinon Press, 1995.

Schooler, Jayne E. *The Whole Life Adoption Book*. Colorado Springs: Pinon Press, 1993.

Sorosky, Arthur D., Annette Baran, and Reuben Pannor. *The Adoption Triangle*. New York: Anchor Press, Doubleday, 1978.

van Gulden, Holly, and Lisa Bartels-Rabb. *Real Parents, Real Children: Parenting the Adopted Child*. New York: Cross Road, 1993.

Wadia-Ells, Susan, editor. *The Adoption Reader: Birth Mother, Adoptive Mothers, and Adopted Daughters Tell Their Stories*. Seattle: Seal Press, 1995.

Watkins, Mary, and Susan Fisher. *Talking with Young Children About Adoption*. New Haven: Yale University Press, 1993.

Books for young children

Banish, Roslyn, with Jennifer Jordan-Wong. *A Forever Family: A Child's Story About Adoption*. New York: Harper Trophy, 1992.

Blomquist, Geraldine and Paul. *Zachary's New Home: A Story for Foster and Adopted Children*. New York: Magination Press, 1990.

Boyd, Brian. *When You Were Born in Korea: A Memory Book for Children Adopted from Korea.* St. Paul, MN: Yeong & Yeong Book Company, 1993.

Brodzinsky, Anne Braff. *The Mulberry Bird.* Indianapolis: Perspectives Press, 1986.

Caines, Jeanette. *Abby.* New York, Harper Trophy, 1973.

Curtis, Jamie Lee. *Tell Me Again About the Night I Was Born.* New York: HarperCollins, 1996.

Gordon, Shirley. *The Boy Who Wanted a Family.* New York: Harper & Row, 1980.

Hicks, Randall. *Adoption Stories for Young Children.* Sun City: Wordslinger, 1995.

Karvoskaia, Natascha. *Dounia.* Brooklyn, NY: Kane/Miller, 1995.

Keller, Holly. *Horace.* New York: Greenwillow Books, 1991.

Koch, Janice. *Our Baby: A Birth and Adoption Story.* Fort Wayne, IN: Perspectives Press, 1985.

Lifton, Betty Jean. *Tell Me a Real Adoption Story.* New York: Alfred A. Knopf, 1993.

MacLachlan, Patricia. *Mama One, Mama Two.* New York: Harper & Row, 1982.

Miller, Kathryn. *Did My First Mother Love Me? A Story for an Adopted Child.* Buena Park, CA: Morning Glory Press, 1994.

Say, Allen. *Allison.* New York: Houghton Mifflin, 1997.

Schaffer, Patricia. *How Babies and Families Are Made: There Is More Than One Way!* Berkeley, CA: Tabor Sarah Books, 1988.

Turner, Ann. *Through Moon and Stars and Night Skies.* New York: HarperCollins, 1990.

Wickstrom, Lois. *Oliver.* Wayne, PA: Our Child Press, 1991.

For older children and teenagers

Cooney, Caroline B. *The Face on the Milk Carton.* New York: Bantam Doubleday, 1990.

Cooney, Caroline B. *Whatever Happened to Janie?* New York: Bantam Doubleday, 1993.

Doherty, Berlie. *The Snake-Stone.* New York: Orchard Books, 1995.

Furlong, Monica. *Wise Child.* New York: Random House, 1987.

Granvelle, Karen, and Susan Fischer. *Where Are My Birthparents?* New York: Walker and Co., 1993.

Krementz, Jill. *How It Feels to Be Adopted.* New York: Knopf, 1982.

Lantz, Francess. *Someone to Love.* New York: Avon, 1997.

Lee, Marie G. *If It Hadn't Been for Yoon Jun.* New York: Houghton Mifflin, 1993.

Lifton, Betty Jean. *I'm Still Me.* New York: Alfred A. Knopf, 1981.

Lowry, Lois. *Find a Stranger, Say Goodbye.* New York: Simon & Schuster, 1978.

Nerlove, Evelyn. *Who Is David?* New York: CWLA, 1985.

Okimoto, Jean Davies. *Molly by Any Other Name.* New York: Scholastic, 1990.

Powledge, Fred. *So You're Adopted.* New York: Scribner, 1982.

Rabe, Berniece. *Magic Comes In Its Time.* New York: Simon & Schuster, 1993.

Rosenberg, Maxine B. *Growing Up Adopted.* New York: Bradbury Press, Macmillan, 1989.

Shreve, Susan. *Zoe and Columbo.* New York: William Morrow, 1995.

Woodson, Jacqueline. *The Dear One.* New York: Dell, 1991.

Support Groups

The following is a partial list of the support groups available throughout the U.S.:

Alabama

Greater Birmingham FPA and North American Council on Adoptable Children Representative
925 26th Street
Birmingham, AL 35244
(205) 925-6655
World Wide Web: http://members.aol.com/nacac

Single Adoptive Parents Support Group
Alabama Friends Adopt.
2407 Titonka Road
Birmingham, AL 35244
(205) 733-0976

Alaska

Anchorage Adoptive Parents Association
550 West Seventh, Suite 1780
Anchorage, AK 99502
(907) 276-1680

North American Council on Adoptable Children
State Representative
1018 26th Avenue
Fairbanks, AK 99701
(907) 452-5397
World Wide Web: http://members.aol.com/nacac

Arizona
Adopt America Network and North American
Council on Adoptable Children Representative
2911 E. Michigan
Phoenix, AZ 85032
(602) 493-1722
E-mail: tseptember@aol.com

Advocates for Single Adoptive Parenting
8702 East Malcomb Drive
Scottsdale, AZ 85250
(602) 951-8310

Arkansas
Adopt America Network and North American
Council on Adoptable Children Representative
1314 N. Boston Avenue
Russellville, AR 72801
(501) 967-9337

AFACT and North American Council on Adoptable
Children
17 McKee Circle
North Little Rock, AR 72166
(501) 758-7061

California
Bay Area Single Adoptive Parent Group
South
385 S. 14th Street
San Jose, CA 95112
(408) 292-1638

Open Door Society and North American Council
on Adoptable Children Representative
170 E. Highland, Room E
Sierra Madre, CA 91204
(818) 355-5920

PACT, an Adoption Alliance
3450 Sacramento Street, Suite 239
San Francisco, CA 94118
(415) 221-6957
Fax: (510) 482-2089
World Wide Web: http://www.pactadopt.org
E-mail: info@pactadopt.org

Post Adoption Support Group
3805 Regent Road
Sacramento, CA 95821
(916) 487-7243

Private Adoption—Where to Begin?
P.O. Box 405
Boulder Creek, CA 95006

Colorado
Adoptive Families of Denver and North American
Council on Adoptable Children Representative
6660 South Race Circle West
Littleton, CO 80121
(303) 795-2890
World Wide Web: http://members.aol.com/nacac

Attachment Center at Evergreen
27618 Fireweed
Evergreen, CO 80439
(303) 674-1910
World Wide Web:
http://www.attachmentcenter.org/

Family Attachment Institute
P.O. Box 1731
Evergreen, CO 80437
(303) 674-0547

Loving Homes and North American Council on
Adoptable Children Representative
4760 Oakland, Suite 700
Denver, CO 80239
(303) 371-9185
Fax: (303) 371-1193
E-mail: Lhomes@aol.com

Connecticut
Attachment Disorder Parents Network of
Connecticut
85 Westward Avenue
Plainville, CT 06062
(860) 669-2750

Casey Family Services
789 Reservoir Avenue
Bridgeport, CT 06606
(203) 372-3722
Fax: (203) 372-3558
Toll-free: (800) 332-6991

North American Council on Adoptable Children
Representative
506 Taylor Road
Enfield, CT 06082
(203) 749-9123

Delaware
Adoptive Families Information and Support and
North American Council on Adoptable Children
Representative
523 Ashland Ridge Road
Hockessin, DE 19707
(302) 239-0727
World Wide Web: http://members.aol.com/nacac

District of Columbia
Families for Private Adoption
P.O. Box 6375
Washington, DC 20015-0375
(202) 722-0338

Florida
Daniel Memorial Adoption Information Center
and North American Council on Adoptable
Children Representative
134 E. Church Street
Jacksonville, FL 32202
(904) 353-0679
Fax: (904) 353-3472

Stars of David South Florida
Ruth Rales Jewish Family Services
21300 Ruth and Baron Coleman Blvd.
Boca Raton, FL 33428
(561) 852-3380
World Wide Web: http://www.starsofdavid.org
E-mail: starsdavid@aol.com

Stressed Out Adoptive Parents
1403 N.W. 40th Avenue
Lauderhill, FL 33313
(954) 797-8368

Georgia

Alliance of Single Adoptive Parents
(Metro Atlanta)
687 Kennolia Drive, S.W.
Atlanta, GA 30310-2363
(404) 755-3280

Central Savannah River Area Council on Adoptable
Children (CSRA-COAC) Parent Support
Coordination Office of Adoptions
North American Council on Adoptable Children
Representative
3739 Roscommon North
Martinez, GA 30907
(706) 863-6241
E-mail: shipesjudy@aol.com

One Church, One Child Program, Inc.
P.O. Box 115238
Atlanta, GA 30310
(404) 766-0383
Toll-free: (800) 662-3651

Single Women Adopting Children
GA
(404) 730-4593

Stars of David
3300 Arborwood Drive
Alpharetta, GA 30202
(770) 992-3422
World Wide Web: http://www.starsofdavid.org/
E-mail: starsdavid@aol.com

Washington County Alliance of Adoptive Parents
P.O. Box 108
Sandersville, GA 31082

Hawaii
Forever Families
7719 Waikapu Loop
Honolulu, HI 96825
(808) 396-9130

Resolve of HI—Kafuai Site
3721-A Omao Road
Koloa, HI 96756
(808) 742-8885

Idaho
Families of MAC (Multicultural Adopted Children)
2820 Shamrock Avenue
Nampa, ID 83686
(208) 463-4040
World Wide Web: http://www.familiesofmac.com
E-mail: kym@familiesofmac.com

North American Council on Adoptable Children
1301 Spokane Street
Post Falls, ID 83854
(208) 773-5629
World Wide Web: http://members.aol.com/nacac

Illinois
Illinois Coalition for TRUTH in Adoption
P.O. Box 4638
Skokie, IL 60076-4638
(217) 664-3342
World Wide Web: http://www.prairienet.org/icta
E-mail: ICTA97@aol.com

North American Council on Adoptable
Children Representative
2426 Austin Drive
Springfield, IL 62704
(217) 787-7367
Fax: (217) 524-3966
World Wide Web: http://members.aol.com/nacac

Single Adoptive Parent Support Group
P.O. Box 578478
Chicago, IL 60657
(847) 604-1974

Special Needs Adoption Support Group
Lifelink/Bensenville Home Society
331 York Road
Bensenville, IL 60106
(630) 766-5800, Ext: 282

Indiana
Adoptive Parents Together and North American
Council on Adoptable Children State
Representative
756 Woodruff Place
Indianapolis, IN 46201
(317) 638-0965

Families Adopting Children Together
RR 1, P.O. Box 151
Gentryville, IN 47537
(812) 925-3341

Indiana One Church One Child Program, Inc.
850 N. Meridian Street
Indianapolis, IN 46204
(317) 684-2181

Iowa

Family Connections and North American Council
on Adoptable Children Representative
66684 110th Street
McCallsburg, IA 50154
(515) 487-7833
Fax: (515) 487-7833
World Wide Web: http://members.aol.com/nacac
E-mail: mcbritco@netins.net

Ours Through Adoption and North American
Council on Adoptable Children Representative
2618 Arlington Avenue
Davenport, IA 52803
(319) 322-6469

Kansas

Families for Russian and Ukrainian Adoptions
Kansas City Area FRUA Chapter
38209 Bethel Church Road
Osawatomie, KS 66064
E-mail: ed@micoks.net

International Families of Mid America
6708 Granada Road
Prairie Village, KS 66208
(913) 722-5697

Special Needs Adoption Project
University of Kansas Medical Center Children's
Rehabilitation Unit
3901 Rainbow Blvd., #5017
Kansas City, KS 66103
(913) 588-5745

Kentucky
Parents & Adoptive Children of Kentucky
139 Highland Drive
Madisonville, KY 42431
(502) 825-2158

SNAP and North American Council on Adoptable
Children State Representative
710 W. High Street
Lexington, KY 40508
(606) 252-1728
World Wide Web: http://members.aol.com/nacac

Louisiana
Louisiana Adoption Advisory Board (LAAB), Inc.
P.O. Box 3318
Baton Rouge, LA 70821
(504) 342-4086

North American Council on Adoptable Children
3528 Vincennes Place
New Orleans, LA 70125
(504) 866-4449
World Wide Web: http://members.aol.com/nacac

Maine
Adoptive Families of Maine
P.O. Box 350
Portage, ME 04708
(207) 435-8018

Adoptive Families of Maine and North American
Council on Adoptable Children
156 Essex Street
Bangor, ME 04401
(207) 941-9500

Central Maine Area Adoption Group
7 Noyer Street
Waterville, ME 04901
(207) 873-6020

Maryland
Adoptive Family Network
P.O. Box 7
Columbia, MD 21045
(301) 984-6133
World Wide Web: http://www.erols.com/giconklin

Barker Foundation Parents of Adopted
Adolescents Group
7945 MacArthur Blvd., Suite 206
Cabin John, MD 20818
(301) 229-8300

Families Adopting Children Everywhere and
North American Council on Adoptable Children
Representative
P.O. Box 28058
Baltimore, MD 21239
(410) 488-2656

Joint Council on International Children's Services
7 Cheverly Circle
Cheverly, MD 20785-3040
(301) 322-1906
Fax: (301) 322-3425
World Wide Web: http://www.jcics.org

Latin America Parents Association of the National
Capital Region
P.O. Box 4403
Silver Spring, MD 20904-4403
(301) 431-3407
World Wide Web: http://www.lapa.com
E-mail: joet@highcaliber.com

National Council for Single Adoptive Parents
P.O. Box 15084
Chevy Chase, MD 20825
(202) 966-6367
World Wide Web:
http://www.adopting.org/ncsap.html

Open Adoption Discussion Group
22310 Old Hundred Road
Barnesville, MD 20838
(301) 972-8579
E-mail: msaasta@hotmail.com

Stars of David c/o Jewish Family and Children's
Service
5750 Park Heights Avenue
Baltimore, MD 21215
(410) 466-9200
World Wide Web: http://www.starsofdavid.org/
E-mail: starsdavid@aol.com

Massachusetts
Adoption Connection
11 Peabody Square, Room 6
Peabody, MA 01960
(978) 532-1261

Boston Single Mothers By Choice
P.O. Box 600027
Newtonville, MA 02160-0001
(617) 964-9949

Family Center Pre- and Post-Adoption Consulting
Team
385 Highland Avenue
Somerville, MA 02144
(617) 628-8815

Open Door Society of Massachusetts and
North American Council on Adoptable Children
State Representative
43 King Street
Groveland, MA 01834
(987) 521-6205
Toll-free: (800) 93A-DOPT

Stars of David of Massachusetts
8 Brook Way
Westboro, MA 01581
(508) 752-2512
World Wide Web: http://www.starsofdavid.org/
E-mail: starsdavid@aol.com

Michigan
Adopt America Network and North American
Council on Adoptable Children
3051 Siebert Road
Midland, MI 48640
(517) 832-8117

Concerned Citizens for International Adoption
P.O. Box 1083
Portage, MI 49082-1083

Families of Latin Kids
P.O. Box 15537
Ann Arbor, MI 48106
(313) 429-4312

Families on the Move and North American
Council on Adoptable Children
18727 Avon
Detriot, MI 48219
(313) 532-0012
Fax: (313) 532-1345

Jewish Family Services of the Jewish Federation of
Washtenew County
2939 Birch Hollow
Ann Arbor, MI 48108
(313) 971-3280
Fax: (313) 677-0109

Michigan Association of Single Adoptive Parents
7412 Coolidge
Centerline, MI 48015
(313) 758-6909

North American Council on Adoptable Children
Representative
23891 Bedford Road
Battle Creek, MI 49017
(616) 660-0448

Orchards Adoptive Parent Support Group
30215 Southfield Road, Suite 100
Southfield, MI 48076
(248) 258-1278

Post Adoption Resources
21700 Northwestern Highway, Suite 1490
Southfield, MI 48075-4901
(248) 423-2770

Psychotherapy Center for Adoptive Families
17500 Northland Park Court
Southfield, MI 48075
(248) 531-9659

Stars of David
4458 Apple Valley Lane
West Bloomfield, MI 48323
(810) 737-3874
World Wide Web: http://www.starsofdavid.org/
E-mail: starsdavid@aol.com

Minnesota
Adoptive Families of America
2309 Como Avenue
St. Paul, MN 55108
(612) 645-9955
World Wide Web: http://www.AdoptiveFam.org/
E-mail: info@AdoptiveFam.org

Contact One-Plus
1316 California Avenue
St. Paul, MN 55108
(612) 644-0728

Families of Multi-Racial Adoptions
1125 Cross Street
North Mankato, MN 56033
(507) 345-4279

Families Under Severe Stress
2230 Como Avenue
St. Paul, MN 55108
(612) 646-6393

Minnesota Adoption Resource Network and
North American Council on Adoptable Children
Representative
2409 W. 66th Street, P.O. Box 39722
Minneapolis, MN 55439
(612) 861-7115
Fax: (612) 861-7112
World Wide Web: http://www.mnadopt.org/
E-mail: MNadopt@aol.com

Minnesota Kinship Caregivers Association
501 East 45th Street
Minneapolis, MN 55409

Parents of Latin American Children
16665 Argon Street, N.W.
Anoka, MN 55304
(612) 427-6277

Partners for Adoption
621 County Road, 10 S.E.
Watertown, MN 55388
(612) 955-2046

Mississippi
F.A.C.E. Adoption Support Group for North
Mississippi
P.O. Box 728
Booneville, MS 38829

North American Council on Adoptable Children
Representative
5722 Michelle Ray Street
Jackson, MS 39209
(601) 922-3989

Missouri
Adoptive Family Support Group
Route 1, Box 84
Millersville, MO 63701
(573) 266-3609

Adoptive Parents of Southwest Missouri
4925 Royal Drive
Springfield, MO 65804
(417) 887-5788

Citizens for Missouri's Children and
North American Council on Adoptable Children
Representative
701 S. Skinner Blvd., Apt. 303
St. Louis, MO 63105-3326
(314) 962-6397
Fax: (314) 434-3936

Montana
Family Support in Adoption Association and
North American Council on Adoptable Children
Representative
7049 Fox Lane
Darby, MT 59829
(406) 349-2872

Montana Adoption Resource Center, Post
Adoption Center
P.O. Box 634
Helena, MT 59624
(406) 449-3266

Nebraska
North American Council on Adoptable Children
Representative
1811 W. 2nd Street
Grand Island, NE 68803
(308) 382-4495
Fax: (308) 382-2582

Voices for Children in Nebraska
7521 Main Street
Omaha, NE 68127
(402) 597-3100

Nevada
North American Council on Adoptable Children
Representative
4125 Wendy Lane
Las Vegas, NV 89115
(702) 643-7574

Southern Nevada Adoption Association and
North American Council on Adoptable Children
Representative
1316 Saylor Way
Las Vegas, NV 89108
(702) 385-5331

New Hampshire
Open Door Society of New Hampshire, Inc.
40 Gerrish Drive
Nottingham, NH 03290
(603) 679-8144

Ours for a United Response of New England
347 Candia Road
Chester, NH 03036
(617) 967-4648

New Jersey
Adoption Information Service, Inc.
12 Roberts Street
Rockaway, NJ 07866
(973) 586-1552

Adoptive Single Parents of New Jersey
73 Tristan Road
Clifton, NJ 07013
(201) 742-9441

Camden County FACES
130 S. Mansfield Blvd.
Cherry Hill, NJ 08034
(609) 784-1081

Central New Jersey Singles Network of Adoptive
Parents
P.O. Box 1012
Flemington, NJ 08822
(908) 782-5500

Concerned Parents for Adoption and
North American Council on Adoptable Children
State Representative
12 Reed Drive North
Princeton Junction, NJ 08550
(609) 799-3269
E-mail: lebfrom nj@aol.com

Rainbow Families
670 Oakley Place
Oradell, NJ 07649
(201) 261-1148

Roots & Wings
P.O. Box 577
Hackettstown, NJ 07840
(908) 813-8252
World Wide Web: http://www.adopt-usa.com/
rootsandwings
E-mail: adoption@interactive.net

Singles Network of Adoptive Parents
8 N. Whittesbog Road
Browns Mills, NJ 08015
(609) 893-7875

Stars of David, Central New Jersey Chapter
P.O. Box 471
Holmdel, NJ 07733
World Wide Web: http://www.starsofdavid.org/
E-mail: starsdavid@aol.com

New Mexico
North American Council on Adoptable Children
Representative
88 Manzano Spring Road
Taijeras, NM 87059
(505) 281-6537
World Wide Web: http://members.aol.com/nacac

Stars of David
13705 Ivy Wood Lane
Silver Spring, NM 20904
(301) 622-4757
World Wide Web: http://www.starsofdavid.org
E-mail: starsdavid@aol.com

New York
Adoptive Families of Older Children, Inc.
149-32A Union Turnpike
Flushing, NY 11367
(718) 380-7234

Adoptive Family Network of Central New York
503 Maple Drive
Fayetteville, NY 13066-1735
(315) 446-5607
E-mail: sferrara@hotmail.com

Capitol District—Albany, Troy, Schenectady,
Saratoga Upstate NY Single Adoptive Parents
38 Shaker Drive Blvd.
Loudonville, NY 12211
(518) 489-4322

Center Kids: The Family Project of the Lesbian
and Gay Community Services Center of NY
1171 Fr. Capodanno Blvd.
Staten Island, NY 10306
(212) 620-7310
Fax: (212) 924-2657

Friends in Adoption Post Placement Group
16 Willey Street
Albany, NY 12203
(518) 452-0271

Grandparents Reaching Out
141 Glen Summer Road
Holbrook, NY 11741
(516) 472-9728

Holt Families Unlimited
P.O. Box 25
Candor, NY 13743
(607) 659-7540

Jewish Child Care Association Foster Parents
3170 Broadway #11B
New York, NY 10027
(212) 316-1762

New Life for Black Children
P.O. Box 11164
Rochester, NY 14611
(716) 436-6075

New York Council on Adoptable Children
Suite 820, 666 Broadway
New York, NY 10012
(212) 475-0222
World Wide Web: http://www.coac.org
E-mail: coac@erols.com

New York Singles Adopting Children
P.O. Box 472
Glen Oaks, NY 11004
(212) 289-1705

New York State Citizens' Coalition for Children
and North American Council on Adoptable
Children Representative
614 W. State Street, 2nd Floor
Ithaca, NY 14850
(607) 272-0034
Fax: (607) 272-0035
World Wide Web: http://www.nysccc.org
E-mail: office@nysccc.org

Open Door Society of Long Island
40 Pennsylvania Avenue
Medford, NY 11763
(516) 758-5571

Private Adoption Support Group/
Western New York
142 Brush Creek Road
Williamsburg, NY 14221
(716) 689-8991

Rochester Attachment Network
227 Aldine Street
Rochester, NY 14619-1204
(716) 527-0514

Single Mothers By Choice
P.O. Box 1642, Gracie Square Station
New York, NY 10028
(212) 988-0993
E-mail: mattes@pipeline.com

Stars of David/Albany Area
RD 1, P.O. Box 88
Duanesburg, NY 12056
(518) 895-8001
World Wide Web: http://www.starsofdavid.org/
E-mail: starsdavid@aol.com

Tri County Families of Korean Children
54 Benneywater Road
Port Jervis, NY 12771
(914) 355-3711

Upstate Adoptive Parents Community Support
Group
4356 Buckingham Drive
Schenectady, NY 12304
(518) 372-2874

Upstate New York Single Adoptive Parent Group
21 Conifer Drive
Saratoga Springs, NY 12866
(518) 581-0891

North Carolina
Adoptive Families Heart to Heart
456 NC Highway 62, East
Greensboro, NC 27406
(336) 674-5024

Family Resources
348 Lake Point Lane
Bellews Creek, NC 27009-9207
(910) 644-1664

North Carolina Friends of Black Children
P.O. Box 494
Sanford, NC 27330
Toll-free: (800) 774-3534

Piedmont Families thru International Adoption
29 Carrisbrooke Lane
Winston-Salem, NC 27104
(336) 765-9064
E-mail: MaMiska@aol.com

Single Adoptive Parent Support Groups
102 South 26th Street
Morehead City, NC 28557
(919) 247-7071

Triad Adoptive Parent Support Group and
North American Council on Adoptable Children
133 Penny Road
High Point, NC 27260
(910) 886-8230

North Dakota

Adopt America Network—VFSC and
North American Council on Adoptable Children
Representative
P.O. Box 9859
Fargo, ND 58106
(701) 235-6433

LSS of North Dakota and North American Council
on Adoptable Children Representative
P.O. Box 389
Fargo, ND 58107
(701) 271-3265
Fax: (701) 235-7359
E-mail: iohnsief@ortel.com

Ohio

ACT Group, Advocates for Children Today
3965 Ganyard
Brunswick, OH 44212
(330) 225-1088

Adopt America Network of Ohio
340 Bank Street
Painesville, OH 44077
(440) 352-3780

Adoptive Families of Greater Cincinnati
4686 Yankee Road
Cincinnati, OH 45044
(513) 539-9787

Attachment and Bonding Center of Ohio
12608 State Road
Cleveland, OH 44133
(440) 230-1960

Attachment Disorders Parents Network
P.O. Box 176
Cortland, OH 44410

Catholic Charities, Diocese of Toledo
1933 Spielbusch Avenue
Toledo, OH 43697-0985
(419) 244-6711

Central Ohio Families with Children from China
(COFCC)
P.O. Box 554
Hillard, OH 43026-0554

Connections
c/o Jewish Family Services
6525 Sylvania Avenue
Toledo, OH 43560
(419) 885-2561

Down Syndrome Association of Cincinnati
5741 Davey Avenue
Cincinnati, OH 45224
(513) 542-3286

Families with Children from China
5141 Morningsun Road
Oxford, OH 45056
(513) 769-7733
E-mail: bgambill-1@cinergy.com

Foreign Adoptive Children—Eastern Suburbs
11875 Laurel Road
Chesterland, OH 44026
(440) 729-2535

Latin American Families
3568 Stoneboat Court
Maineville, OH 45039
(513) 677-1732

North American Council on Adoptable Children
Representative
1371 Virginia Avenue
Columbus, OH 43212
(614) 299-0177
E-mail: TimOHanlon@aol.com

Open Adoption Support Group
541 Brandywynne Court
Dayton, OH 45406
(513) 275-9628

Parents Supporting Parents
19306 Boerger Road
Marysville, OH 43040
(937) 349-7105

Single Parent by Adoption Support System
2547 Talbott Avenue
Cincinnati, OH 45211
(513) 661-5170

Stars of David
26001 S. Woodland
Beachwood, OH 44122
(216) 831-0700
World Wide Web: http://www.starsofdavid.org/
E-mail: starsdavid@aol.com

Oklahoma
Attachment Network
P.O. Box 532
Broken Arrow, OK 74013
(918) 251-7781

Babb Enterprises and North American Council on
Adoptable Children Representative
488 Claremont
Norman, OK 73069
(405) 329-9294
E-mail: annebabb@homes4kids.org

Concerned Families Reaching Out
615 E. First Street
Watonga, OK 73772
(580) 623-8622

North American Council on Adoptable Children
Representative
P.O. Box 25
Harrah, OK 73045
(405) 454-1179
Fax: (405) 454-1179
E-mail: rlaws@homes4kids.org

Oklahoma Council on Adoptable Children and
North American Council on Adoptable Children
2609 N.W. 38th Street
Oklahoma City, OK 73112
(405) 942-0810

Oregon

North American Council on Adoptable Children
Representative
357 Alta Street
Ashland, OR 97520
(541) 482-7288
World Wide Web: http://members.aol.com/nacac
E-mail: linsday@wave.net

Northwest Adoptive Families Association and
North American Council on Adoptable Children
Representative
5737 S.W. Pendleton
Portland, OR 97122-1762
(503) 246-3236
Fax: (503) 246-6264
World Wide Web: http://members.aol.com/nacac
E-mail: kgstocker@aol.com

Single Adoptive Parents Support Group
5621 S.E. Oak Street
Portland, OR 97215
(503) 234-7042

Pennsylvania

After Adoption and Parenting Services for Families
5500 Wissahickon Avenue, Alden Park Manor,
A-202
Philadelphia, PA 19144
(215) 844-1312

Council on Adoptable Children of Southwestern
Pennsylvania and North American Council on
Adoptable Children State Representative
224 S. Aiken Avenue
Pittsburgh, PA 15206
(412) 471-8722

International Adoptive Families
402 Pebblecreek Drive
Cranberry Township, PA 16066
(814) 772-5787

National Adoption Center
1500 Walnut Street, Suite 701
Philadelphia, PA 19102
(215) 735-9988
World Wide Web:
http://www.adopt.org/adopt/nac/nac.html
E-mail: nac@adopt.org

Parents of Adopted African Americans
544 W. 31st Street
Erie, PA 16508-1743
(814) 455-2149

Pre- and Post-Adoption Consultation and
Education
47 Marchwood Road, Suite 1E
Exton, PA 19341
(610) 524-9060

Single Adoptive Parents of Delaware Valley
2239 Strahle Street, 2nd Floor
Philadelphia, PA 19152
(215) 745-2855

Stars of David—Central PA Chapter
C/O Jewish Fam. Svc. Of Harrisburg, 3333 N.
Front Street
Harrisburg, PA 17110
(717) 233-1681
Fax: (717) 234-8258
World Wide Web: http://www.starsofdavid.org/
E-mail: starsdavid@aol.com

Rhode Island

Adoption Rhode Island and North American
Council on Adoptable Children Representative
500 Prospect Street
Pawtucket, RI 02860
(401) 724-1910
Fax: (401) 724-1910
World Wide Web: http://www.adoptionri.org
E-mail: adoptionri@ids.net

Jewish Family Services Adoptive Parent Support
Group
229 Waterman Avenue
Providence, RI 02906
(401) 331-1244

South Carolina

Center for Child and Family Studies
Post-Legal Adoption Education and Training
University of South Carolina
Columbia, SC 29208
(803) 777-9408

Single Adoptive Parents of South Carolina
P.O. Box 417
Norway, SC 29113-0417
(803) 263-4502

South Carolina Council on Adoptable
Children/South Carolina Seedlings and North
American Council on Adoptable Children
Representative
P.O. Box 1453
Greenville, SC 29602
(864) 239-0303
World Wide Web: http://members.aol.com/nacac

South Dakota
Families Through Adoption
P.O. Box 851
Sioux Falls, SD 57101
(605) 371-1404

North American Council on Adoptable Children
State Representative
c/o Native American Child and Family
Resource Center
29758 202nd Street
Pierre, SD 57501
(605) 224-9045
World Wide Web: http://members.aol.com/nacac

Tennessee
Council on Adoptable Children and
North American Council on Adoptable Children
State Representative
7630 Luscomb Drive
Knoxville, TN 37919
(423) 693-8001

Mountain Region Adoption Support Group
4428 Fieldstone Drive
Kingsport, TN 37664
(423) 523-7206

North American Council on Adoptable Children
Representative
27 Windhaven Lane
Oak Ridge, TN 37830
(423) 482-5264

Parents of International Children (PIC)
615 Tidesbridge Court
Murfreesboro, TN 37128
(615) 848-5278
World Wide Web: http://www.parentsofintchildren.
com

Texas
Adopting Children Together
8330 Meadow Road, Suite 218
Dallas, TX 75231
(214) 373-8348

Adopting Children Together and North American
Council on Adoptable Children Representative
1701 Los Prados Trail, P.O. Box 120966
Arlington, TX 76012-9066
(817) 265-3496
Fax: (817) 795-6009

Circle of Hope
c/o Hope Cottage
4209 McKinney
Dallas, TX 75205
(214) 526-8721

Council on Adoptable Children and North
American Council on Adoptable Children
Route 2, Box 77-F
Edinburg, TX 78539
(956) 383-2680
Fax: (956) 381-2177

Council on Adoptable Children and
North American Council on Adoptable Children
Representative
808 Woodlawn Drive
Harker Heights, TX 76543
(254) 690-3317
World Wide Web: http://members.aol.com/nacac

National Adoption Network
P.O. Box 2130
Coppell, TX 75019
(214) 335-0906
Toll-free: (800) 246-4237

Single Adoptive Parent Support Group
12751 Whittington, Apartment 136
Houston, TX 77077
(713) 496-2855

Utah
Catholic Community Services Parent Support
Group—Waiting Families
2300 West, 1700 South
Salt Lake City, UT 84104
(801) 977-9119

Families for Children and North American Council
on Adoptable Children State Representative
1219 Windsor Street
Salt Lake City, UT 84105
(801) 487-3916
World Wide Web: http://members.aol.com/nacac

Parents for Attachment (PFA)
603 West 3750 North
Pleasant View, UT 84414
(801) 782-2727

Utah State Adoption Support Group
645 East, 4500 South
Salt Lake City, UT 84117
(801) 264-7598

Vermont
Casey Family Services
7 Palmer Court
White River Junction, VT 05001-3323
(802) 649-1400

Family Life Services
72 Main Street
Vergennes, VT 05491
(802) 877-3166

Friends in Adoption
Buxton Avenue, P.O. Box 7270
Middletown Springs, VT 05757

Vermont Children's Aid Society Lifetime
Adoption Project
P.O. Box 127
Winooski, VT 05404-0127
(802) 655-0006
Toll-free: (800) 479-0015

Virginia
Adoption Resource Exchange for Single Parents
(ARESP)
P.O. Box 5782
Springfield, VA 22150
(703) 866-5577
Fax: (703) 912-7605
World Wide Web: http://www.aresp.org
E-mail: aresp@aol.com

Annandale Adoption and Attachment Partners
4300 Evergreen Lane, Suite 300
Annandale, VA 22003
(703) 658-7103

Association for Single Adoptive Parents
P.O. Box 3618
Merrifield, VA 22116-9998
(703) 521-0632

Friends of Children Services
2312 N. Wakefield Street
Arlington, VA 22207
(703) 528-6159

North American Council on Adoptable Children
Representative
Route 1, P.O. Box 417
McGaheysville, VA 22840
(540) 289-9535
World Wide Web: http://members.aol.com/nacac

Virginia One Church, One Child
1214 W. Graham Road, Suite 2
Richmond, VA 23220
(804) 329-3420
Fax: (804) 329-3906

Washington
Advocates for Single Adoptive Parents
11634 S.E. 49th Street
Bellevue, WA 98006
(425) 644-4761

Advocates for Single Adoptive Parents—NW
5706 NE 204th Street
Seattle, WA 98155
(435) 485-6770

North American Council on Adoptable Children
1229 Cornwall Avenue, #206
Bellingham, WA 98225
(425) 676-5437
World Wide Web: http://members.aol.com/nacac

One Church, One Child and North American
Council on Adoptable Children Representative
451 SW 10th Street, Suite 120
Renton, WA 98055-2981
(425) 235-4472
Fax: (425) 235-4863
Toll-free: (800) 882-4453

West Virginia
Appalachian Families for Adoption
P.O. Box 2775
Charleston, WV 25330-2775
(304) 744-4067

North American Council on Adoptable Children
1511 Byng Drive
South Charleston, WV 25303
(304) 744-9602
World Wide Web: http://members.aol.com/nacac

Parents Adopting and Learning to Support
301 High Street
Belington, WV 26250
(304) 823-3015

Wisconsin
Adoptive Families of Wisconsin
P.O. Box 575, Route 3
Galesville, WI 54630

Adoptive Moms Discussion Group
Jewish Community Center
6255 N. Santa Monica Blvd.
Whitefish Bay, WI 53217
(414) 964-4444

Adoptive Parent Group of Southern Wisconsin
1408 Vilas Avenue
Madison, WI 53711
(608) 251-0736

Friends of Adoption
1702 Old A Road
Spooner, WI 54801
(715) 468-2881

Inter-Racial Families Network
2120 Fordem Avenue
Madison, WI 53704

Special Needs Adoptive Parents
Route 1, P.O. Box 230C
Scandinavia, WI 54977

Special Needs Adoptive Parents (SNAP)
5209 Airport Road
Stevens Point, WI 54481
(715) 341-5291

United States Chilean Adoptive Families (USCAF)
1239 East Broadway
Waukesha, WI 53186
(414) 547-0671

Wisconsin Association of Single Adoptive Parents
4520 N. Bartlett Avenue
Shorewood, WI 53211-1509
(414) 962-9342

Wisconsin Open Door Society
2841 North Stowell Avenue
Milwaukee, WI 53211
(414) 963-0273

Wisconsin Single Parents of Adopted Children
810 Richards Avenue
Watertown, WI 53094
(920) 262-2540

Wyoming
Adoptive Parent Group of Cheyenne
Wyoming Children's Society
714 Randall
Cheyenne, WY 82001
(307) 686-6412

Northern Wyoming Adoptive Parents and
North American Council on Adoptable Children
State Representative
P.O. Box 788
Basin, WY 82410
(307) 568-2729

Support groups for gay and lesbian adoptive parents

Arizona
Gay and Lesbian Parent Support Network
P.O. Box 66823
Phoenix, AZ 85082-6823
(602) 256-9173

California
Gay Fathers of Long Beach
c/o The Center
2017 East Fourth Street
Long Beach, CA 90814

Lesbian Mothers Group of Long Beach
2017 E. 4th Street
Long Beach, CA 90814
(310) 434-4455

The Lyon-Martin Women's Health Clinic
1748 Market Street, Suite 201
San Francisco, CA 94102
(415) 565-7674

Outreach for Couples
405 W. Washington Street, #86
San Diego, CA 92103

Gay and Lesbian Parents of Los Angeles
7985 Santa Monica Blvd.
Suite 109-346
West Hollywood, CA 90046
(213) 654-0307

Colorado
Gay and Lesbian Parents—Denver
P.O. Box Drawer E
Denver, CO 80218
(303) 937-3625

District of Columbia
Gay Fathers Coalition of Washington, DC
P.O. Box 19891
Washington, DC 20036
(202) 583-8029

Florida
Gay and Lesbian Parents Coalition
P.O. Box 618132
Orlando, FL 32861-8132
(407) 420-2191

Indiana
Evansville GLPC
P.O. Box 8341
Evansville, IN 47716

Maryland
Gay and Lesbian Parenting Coalition of
Metropolitan—Washington
14908 Piney Grove Court
North Potomac, MD 20878
(301) 762-4828

Massachusetts
Lesbian/Gay Family Parenting Services
Fenway Community Health Center
7 Haviland Street
Boston, MA 02115

Gay Fathers of Greater Boston
P.O. Box 1373
Boston, MA 02205

New York
Center Kids
208 West 13th Street
New York, NY 10011
(212) 620-7310

Gay Fathers Coalition of Buffalo
Westside Station
P.O. Box 404
Buffalo, NY 14213
(716) 633-2692

Gay Fathers NY
Church Street Station
P.O. Box 2553
New York, NY 10008-7727

Gay Fathers Forum of Greater New York
Midtown Station
P.O. Box 1321
New York, NY 10018-0725
(212) 721-4216

Gay Fathers of Long Island
P.O. Box 2483
Patchogue, NY 11772-0879

North Carolina
GLP/Queen City—Charlotte
4417-F Sharon Chase Drive
Charlotte, NC 28215

Ohio
Gay and Lesbian Parenting Group of Central Ohio
P.O. Box 16235
Columbus, OH 43216

Gay Fathers
1319 W. 106th Street
Cleveland, OH 44102
(216) 228-4550

Lesbian Mothers/Co-Parents Support Group
Cincinnati, OH
(513) 631-5812

Momazons
P.O. Box 02069
Columbus, OH 43202
(614) 267-0193

Pennsylvania
CALM, Inc. (Custody Action for Lesbian Mothers)
P.O. Box 281
Narberth, PA 19072
(215) 667-7508

Texas

Gay Fathers of Austin
c/o Robert H. Havican
P.O. Box 16181
Austin, TX 78761-6181

Gay Fathers/Fathers First of Houston
P.O. Box 981053
Houston, TX 77098-1053
(713) 782-5414

Houston Gay and Lesbian Parent Support
P.O. Box 35709-262
Houston, TX 77235
(713) 666-8260

SAGL Parents
P.O. Box 15094
San Antonio, TX 78212
(512) 828-4092

Important Statistics

The following statistics were provided by the National Adoption Information Clearinghouse.

Adoption: Numbers and Trends. In 1992, there were 127,441 children adopted in the United States (Flango and Flango, 1994). In the 1990s, there are approximately 120,000 adoptions of children each year. This number has remained fairly constant in the 1990s, and is still relatively proportionate to population size in the U.S. (Flango and Flango, 1994).The estimated total number of adoptions has ranged from a low of 50,000 in 1944 to a high of 175,000 in 1970 (Maza, 1994).

ADOPTION FROM FOSTER CARE (Estimates as of 1/99)

The American Public Human Services Association (APHSA) [formerly the American Public Welfare Association (APWA)] continues to collect national data on adoption through the Voluntary Cooperative Information System (VCIS). Since 1983, the VCIS system has estimated the number of children in foster care based on data submitted voluntarily by participating states.

Based on 1999 estimates, there are approximately 520,000 children currently in foster care in the United States. Of these, 110,000 are eligible for adoption (U.S. HHS, 1999).

Who are the children in foster care?

The most recent complete data on children in foster care, summarized below, was released in January 1999 by the Children's Bureau, U.S. Department of Health and Human Services. Many states have not yet submitted complete data for each area.

Children in foster care, October 1, 1997 to March 31, 1998:

Age The ages of children in foster care are relatively evenly distributed: Twenty-seven percent are 1 to 5; 28 percent are 6 to 10; 26 percent are 11 to 15. A disproportionate number, 13 percent, are 16 to 18, while only 4 percent are under 1 year old and 1 percent are 19 and older.

Gender Fifty-one percent are male, while 49 percent are female.

Race/Ethnicity Sixty-one percent of children in foster care are of minority background; 35 percent are White. Forty-six percent of all foster children are Black; 13 percent are Hispanic; 1 percent are American Indian; 1 percent are Asian/Pacific Islander; and 4 percent are unknown.

Who are the children adopted from foster care?

Thirty-one thousand children were adopted from the public foster care system in fiscal year 1997 (October 1, 1996 through September 30, 1997). Children adopted from foster care, October 1, 1997 to March 31, 1998.

Age of Children Adopted
Forty-four percent were 1 to 5 years old; 37 percent were 6 to 10 years old; 15 percent were 11 to 15 years old; 2 percent were 16 to 18 years old; and 2 percent were under 1 year old when adopted from the public welfare system.

Gender of Children Adopted
The children adopted from foster care are equally distributed between males and females (50 percent each).

Race/Ethnicity of Children Adopted
Forty percent of the children in foster care are White, while a majority (59 percent) are of minority background. Of these, 44 percent of all children are Black; 13 percent are Hispanic; 1 percent are American Indian; and 1 percent are Asian/Pacific Islander.

The Relationship of the Adoptive Parent(s)
Sixty-four percent of the children adopted from foster care are adopted by former foster parents; 14 percent by relatives; approximately 21 percent by people unrelated to them; and fewer than 1 percent by stepparents (U.S. HHS, 1999).

Who are the children waiting to be adopted?
One hundred and ten thousand children in foster care are waiting to be adopted.

Age of Waiting Children on March 31, 1998
Two percent were less than 1 year old; 33 percent were 1 to 5 years; 36 percent were 6 to 10 years; 23 percent were 11 to 15 years; and 5 percent were 16 to 18 years old.

Gender of children waiting to be adopted
Fifty-two percent are male, while 48 percent are female.

Race/Ethnicity
Approximately 67 percent of children waiting in foster care are of minority background; 28 percent are White. Fifty-six percent of all foster children waiting for adoption are Black; 9 percent are Hispanic; 1 percent are American Indian; 1 percent are Asian/Pacific Islander; and 5 percent are unknown/unable to determine.

How many families are adopting transracially?
The most recent estimate of transracial adoption was performed in 1987 by the National Health Interview Survey (NHIS). The findings revealed that only 8 percent of all adoptions include parents and children of different races.

- One percent of white women adopt black children.

- Five percent of white women adopt children of other races.

- Two percent of women of other races adopt white children (estimates include foreign-born) (Stolley, 1993).

Of the 31,000 children adopted from the public welfare system in fiscal year 1997, slightly fewer than 10,000 children were adopted transracially or transculturally (U.S. DHHS, 1999).

Intercountry adoptions:
For fiscal year 1998, Number of Immigrant Visas issued to orphans coming to the United States:

Total	15,774
Russia	4,491
China	4,206
South Korea	1,829
Guatemala	911
Vietnam	603
Other	3,734

For fiscal year 1997, Number of Immigrant Visas issued to orphans coming to the United States:

Total	13,620
Russia	3,816
China	3,597
South Korea	1,654
Guatemala	788
Romania	621
Other	2,784

What is Open Adoption?

The term "open adoption" refers to the sharing of information and/or contact between the adoptive and biological parents of an adopted child. This can occur before, during, and/or after the placement of the child (Barman and Pannor, 1993).

The Continuum of Openness (Grotevant and McRoy, 1998)

Confidential ⟷ Mediated ⟷ Fully Disclosed

Confidential: Minimal information is shared between adoptive and birth family members and is never transmitted directly; any exchange of information typically stops with the adoptive placement or shortly thereafter.

Mediated: Non-identifying information is shared between parties through adoption agency personnel, who serve as go-betweens; sharing could include exchange of pictures, letters, gifts, or infrequent meetings at which full identifying information is not revealed.

Fully disclosed: Involves full disclosure of identifying information between adoptive and birth families; may involve direct meetings in each others' homes or in public places, phone calls, letters, and sometimes contact with the extended family.

Placing children for adoption

Two percent of unmarried women at any age place their child for adoption (ChildTrends, 1995). The percentage of premarital births placed for adoption has decreased since the 1970s. Analyses of three cycles of the National Survey of Family Growth show the following trend:

- From 1952 to 1972, 8.7 percent of all premarital births were placed for adoption.
- From 1973 to 1981, this percentage fell to 4.1 percent.
- From 1982 to 1988, it fell further to 2 percent (Bachrach, Stolley, London, 1992).

Women who voluntarily place their children for adoption are likely to have greater educational and vocational goals for themselves than those who keep their children. Women making adoption plans often come from higher socioeconomic backgrounds. These women come from intact families which are supportive of the placement, and which have not experienced teenage pregnancies by other family members (Stolley, 1993). Women whose mothers completed at least one year of college were three times more likely to place their babies for adoption than women whose mothers did not complete high school (Bachrach, Stolley, London, 1992). The 1995

National Survey of Family Growth found that 15 percent of recent births to never-married women and 18 percent of those to formerly married were unwanted by the mother at time of conception (Freundlich, 1998). The influences on the number of children available for adoption:

Declining numbers of women placing children for adoption: The decline in the number of women placing their children for adoption is primarily due to the declining numbers of white women placing their children for adoption; rates for minority women who place their children have remained relatively stable (Bachrach, Stolley, London, 1992). The initial drop in placement rates among white women reflected the increase in abortion rates after the legalization of abortion in 1973 (Bachrach, Stolley, London, 1992).

Declining stigma of unwed motherhood: The continuing decline in placement rates reflects the diminishing stigma attached to unwed parenthood (Bachrach, Stolley, London, 1992).

Declining numbers of teens placing children for adoption: The proportion of teens placing their children for adoption has declined sharply over recent decades (ChildTrends,1995). When they become pregnant, very few teens choose to place their children for adoption. In a 1995 survey, 51 percent of teens who become pregnant give birth; 35 percent seek abortions; 14 percent miscarry. Fewer than 1 percent choose to place their children for adoption (ChildTrends, 1995). The age of unmarried mothers has increased with time. In 1970, half of non-marital births were to teens; by 1993, the highest proportion of unmarried mothers were women in their twenties, a significant change. The birth rate for unmarried teens declined in 1995. Teen mothers, however continued to make up the largest single group of all first births to unmarried women (Freundlich, 1998).

Declining pregnancy rate:
Pregnancy rates declined by 1 percent for white women and by 5 percent for women of all other races between 1980 to 1991 (NCHS, 1995).

Increasing use of contraceptives:
Four percent of never-married women relied on their partners to use condoms in 1982; this number increased to 8 percent in 1988, and to 14 percent in 1995—a more than three-fold increase (NCHS, 1997). In 1995, 10.7 million women were using female sterilization, 10.4 million were using the birth control pill, 7.9 million used condoms, and 4.2 million were using male sterilization as a contraceptive technique (NCHS, 1997).

Declining abortion rate:
There has been no research showing that women are choosing to abort their children rather than place these children for adoption. Although the adoption rate has remained relatively steady, nationwide abortion rates have continued to decline since 1990 (Freundlich, 1998).

Are there any statistics on birthfathers?
Experts point out that only a very small percentage of birthfathers historically have taken an active part in the decisions surrounding adoption, but some agencies report that in recent years, a quarter or more relinquishments have included active involvement of birthfathers (Freundlich, 1998).

Those who adopt:
Of the 500,000 women seeking to adopt, only 100,000 had actually applied to adopt a child (National Center for Health Statistics, 1997). The 1995 National Survey of Family Growth found that 232,000 women took concrete steps toward adoptions, compared to 204,000 in 1988 (National Center for Health Statistics, 1999). About 2 percent of never-married women aged 15 to 44 have ever adopted a child; this statistic has remained stable since the 1970s (Bachrach, Adams, Sambrano, London, 1990).

Single adoptive parents

How many singles seek to adopt?
Research in the 1970s found that an estimated 4 to 5 percent of persons completing adoptions were single. Studies in the 1980s found from 8 to 34 percent of adopters were single (Stolley, 1993). Across the country the number of single-parent placements slowly and steadily continues to increase, both in domestic and intercountry adoption (Feigelman and Silverman, 1993).

Who are they?
Most single adoptive parents are female, are most likely to adopt older children than infants, and are less likely to have been a foster parent to the adopted child (Stolley, 1993). As a group, the single-parent adopters of U.S. children tended to adopt "special needs" children who were older, minority, and/or handicapped children (Feigelman and Silverman, 1993).

Drug-exposed infants

Skyrocketing use of drugs and alcohol, leading to higher numbers of drug-exposed children, has been targeted as a primary factor in the increase in children placed in out-of-home care in the late 1980s and 1990s. Studies estimating the incidence of prenatal alcohol and drug exposure do not agree upon a precise incidence level:

Alcohol

2.6 million infants each year are prenatally exposed to alcohol (Gomby and Shiono, 1991).

Fetal Alcohol Syndrome (FAS) affects between 1.3 and 2.2 children per 1,000 live births in North America each year (Streissguth and Guiunta, 1988; U.S. DHHS, 1990).

Cases of Alcohol Related Birth Defects (ARBD) outnumber cases of FAS by a ratio of 2 to 3 to 1 (Abel and Dintcheff, 1984; Streissguth and Guiunta, 1988).

Illicit Drugs

Each year, 11 percent of all newborns, or 459,690, are exposed to illicit drugs (Chasnoff, 1989).

More than 739,000 women each year use one or more illicit drugs during pregnancy (Gomby and Shiono, 1991).

A substance-exposed infant is born more frequently than once every 90 seconds (Schipper, 1991).

Services

How many adoptions disrupt?

Most adoptions do not disrupt before legalization; over 80 percent remain intact (Groza and Rosenberg, 1998). Most adoptions do not dissolve; over 98 percent are not terminated after legalization (Groza and Rosenberg, 1998). Very few adoptions are contested: fewer than 1 percent each year (Groza and Rosenberg, 1998). Adoption disruption and dissolution rates have remained relatively consistent over the past 15 years, ranging between 10 and 20 percent, depending on the type of adoption (Barth and Berry, 1988). Disruption can range as widely as 3 to 53 percent, depending on the group being studied and the calculating techniques being used (Stolley, 1993).

Disruption and dissolution

What kinds of adoptions disrupt?

Fewer than 1 percent of infant adoptions disrupt (Barth and Berry, 1988). Ten to 12 percent of adoptions of children aged 3 and older disrupt (Barth and Berry, 1990). Of children placed for adoption at ages 6 to 12, the disruption rate is 9.7 percent (Barth, 1988). Of children placed for adoption at ages 12 to 18, the disruption rate is 13.5 percent (Barth, 1988). Of children of any age with special needs placed for adoption, the disruption rate is 14.3 percent (Groza, 1986). Placements of older children and children with histories of previous placements and longer stays in the foster care system are more likely to disrupt (Stolley, 1993). The disruption rate increases as the age of the child at the time of adoption increases (Boyne et al., 1984; Barth and Berry, 1988). The overall decrease in disruption percentages from 1984 to 1988 can be traced to the introduction of post-adoption services, an important factor in containing the number of adoption disruptions (Barth and Berry, 1988).

Searching for birth relatives

How many adoptees search?

Between 2 and 4 percent of all adoptees searched in the year 1990 (American Adoption Congress, 1996). A survey conducted in the late 1980s estimated that 500,000 adult adoptees were seeking for or had found their birth families (Groza and Rosenberg, 1998).

Why do adoptees search?

In a study of American adolescents, the Search Institute found that 72 percent of adopted adolescents wanted to know why they were adopted; 65 percent wanted to meet their birthparents; and 94 percent wanted to know which birthparent they looked like (American Adoption Congress, 1996). The psychological literature has established that the desire of 60 to 90 percent of adoptees wanting to obtain identifying information regarding their biological parents is a normative aspect of being adopted (American Adoption Congress, 1996).

Infertility/impaired fecundity

What is infertility?

The term "infertility" is the failure to conceive for a period of 12 months or longer due to a deviation from or interruption of the normal structure or function of any reproductive part, organ, or system.

What is impaired fecundity?

The term "impaired fecundity" is defined as difficulty conceiving or in carrying a child to term.

How many Americans are affected?

About 6.1 million women experienced impaired fecundity in 1995, compared with 4.9 million in 1988. The percent with impaired fecundity increased to 10.2 percent in 1995 from 8.4 percent in 1988. Some of this increase is due to the aging of the Baby Boom generation (Fertility, Family Planning, and Women's Health, 1997). There were 2.1 million infertile couples in 1995, compared to 2.3 million in 1988 and 2.4 million in 1982 (Freundlich, 1998).

Who is affected?

Almost one-third of infertile childless married women were in the 35-to-44-year-old age group (Freundlich, 1998). Impaired fecundity is no more prevalent in any one race or socioeconomic group, but those in higher socioeconomic groups use infertility services far more often (Mosher and Bachrach, 1996). Older women, childless women, and married women are significantly more likely to report impaired fecundity, but differences by race or ethnicity are not significant (Barth, Brooks, Iyer, 1995). The trends with regard to impaired fecundity and infertility among older childless women appear to be associated with two factors: delayed child bearing and the very large numbers of Baby Boom women who have moved into their reproductive years. One demographer has estimated that the number of women with impaired fecundity may drop to 4.7 million in 2015 and then rise again to between 4.8 million and 5.9 million in 2020 (Freundlich, 1998).

Why pursue services?

Families who give birth as a result of donor insemination chose the procedure primarily because of their dissatisfaction with the adoption process on three counts:

- Long waiting lists
- Grueling and demeaning selection process
- Worries about adoption laws and the security of adoptions (Barth, Brooks, Iyer, 1995)

Like treatment for infertility, the adoption process is viewed by many infertile couples as time-consuming, intrusive, and beyond the control of the couple (Bachrach, London, Maza, 1991).

A

Adolescent and children's support groups, 310–11

Adoptalk, 431

Adopted Child (publication), 431

Adopted Child Syndrome, 238

Adoption and Foster Care Analysis and Reporting System (AFCARS), 66

Adoption and Safe Families Act (ASFA), 65–66, 72, 131–35
  permanent placement encouraged by, 133
  requirements of, 132–33

Adoption Awareness Month (AAM), 319–20

Adoption Exchange Association, 115

Adoption Resource Center, 170

Adoption Tax Credit Act, 163–64

Adoptive families. *See* Families, adoptive

Adoptive Families of America (AFA), 311, 312, 428

Adoptive Families (publication), 432

Adoptive parent groups, 307–9. *See also* Support groups

Adoptive Parents Committee, 308

Advertising, for birthmothers, 58–60

Advocacy for change, 318–22

Advocate groups, 314

African-American babies, waiting period for, 37

Age, 145
  of adopted child, 6, 145. *See also* Older children, adoption of
  of adoptive parents, 11–13, 145

Agencies, adoption (agency-assisted adoptions), 23–38. *See also* Post-adoption support services
  advantages of using, 25–26
  application to, 178–79
  autobiographical statement required by, 180–81
  counseling offered by, 26
  decision not approve adoption, 198
  disadvantages of, 27–29

Get the inside scoop...with the *Unofficial Guides*™!

Health and Fitness

The Unofficial Guide to Alternative Medicine
ISBN: 0-02-862526-9 Price: $15.95

The Unofficial Guide to Conquering Impotence
ISBN: 0-02-862870-5 Price: $15.95

The Unofficial Guide to Coping with Menopause
ISBN: 0-02-862694-x Price: $15.95

The Unofficial Guide to Cosmetic Surgery
ISBN: 0-02-862522-6 Price: $15.95

The Unofficial Guide to Dieting Safely
ISBN: 0-02-862521-8 Price: $15.95

The Unofficial Guide to Having a Baby
ISBN: 0-02-862695-8 Price: $15.95

The Unofficial Guide to Living with Diabetes
ISBN: 0-02-862919-1 Price: $15.95

The Unofficial Guide to Overcoming Arthritis
ISBN: 0-02-862714-8 Price: $15.95

The Unofficial Guide to Overcoming Infertility
ISBN: 0-02-862916-7 Price: $15.95

Career Planning

The Unofficial Guide to Acing the Interview
ISBN: 0-02-862924-8 Price: $15.95

The Unofficial Guide to Earning What You Deserve
ISBN: 0-02-862523-4 Price: $15.95

The Unofficial Guide to Hiring and Firing People
ISBN: 0-02-862523-4 Price: $15.95

Business and Personal Finance

The Unofficial Guide to Investing
ISBN: 0-02-862458-0 Price: $15.95

The Unofficial Guide to Investing in Mutual Funds
ISBN: 0-02-862920-5 Price: $15.95

The Unofficial Guide to Managing Your Personal Finances
ISBN: 0-02-862921-3 Price: $15.95

The Unofficial Guide to Starting a Small Business
ISBN: 0-02-862525-0 Price: $15.95

Home and Automotive

The Unofficial Guide to Buying a Home
ISBN: 0-02-862461-0 Price: $15.95

The Unofficial Guide to Buying or Leasing a Car
ISBN: 0-02-862524-2 Price: $15.95

The Unofficial Guide to Hiring Contractors
ISBN: 0-02-862460-2 Price: $15.95

Family and Relationships

The Unofficial Guide to Childcare
ISBN: 0-02-862457-2 Price: $15.95

The Unofficial Guide to Dating Again
ISBN: 0-02-862454-8 Price: $15.95

The Unofficial Guide to Divorce
ISBN: 0-02-862455-6 Price: $15.95

The Unofficial Guide to Eldercare
ISBN: 0-02-862456-4 Price: $15.95

The Unofficial Guide to Planning Your Wedding
ISBN: 0-02-862459-9 Price: $15.95

Hobbies and Recreation

The Unofficial Guide to Finding Rare Antiques
ISBN: 0-02-862922-1 Price: $15.95

The Unofficial Guide to Casino Gambling
ISBN: 0-02-862917-5 Price: $15.95

All books in the *Unofficial Guide* series are available at your local bookseller, or by calling 1-800-428-5331.

The *Unofficial Guide*™ Reader Questionnaire

If you would like to express your opinion about adopting a child or this guide, please complete this questionnaire and mail it to:

The *Unofficial Guide*™ Reader Questionnaire
IDG Lifestyle Group
1633 Broadway, floor 7
New York, NY 10019-6785

Gender: ___ M   ___ F

Age: ___ Under 30   ___ 31–40   ___ 41–50
___ Over 50

Education: ___ High school   ___ College
___ Graduate/Professional

What is your occupation?

_____

How did you hear about this guide?
___ Friend or relative
___ Newspaper, magazine, or Internet
___ Radio or TV
___ Recommended at bookstore
___ Recommended by librarian
___ Picked it up on my own
___ Familiar with the *Unofficial Guide*™ travel series

Did you go to the bookstore specifically for a book on adopting a child? Yes ___   No ___

Have you used any other Unofficial Guides™?
Yes ___   No ___

If Yes, which ones?

_____
_____
_____

What other book(s) on adopting a child have you purchased? _____

_____

_____

Was this book:
___ more helpful than other(s)
___ less helpful than other(s)

Do you think this book was worth its price?
Yes ___   No ___

Did this book cover all topics related to adopting a child adequately?
Yes ___   No ___

Please explain your answer:

_____

_____

_____

Were there any specific sections in this book that were of particular help to you?   Yes ___   No ___

Pl

DATE DUE

JAN 25 2005			
OCT 0 5 2006			

Or_____ing,
ho_____

Wl_____d in
the_____

_____

_____

Ar_____
ar_____

Ou_____

_____

_____

_____

GAYLORD   PRINTED IN U.S.A.